RETIREMENT STRATEGIES FOR WOMEN

RETIREMENT STRATEGIES FOR WOMEN

Turning Dreams into Reality

SANDY CIMORONI, BETH GRUDZINSKI, AND PATRICIA LOVETT-REID

Canadian Cataloguing in Publication Data

Cimoroni, Sandy
    Retirement strategies for women : turning dreams into reality

Includes index.
ISBN 1-55013-920-7

1. Women – Finance, Personal. 2. Women – Retirement – Planning.
I. Grudzinski, Beth. II. Lovett-Reid, Patricia. III. Title.

HG179.C587 1997   332.024′042   C97-931301-5

THE CANADA COUNCIL | LE CONSEIL DES ARTS
FOR THE ARTS | DU CANADA
SINCE 1957 | DEPUIS 1957

The publisher gratefully acknowledges the support of the Canada Council for the Arts and the Ontario Arts Council for its publishing program.

Key Porter Books Limited
70 The Esplanade
Toronto, Ontario
Canada M5E 1R2

Design: Jean Lightfoot Peters
Illustrations: Linda Montgomery

Printed and bound in Canada

98 99 00 6 5 4 3 2

CONTENTS

INTRODUCTION

All your life you've worked towards specific goals: learning new skills, being happy with your work, raising a family—the list goes on. Maybe you thought about your retirement, but for so many years it seemed more like a far-off concept than an eventual reality. As hard as it is to believe, your retirement years are quickly approaching, bringing with them new opportunities and new challenges. It's important to think about what's ahead. How will you spend your time? Will you continue to work part-time; do you want to travel, spend more time with family and friends? Now is the time to take stock, set new goals, and start planning.

No matter how well you've saved over the years, possibly one nagging question persists in the back of your mind: *Will I have enough money to see me through my retirement years?* You are not alone. Millions of Canadian women on the eve of retirement share the same concern.

Why Should Women Be Concerned about Retirement Planning?

Studies have shown that women's financial futures tend to be less secure than men's, perhaps because they have not handled their own or their family's investments in the past. Or perhaps because in many cases women face different challenges than men when planning their retirements. Consider these facts:

- **Women have longer retirements.** Women generally retire long before the age of 65, and live, on average, seven years longer than men.
- **Many women will live alone for at least part of their retirement.** The fact that women are retiring earlier and living longer than men means most women will likely need to look after their own finances at some time during their retirement.
- **Women earn less than men.** Though women have made great strides towards closing the gender gap with respect to salaries, they still make less than men on the whole. This means that over a lifetime women have had less income available to put towards retirement saving.
- **Few women have an adequate company pension plan.** The responsibility of raising a family generally leads to three results: women are in the workforce fewer years; fewer women have been promoted to senior higher-paying positions; women often choose part-time work. Given that most company pensions are formulated on salary and number of years working, the net effect is a lower pension.

When you stack up all the statistics the bottom line is startlingly clear—women need to take a more active role in planning and preparing for their retirement to ensure that they don't outlive their savings!

Taking charge of your finances and learning to maximize your investments will be the key to a successful retirement. Achieving this success requires the realization that as investors, and women, you must have a good understanding of the ever-changing social and work environment and how it will affect your retirement goals. As companies and governments increasingly transfer more and more responsibility for retirement planning to the individual, it is essential that you stay informed to protect yourself from the consequences of these changes. Now more than ever, successful retirement depends on your ability to set realistic goals and manage your resources effectively.

This book is designed to take you through a step-by-step planning process for your retirement—with an emphasis on turning your retirement dreams into a reality.

A Three-Step Program

In Step 1, you will identify your retirement goals, analyse your current financial situation, and estimate the costs associated with your retirement. In Step 2, we will review the essentials of retirement planning. You will learn about your potential retirement income sources and how to invest wisely by maximizing your income through key strategies. We will discuss how to preserve your hard-earned assets through estate planning. Finally, in Step 3, you can follow our Retirement Action Plan to a comfortable and fulfilling retirement. And because your retirement is more than just personal finances, we've added some tips to inspire you to stay healthy and active.

MEET MARIE, JESSIE, AND RUTH.

Marie and Jessie are friends. They both enjoy music and met when they were members of the same choral group. They have maintained their friendship, and both talk about rekindling their interest in music and rejoining a choir when they retire. Ruth is Marie's aunt. When Marie was growing up, she spent most of her summers at Ruth's family cottage. They share a special family bond.

Marie

Marie is 49 years old and recently resumed full-time employment as a dental assistant, earning $30,000 a year. While her children were in high school, she worked only part-time. John, her husband, is 53 years old and is employed as a fire fighter, at $60,000 per year. They have a 19-year-old daughter, Ann, and a 21-year-old son, George. George is in his last year of a computer science degree at the local community college; Ann will start university this fall. Both children are living at home. Marie enjoys music and spends much of her free time perfecting her pottery skills. She is planning to retire from her job in five years.

Jessie

Jessie is 54 years old and is a full-time nurse at a local hospital, earning $50,000 a year. She has been divorced for seven years. She has one daughter, Sandy, who is 28 years old. Last year there was a lot of excitement at the house because of Sandy's wedding! Jessie is planning to retire in two years, and is looking forward to spending more time relaxing in her garden, travelling, and enjoying a choir group with Marie.

Ruth

Ruth is 64 years old and retired just last year. Prior to retiring she was an office manager for a local real estate office. Ruth is widowed; her husband died very suddenly last year. Ruth has four children, and all are married with their own children. She has six grandchildren! She enjoys spending time with her family and painting at the cottage in the summertime. She has been playing more bridge recently and is interested in participating in competitive tournaments, which may require travel to different cities.

You'll read more about these women throughout this book, and understand the retirement options available to them—and yourself!—through their experiences.

STEP 1
PLANNING YOUR RETIREMENT

Planning your retirement is somewhat like planting a garden. First you dream about your beautiful landscape and read about which plants grow best under different conditions. Then you plan how to arrange your garden and consider what you may already have growing that's worth keeping. Next you invest in a few annuals and perennials, maybe a rock here and there, and consult an expert. Finally you water and weed regularly, and watch your garden grow. The first year you may not see significant changes, but just wait a few years. Your garden will be brimming with flowers and you'll be able to enjoy the rewards of your careful planning and diligent attention to details.

In Step 1, we invite you to start thinking about that dream garden. Begin by considering the landscape. In financial planning terms, that equates to assessing your current situation.

How does your garden grow?

Whether you're an expert gardener or just digging in, you're part of a growing trend to spend more time in your own backyard. Not only does a beautiful garden lift your spirits, it boosts your home's curb appeal if you decide to sell it in the future.

WHAT IS RETIREMENT PLANNING?

Retirement planning is the process of understanding and managing your financial resources so that you can use them most effectively for your future. It is an ongoing process that involves setting goals, assessing options, and developing a strategy. As your needs and goals change over time, your financial plan will too.

Many of us put off doing our financial homework, from balancing the cheque book to paying down debts. In our gardening analogy it's akin to weeding. Why the procrastination? Well, there are simply not enough hours in the day, after work and family commitments. Or perhaps you view it as an insurmountable task. But the need to map out your finances and plan for the future is not going to disappear.

A sound retirement plan doesn't necessarily mean sacrificing today's lifestyle for tomorrow's security. It means finding a balance between what you earn and what you spend, preparing yourself for unexpected expenses, and investing to achieve your goals.

Retirement planning doesn't have to consume all your time, nor do you require a PhD in economics. You'll find that a little knowledge will carry you a long way as you become more comfortable with the process. Finding out where you are financially and making a plan to move forward can be very satisfying. As you watch your investments grow, you will feel secure in knowing you have planned your garden with care and foresight.

Take the time to define your current financial situation, your future goals, and the options available to help you achieve these goals. You will soon realize how powerful retirement planning can be and how comforting it is to know you are in control of your future.

What Are Your Retirement Goals?

Now that you have been introduced to the concept of retirement planning, let's begin the process by establishing your retirement goals. Quite simply, what do you plan to do when you retire? Or, if you've already retired, what goals do you have for your retirement?

You can look forward to slowing down your pace. With your new-found abundance of time, you'll be able to relax more. In fact, if you worked full-time, your average work week translates into 2,000 hours per year—just imagine what you can do with that extra time! Travel through Europe, join a new club, volunteer at the local hospital, learn a new sport, or master an old one. You need to think about *how* you're going to spend your retirement time before you can determine your financial needs.

So, to turn your retirement dreams into a reality, begin by listing your retirement goals on the worksheet in order of importance. These will likely include a combination of lifestyle and financial goals.

Your Retirement Goals Worksheet

Financial Goals:	When is money needed?	Amount needed?
1. _____	_____	$_____
2. _____	_____	$_____
3. _____	_____	$_____

Lifestyle Goals:

1. _____
2. _____
3. _____

As you envision your retirement lifestyle, you may find not all of your goals require money; for example, taking nature walks, reading more books, or spending time with family and friends. However, many of your dreams will require financial resources. Your financial goals should be clearly defined and measurable to ensure that you can monitor your progress. Knowing what you want to do will help you find the strategies to do it.

Marie's Retirement Goals

Financial Goals:	When is money needed?	Amount needed?
1. Retire debt free. To do this, John and I will need to:		
Pay off mortgage	5 years	$8,500
Pay off line of credit		$4,000
2. Maintain current income throughout retirement.	5 years	$30,000/ annum
3. Move pottery studio from basement to renovated attic, where it will be brighter.	4 years	$5,000
4. Put money away for my children's weddings or to help them with the downpayment on a home.	5 years	$10,000

Lifestyle Goals:

1. Start a new fitness routine and stick with it!
2. Rekindle an interest in music, join a choir.

Home is where the heart is

One of the biggest retirement lifestyle decisions you'll make is determining where you will retire. The family cottage, a Florida retirement community, or a smaller house in your current community are just some of your options. For many, the family home seems like the best place to welcome children and grandchildren home for the holidays. Here are some considerations if you decide to move from your current home:

• *The family cottage.* Moving to a quiet rural community may be ideal for some people. But don't commit yourself unless solitude is what you crave. Also, consider the expenses you may have to incur to winterize your home and perhaps even bring in phone lines. How accessible will it be in the winter? Will you have a long driveway to shovel? A trial run in the dead of winter is a good idea.

• *Sun belt retirement community.* Before buying in any new community, try it on for size. Spend more than a vacation there to get a really good feel for the people, the climate, the cost of living, and activities. In addition, moving to another country for more than six months of the year may expose you to dual tax and may jeopardize your Canadian benefits.

• *A smaller home in your community.* This option has its advantages—same friends, same amenities, and less house and yard to look after. Be realistic about how much space you can afford to lose. If you plan to do a lot of entertaining, you will still want lots of living and dining space, but perhaps you can spare a bedroom or two. On the other hand, if you anticipate having regular overnight guests, you may want to have extra beds available.

ASSESSING YOUR CURRENT SITUATION

After you have an idea how you'd like your garden to look, it's important to take stock of what plants you already have growing and what weeds you'd like to eliminate. In the world of retirement planning, your existing plants are your current investments, and the weeds are your debts. And just as we use hoes and spades to tend to the land, we use tools in retirement planning to assess our current financial situation. There are two tools used to establish a clear picture of where we stand today:

• Net Worth Statement
• Cash In/Outflow Worksheet

The Net Worth Statement

Ease the garden strain
A day spent weeding, pruning, and planting is good exercise. And hard work. To avoid back strain, make sure you stretch often. To protect your knees from injury, use a rolled-up towel or, even better, knee pads.

To get a sense of your financial situation, it's helpful to assess your net worth, which is the difference between your assets (what you own, such as cash, investments, or property) and your liabilities (what you owe, such as a mortgage, car loan, or credit card balances). Your net worth will give you a snapshot of your financial situation by creating a personal inventory. You may be surprised to see exactly how much you have managed to save over the years.

Why complete a net worth statement? It forms the necessary foundation for all of your financial plans by providing a means for monitoring the value of your assets over time, as you get closer to retiring or throughout your retirement. Your net worth should be re-examined every year and compared with the previous year's to maintain an accurate inventory of your personal finances. As you approach retirement, your primary objective should be to maximize your assets and eliminate as many of your liabilities as possible. And, once you're in retirement, adhering to this strategy will be critical to your plan. As well, in retirement, your primary objective will most likely shift from growing your assets to preserving your assets. The completion of your Net Worth Statement allows you to monitor your progress and feel confident about your financial future.

Tips for Completing Your Net Worth Statement

- To find the current value of your investments, refer to your most recent account or investment statements. Store these statements for quick reference.
- For real estate assets, use the most recent appraised value or check with your local realtor.
- For vehicles, remember to deduct depreciation from your original cost.
- For jewellery, art, and collectibles, use the appraised value or your best estimate.
- For other assets, use your best estimate of its resale value.
- Record the current interest rate being charged on all liabilities listed. Look for opportunities to reduce the cost of borrowing by paying the most expensive debt first, or by consolidating debt.

YOUR NET WORTH STATEMENT

ASSETS	CURRENT VALUE	LIABILITIES	CURRENT VALUE	INTEREST RATE %
A. Liquid Assets				
Chequing accounts	$ _____	Credit cards	$ _____	_____
Savings accounts	_____		_____	_____
GICs & T-Bills	_____	Auto loans	_____	_____
Cash value of life insurance	_____		_____	_____
Money market mutual funds	_____	Education loans	_____	_____
Other *(e.g., money owed to*	_____		_____	_____
you, tax refund, etc.)	_____		_____	_____
Total Liquid Assets	$ _____ **(A)**	Investment loans	_____	_____
			_____	_____
		Other loans	_____	_____
B. Long-Term Assets			_____	_____
Mutual funds		Mortgage	_____	_____
(non-money market)	$ _____		_____	_____
Stocks	_____		_____	_____
Bonds	_____	Other	_____	_____
RRSPs/RRIFs/RESPs	_____			
Company pension plan	_____			
Other	_____	**TOTAL PERSONAL**		
Total Long-Term Assets	$ _____ **(B)**	**LIABILITIES** $_____		
C. Property Assets				
Residence	$ _____			
Vacation property	_____			
Vehicles	_____			
Jewellery/Art/Collectibles	_____			
Other *(e.g., furniture)*	_____			
Total Property Assets	$ _____ **(C)**			

> **DEFINITIONS**
> Personal Assets: What you own
> Personal Liabilities: What you owe

TOTAL PERSONAL ASSETS $ _____
(A+B+C)

YOUR PERSONAL NET WORTH

TOTAL PERSONAL ASSETS	$ _____
LESS: TOTAL PERSONAL LIABILITIES	–$ _____
EQUALS:	
YOUR PERSONAL NET WORTH	$ _____

The Cash In/Outflow Worksheet

The Cash In/Outflow Worksheet is also an essential component to assessing your financial situation. While it illustrates where your money comes from and where it goes, it does double duty as a budgeting tool, helping you identify potential funds for retirement investing. By updating this worksheet every year, you will also have a stronger grasp of your personal expenses, which goes a long way towards understanding how much money you need to maintain your current lifestyle. This will be the base for estimating what your retirement lifestyle will cost.

Start by listing, under **Cash Inflow**, all sources of income, such as salary, rental income, and investment income. Then, under **Outflow**, record your expenses according to the categories indicated. Tally your monthly and yearly cash inflow and outflow. If your inflow exceeds your outflow, you have a cash surplus. You can now invest this money towards your retirement. But if your outflow exceeds your inflow, you have a deficit. Consider some of the following tips to help you manage your budget and work towards achieving a surplus.

Tips for Managing Your Budget

- **Pay Yourself First.** Invest some money automatically from your paycheque—most financial advisors recommend at least 10% of after-tax income. Over time you will be pleased with the amount you are accumulating for retirement.
- **Spend less now.** Use your Cash In/Outflow Statement to identify some areas where you can reduce your spending, such as taking advantage of discounts for entertainment or subscribing to your favourite magazine instead of buying from the newsstand.
- **Earn more.** Consider turning a hobby into a little extra cash. Also, invest wisely, which equates to earning a better rate of return on your money.
- **Track your spending.** Know how much you are spending; file grocery bills, gas receipts, and other payments for a month or two to fine-tune your cash outflow.
- **Equalize payments.** For budgeting purposes, you can opt to pay your hydro bill or insurance premium, for example, by equal monthly payments instead of one or two large payments a year. This makes it easier to track your spending and to manage your larger expenses over time.

YOUR CASH IN/OUTFLOW WORKSHEET

CASH IN/OUTFLOWS	MONTHLY	ANNUALLY

CASH INFLOWS

	MONTHLY	ANNUALLY
Net salary (Gross salary − Income taxes)	$ _____	$ _____
Interest income	_____	_____
Dividends	_____	_____
Capital gains	_____	_____
Rental income	_____	_____
Other income	_____	_____

(e.g., RRSP, RRIF or pension income, government benefits, or a tax refund)

	MONTHLY	ANNUALLY
TOTAL CASH INFLOWS	$ _____	$ _____

CASH OUTFLOWS

A.   Living Expenses

	MONTHLY	ANNUALLY
Mortgage/Rent	$ _____	$ _____
Property taxes	_____	_____
Heat	_____	_____
Water	_____	_____
Electricity	_____	_____
Cable TV	_____	_____
Telephone	_____	_____
Home insurance	_____	_____
Other	_____	_____
Auto maintenance	_____	_____
Auto insurance	_____	_____
Gas	_____	_____
Parking	_____	_____
Other transit	_____	_____
Groceries	_____	_____
Clothing	_____	_____
Health and dental care	_____	_____
Pet care	_____	_____
Other	_____	_____

(e.g., union dues, professional fees, etc.)

	MONTHLY	ANNUALLY
Total Living Expenses	$ _____ (A)	$ _____ (A)

YOUR CASH IN/OUTFLOW WORKSHEET

CASH IN/OUTFLOWS	MONTHLY	ANNUALLY
B. **Debt Payments**		
Auto loan	$ _____	$ _____
Credit card	_____	_____
Other	_____	_____
Total Debt Payments	$ _____ (B)	$ _____ (B)
C. **Investment Programs**		
Life and disability insurance	$ _____	$ _____
RRSP contributions	_____	_____
Emergency fund	_____	_____
Other investment savings	_____	_____
Total Investment Programs	$ _____ (C)	$ _____ (C)
D. **Discretionary Expenses**		
Entertainment	$ _____	$ _____
Vacation	_____	_____
Subscriptions	_____	_____
Membership fees	_____	_____
Gifts	_____	_____
Charitable donations	_____	_____
Household purchases	_____	_____
Tuition	_____	_____
Other	_____	_____
Total Discretionary Expenses	$ _____ (D)	$ _____ (D)
TOTAL CASH OUTFLOWS (A+B+C+D)	$ _____	$ _____

AVAILABLE FOR INVESTMENT

	MONTHLY	ANNUALLY
TOTAL CASH INFLOWS	$ _____	$ _____
LESS: TOTAL CASH OUTFLOWS	–$ _____	–$ _____
EQUALS: **TOTAL SAVINGS AVAILABLE FOR YOUR RETIREMENT GOALS**	$ _____	$ _____

Debt Management

Debt management is your ability to handle your current debt. By using your Net Worth Statement, you can compare your assets to your liabilities from year to year. This will help you gauge how well you are managing your current debt.

Most people can't afford large purchases, such as a house or a car, without the help of a lender. At retirement, however, you probably won't be assuming such large debts.

For many, reducing debt often ranks as a primary financial goal. Paying off an existing mortgage, combined with other loans, can take years. And with the push to put money away for your retirement, it's hard to know which is more important—getting out of debt or maximizing your investment potential.

The answer is both. It's important you manage your debt responsibly and lower the cost of borrowing money as much as possible by meeting payments and taking advantage of low interest rates. Eventually that will free up more money for retirement savings, and it will also ensure you are debt-free, or close to it, when you retire or while in retirement.

> Ruth noticed how high the balance on her department store credit card was climbing. She was carrying a $2,000 balance with interest at an after-tax rate of 24% per annum. She knew that merely paying the minimum monthly payments of $40 meant she'd be years paying this debt. For Ruth to be a *Woman In The Know*, we recommend she take the money that is available in her savings account to pay off the credit card balance so she can save the large amount of interest she is being charged. Ruth would still have sufficient funds in her account in case of emergencies.

HOW CAN YOU MANAGE DEBT EFFECTIVELY?

Here are a few strategies:

- **Carry a limited number of credit cards.** Many people have several credit cards, including retail store cards, gas cards, and major credit cards. There is no reason to have several cards. By having only one major credit card, you'll pay a lower rate of interest, if you carry any surplus balance, than you will with most store and gas cards. You'll simplify your bookkeeping at the same time.
- **Consider lump sum payments for loans and mortgages.** Even if it's only once a year, earmarking a Christmas bonus or a tax refund as a lump sum payment can make a significant difference in reducing both principal and interest amounts outstanding.

- **Evaluate your Net Worth Statement.** Look for opportunities to use your accessible assets to pay down or eliminate outstanding debt. If this is an option, be sure to compare the amount of income being earned on the asset to the amount of interest being charged on the loan or line of credit before the asset is used to pay down debt.
- **Arrange for a line of credit.** If you have ongoing credit needs, you can save time and money by arranging a personal line of credit. You only need to apply once. You can use the line of credit as often as you like for large or small amounts (up to your limit), and the interest rate charged is generally lower than that for most credit cards.
- **Consolidate existing debt.** Budgeting is much simpler when the number of credit payments is reduced. Consider a line of credit to consolidate existing debt. In addition, the interest rate may be lower, especially when used to consolidate credit card balances.

Emergency Fund

You may know someone who has suffered financially when disaster struck—a flooded basement, a car accident. Many don't prepare for those unexpected emergencies and almost always wish they had. Simply having an emergency fund could have made these financial crises less stressful.

Your Net Worth Statement should include your emergency fund. Aim to have the equivalent of three to six months of your expenses saved.

An emergency fund should consist of safe and accessible investments. The following are some good options:

- a money market mutual fund
- a savings account
- Canada Savings Bonds

Alternatively, a line of credit is a viable option for many people who do not want to leave their money in low-interest accounts or investments. Establishing a line of credit for an emergency fund requires discipline to ensure it is used only for true emergencies.

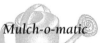

Mulch-o-matic

Don't rake up grass clippings. They are an ideal mulch for your lawn, help deter weeds, and retain moisture. Leave the clippings on the lawn, and by the time you mow again, they'll already be doing their magic.

PROJECTING YOUR RETIREMENT CASH OUTFLOWS

After completing your Cash In/Outflow Worksheet, the next step is to project those figures into the future. In today's dollars, estimate how much you think you will need to live on in retirement. The common recommendation is somewhere between 60% and 80% of your current gross (pre-tax) income. However, as you get closer to retirement it is better to estimate your income needs on the basis of specific retirement expenses.

The Projected Annual Retirement Cash Outflow Worksheet

By completing the worksheet you will be able to more accurately project your retirement cash outflow, which will help you plan your retirement needs. Besides the cost of your specific retirement goals, your basic cost of living will probably change, whether you plan to retire immediately or a few years down the road. There are many variables to consider, depending on your retirement dreams. As you prepare your Projected Annual Retirement Cash Outflow Worksheet, consider these potential changes to your expenses.

	Potential to Decrease	**Potential to Increase**
Living Expenses		
MORTGAGE/RENT	Hopefully you are close to eliminating your mortgage.	If you are considering selling your home, there will be legal and real estate commission costs.
AUTO COSTS/ OTHER TRANSIT	No more driving or taking public transit to and from work. Watch for seniors' fares on public transit.	You may be taking a few more weekend jaunts.
CLOTHING	You may no longer need to maintain a business wardrobe.	You may find you need more casual clothes.
HEALTH AND DENTAL CARE	Take advantage of reduced dispensing fees for seniors at drugstores.	Unless your pension plan offers dental and pharmaceutical care, you may incur drug and dental expenses.
OTHER	Take advantage of available seniors' discounts.	Membership and association fees previously covered by your employer may need to be covered by you.
Investment Programs		
INSURANCE	With greater assets and fewer dependent obligations, your overall life insurance needs will likely be reduced.	With increased assets your insurance needs may also increase to cover costs associated with settling your estate.
RRSP CONTRIBUTIONS	Once you are no longer eligible to make a contribution, this expense will decrease.	Ensure that you maximize any unused contribution room annually before you stop working or before turning 69.

	Potential to Decrease	Potential to Increase
Discretionary Expenses		
ENTERTAINMENT	Watch for and take advantage of seniors' ticket prices at movie theatres, or discounts at restaurants. Miscellaneous spending on morning coffee breaks and lunch meetings will also disappear.	With more time for leisure pursuits, you may attend more theatre, more movies, have dinner at a favourite restaurant.
MEMBERSHIPS	Most clubs reduce membership fees for seniors.	With more time you may decide to join a new club.
OTHER (CLASSES, HOBBIES)	Classes may have senior's discounts.	Whether you want to devote more time to a craft or would like to learn a new one, you're probably going to have to spend a few dollars to get set up.

YOUR PROJECTED ANNUAL RETIREMENT CASH OUTFLOW WORKSHEET

CASH OUTFLOWS	ESTIMATED MONTHLY	ESTIMATED ANNUALLY
A. Living Expenses		
Mortgage/Rent	$ _____	$ _____
Property taxes	_____	_____
Heat	_____	_____
Water	_____	_____
Electricity	_____	_____
Cable TV	_____	_____
Telephone	_____	_____
Home insurance	_____	_____
Other	_____	_____
Auto maintenance	_____	_____
Auto insurance	_____	_____
Gas	_____	_____
Parking	_____	_____
Other transit	_____	_____
Groceries	_____	_____
Clothing	_____	_____
Child care	_____	_____

CASH OUTFLOWS	ESTIMATED MONTHLY	ESTIMATED ANNUALLY
Health and dental care	_____	_____
Pet care	_____	_____
Other	_____	_____
(e.g., union dues, professional fees, etc.)		
Total Estimated Retirement Living Expenses	$ _____ (A)	$ _____ (A)
B. Debt Payments		
Auto loan	$ _____	$ _____
Credit card	_____	_____
Other	_____	_____
Total Estimated Debt Payments	$ _____ (B)	$ _____ (B)
C. Investment Programs		
Life and disability insurance	$ _____	$ _____
RRSP contributions	_____	_____
Education savings plan	_____	_____
Emergency fund	_____	_____
Other investment savings	_____	_____
Total Estimated Investment Programs	$ _____ (C)	$ _____ (C)
D. Discretionary Expenses		
Entertainment	$ _____	$ _____
Vacation	_____	_____
Subscriptions	_____	_____
Membership fees	_____	_____
Gifts	_____	_____
Charitable donations	_____	_____
Household purchases	_____	_____
Tuition	_____	_____
Other	_____	_____
Total Estimated Discretionary Expenses	$ _____ (D)	$ _____ (D)
TOTAL ESTIMATED RETIREMENT CASH OUTFLOWS (A+B+C+D)	$ _____ (E)	$ _____ (E)

You will need to adjust your Total Retirement Cash Outflow amount to take into account the effects of income tax expense. From the table below, select the factor that corresponds to the annual cash outflow amount calculated on Line (E).

Total Estimated Retirement Cash Outflow (Annual amount from Line (E))	$0–$25,000	$25,000–$50,000	Greater than $50,000
Approximate Income Tax Gross-up Factor*	1.35	1.5	1.6

Income Tax Factor _____ (F)

ADJUSTED RETIREMENT CASH OUTFLOW
Multiply Line (E) by Line (F)

_____ (G)

(Adjusted for Taxes)

For a more accurate estimate of your combined federal and provincial marginal tax rate, applicable to the various sources of income, please consult your local Revenue Canada office or the Income Tax Guide.

Before Ruth retired three years ago, she spent about $2,000 a year on clothing, half that amount going towards clothing for work. Now that she's retired, she spends about $1,200 a year updating her wardrobe with more casual wear. Ruth has also found her car expenses have decreased in retirement. Her gasoline bill is down by $600 without her daily commute, and her auto insurance premium has decreased by $500 now that she only drives her car for pleasure.

At the end of Step 1, you should have a comfort level with your current situation, knowing where you are today financially and where you want to be in the future. This information will help you determine what retirement options, discussed in Step 2, are appropriate for your goals and needs.

STEP 2
EXPLORING YOUR
RETIREMENT ALTERNATIVES

Your garden

Improve your garden (and benefit the greater environment too!) by composting your non-perishable uncooked kitchen garbage. It makes a great organic compost for vegetable and flower beds.

A s with every successful garden, preparation accounts for most of the work. With your garden well established in your mind's eye, it's time to till the earth, rake in some compost, and plant some seeds for the future. Though you may be tempted to sit back and watch your seeds blossom forth, don't get too comfortable. A garden, like your retirement plan, requires ongoing regular attention. And the more knowledge you acquire, the more secure you will feel. In Step 2, we review the following topics:

- determining your retirement income sources
- learning to invest wisely
- assessing your post-retirement income options
- strategies to maximize your retirement income
- protecting your assets through estate planning

DETERMINING YOUR RETIREMENT INCOME SOURCES

Once you have established your retirement goals and have looked at your current financial situation, you will want to figure out how much retirement income you can expect to receive and from what sources.

Your retirement income will usually come from a combination of three main sources:

- government benefits
- company pension plans
- personal savings

Government Benefits

Rules and benefit levels of government programs are always changing. To ensure you get the most accurate tally of your projected retirement income, check with the appropriate government branches as you approach retirement.

Tip

To find out your estimated government benefit amounts, contact the Income Security Programs division of Human Resources Development Canada. For QPP benefits, apply to the Régie des rentes du Québec. Check the blue pages in your local telephone directory for your nearest branch.

The following pages give details of the various government benefits for which you may be eligible. There are two primary plans that are funded by the federal government: Canada Pension Plan and Old Age Security Benefit.

CANADA PENSION PLAN (AND QUEBEC PENSION PLAN)

WHAT IS IT?

The Canada Pension Plan (CPP) provides a monthly retirement pension based on your employment earnings over your lifetime; residents of Quebec receive payments from the Quebec Pension Plan (QPP). To qualify for CPP pension payments you must have

- contributed to the plan for at least one year
- reached age 65, unless electing retirement at age 60

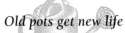

Old pots get new life
If you plant annuals in terra-cotta pots, you know they don't last forever. Break up broken planters into one-inch pieces and use them as drainage in new container gardens.

You can apply for CPP as early as age 60, provided you can show you "substantially" ceased to be a paid employee and earn less than the maximum annual CPP payable at age 65. Your benefit will be reduced by 0.5% a month if you start collecting before the age of 65, and will not return to the 100% level for the rest of your life. You can delay CPP payments until you turn 70, at which point you would receive 0.5% a month more on your benefit payment for every month you delayed payment after turning 65. CPP benefits are taxable and are adjusted each quarter by the rate of inflation, as measured by the Consumer Price Index (CPI). Similar provisions are in effect under QPP.

Although Jessie plans to retire in two years, she has not until now explored potential sources of retirement income, including government benefit programs. Jessie has just checked with the government agency (Income Securities Programs of Human Resources Development), where she was told that she is eligible to receive CPP benefits as early as age 60 or at the normal eligibility age of 65.

The government told her that, based on her earnings from work and participation in CPP for 29 years, she would be eligible to receive a maximum monthly benefit beginning at age 65 of $736.81 (1997 maximum). If she elects to receive her CPP benefit before age 65, for instance, age 60, her monthly benefit would be reduced by $221.

1997 maximum of $736.81 × 30%* = $221.04

Therefore, Jessie's monthly benefit amount would be $516.

$736.81 − $221.04 = $515.77

*30% = 0.5% per month × 60 months (12 months × 5 years)

WHAT ARE THE BENEFITS?

You're entitled to receive 25% of your pensionable earnings each month, up to a maximum monthly payment.

ARE THERE OTHER CONSIDERATIONS?

You may still be eligible for CPP if you lived outside Canada and have contributed to the social security system of a country that has a reciprocal social security agreement with Canada. These agreements, which Canada has with numerous countries, have been formed to recognize the significant number of immigrants residing in Canada. Your Canada Pension benefits can be split between you and your spouse provided you are both 60 years old. The amount received will depend on the number of years you have been married and how many years the higher-pension earner has contributed to the plan.

CPP ALSO OFFERS OTHER PENSION BENEFITS:

- **Disability Pension.** If you become disabled before age 65, CPP may provide monthly benefits until you turn 65 (at which time regular CPP begins) or until you recover from the disability.
- **Child's Benefit for Disabled Pensioner.** If you are disabled and you have a child or children under age 18, or under age 25 and enrolled in school full-time, they may be eligible to receive a flat-rate monthly pension.
- **Death Benefit.** You may be eligible for a lump sum benefit to help pay funeral expenses.
- **Survivor's Pension.** If you are a widow of a CPP pensioner, you may also receive a maximum of 60% of the deceased spouse's retirement benefit in monthly payments.
- **Orphan's Benefit.** An orphan of a deceased CPP contributor can receive a monthly orphan's benefit if under age 18, or under age 25 and enrolled full-time in school.

Current CPP Benefits (1997)	
Type of Benefit	**Maximum Monthly Benefit**
Retirement (age 65)	$736.81
Disability	$883.10
Survivors under age 65	$405.25
over age 65+	$442.09
Children of Disabled	$166.63
Orphans	$166.63
Death Benefit	$3,580.00 (lump sum)

OLD AGE SECURITY BENEFIT

WHAT IS IT?

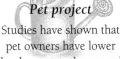

Pet project
Studies have shown that pet owners have lower blood pressure than people who don't own pets. Dogs have the added benefit of getting you out of the house for regular walks, a great way to stay fit. If you don't have the time to house-train a dog or stay with a kitten, why not get an older animal from the Humane Society?

The Old Age Security (OAS) plan is administered and funded by the federal government with income tax dollars. The plan pays a monthly retirement benefit based on your age and the length of time you have lived in Canada. The plan includes:

- a basic OAS benefit, available to anyone who is 65 and who has lived in Canada for
  - 40 years after turning 18, or
  - for the 10 consecutive years before applying for the benefit;

  To receive a pro-rated OAS benefit you must have lived in Canada for at least 10 years after age 18.
- a Guaranteed Income Supplement (GIS) provides an additional benefit to low-income individuals;
- a Spouse's Allowance (SPA)/Widowed Spouse's Allowance extends benefits to spouses of OAS pensioners and spouses of deceased OAS pensioners

who do not qualify for benefits on their own and are
- between the ages of 60 and 65, and
- residents of Canada for at least 10 years after reaching age 18.
Payments stop when the spouse reaches age 65 or remarries, at which point he or she can personally claim OAS and GIS benefits.
- All OAS benefits, except the GIS payment, are included as income for tax purposes.

WHAT ARE THE BENEFITS?

The maximum basic benefit is paid monthly and is adjusted each quarter by the rate of inflation, as measured by the Consumer Price Index (CPI).

Current OAS Benefits (1997)

Type of Benefit	Maximum Monthly Benefit
Old Age Security Benefit	$400.71
Guaranteed Income Supplement	
Single	$476.20
Married to a non-pensioner	$476.20
Married to a pensioner	$310.18
Married to a SPA recipient	$310.18
Spouse's/Widowed Spouse's Allowance	
Spouse	$710.89
Widowed spouse	$784.82

OAS payments are subject to a special tax if your personal income is above a set level. This level has remained the same since 1995, at $53,215, but is subject to government change at any time. If your income exceeds this amount, you must pay 15% of the amount exceeding the threshold up to the maximum OAS benefit. The government will calculate the special tax and deduct it directly from your monthly benefit cheque. Because the calculation is based on your previous year's income, you may be faced with an adjustment that you will be required to file on your tax return. Once you exceed the threshold of $84,000 (which, like the above, has remained the same since 1995), you will not be eligible for any OAS benefit.

ARE THERE OTHER CONSIDERATIONS?

To receive OAS benefits, you must apply at least six months before you turn 65, at which point a flat-rate monthly pension begins. Retroactive payments can be made for up to one year. If you leave Canada for longer than six months after your OAS payments begin and you have lived in Canada for less than 20 years, you will receive OAS payments only for the month of departure from Canada and for six additional months, after which payment is suspended. Payments resume when you return to Canada.

PROPOSED SENIORS BENEFIT

WHAT IS IT?

The new Seniors Benefit was proposed in the 1996 federal budget to replace the Old Age Security and GIS benefits and to eliminate two tax credits: the pension income tax credit and the age tax credit. It is to go into effect in 2001 and will apply to anyone who hasn't reached 60 years of age by December 31, 1995, and their spouses. All Canadians who meet the residency requirements of the previous OAS are eligible to apply for the Seniors Benefit. How much you may receive will depend on your income. Essentially, the more retirement income you receive from all sources, the lower your benefit amount.

WHAT ARE THE BENEFITS?

Single seniors with no other income will be entitled to $11,420 a year. Married seniors with no other income will receive $18,400 a year to be divided evenly between spouses. Seniors receiving income from CPP/QPP and other sources will receive the following benefits based on their income:

Get in the swing
If you're just starting to play golf, do yourself a favour and invest in some lessons. Be sure to include golfing gloves (to prevent getting blisters on your hands), as well as a hat, water bottle, and sunscreen.

Projected Seniors Benefit in 2001

| Income from | Maximum tax-free benefit | |
other sources	Single	Couples
$ 0	$11,420	$18,440
5,000	8,920	15,940
10,000	6,240	13,440
15,000	5,160	10,940
20,000	5,160	10,320
25,000	5,160	10,320
30,000	4,350	9,510
35,000	3,350	8,510
40,000	2,350	7,510
45,000	1,350	6,510
50,000	350	5,510
60,000	—	3,510
70,000	—	1,510
80,000	—	—

ARE THERE OTHER CONSIDERATIONS?

The Seniors Benefit has not yet been legislated. However, it seems likely the proposed change will be approved. Watch financial reports for updates on the Seniors Benefit and be aware of the impact it may have on your sources of retirement income.

Company Pension Plans

A company pension plan is established by your employer and allows contributions from you, your employer, or both, to accumulate on a tax-deferred basis until you retire.

After a specified length of time, known as a vesting period, the contributions made by your employer become portable. In other words, if you leave your employer you have the ability to transfer the vested amount to another registered retirement plan. Most vesting periods are approximately two years.

We will discuss two company pension plans:

- Defined Benefit Plan
- Defined Contribution Plan

DEFINED BENEFIT PLAN

WHAT IS IT?

A defined benefit plan is a pension plan whereby your benefits are calculated using a formula based on such factors as your earnings, job classification, and years of service. These factors are described in the pension plan document given to the members. The employer administers the pension and determines the amount of benefit for which you are eligible. Yearly contributions are made by the employer and often by the employees, who are either allowed or required, depending on the plan, to contribute an amount based on a fixed percentage of their salary.

WHAT ARE THE BENEFITS?

Your benefit amount will depend on your company's type of plan. There are three common types of defined benefit plans:

- **Career average pension benefit.** This is based on a formula that calculates a percentage of an employee's average career earnings while a participant of the plan.
- **Final average pension benefit.** This is based on the employee's average earnings over a certain number of years, possibly the best or last years, as defined in the pension and the number of years the employee was a participant in the plan.
- **Flat benefit pension plan.** This provides a monthly pension amount based on a specified flat rate for each year the employee was with the company, regardless of the difference in salary levels among employees.

ARE THERE OTHER CONSIDERATIONS?

Before you retire, meet with your pension administrator to find out exactly how much you will be receiving and to discuss any other options that may be available to allow you to increase your pension benefits.

Jessie has spoken with the pension administrator at the hospital about the approximate amount she can expect to receive from her pension when she retires in two years. Her defined benefit pension plan is calculated using the *final average* of the last five years of her earnings. Jessie is a *Woman In The Know* for finding out details about her pension plan. She learned how her particular pension benefit would be calculated:

Average annual eligible salary × 2% × credited years of service = annual pension amount

Therefore, Jessie's annual pension amount is $28,420.

$49,000 × 2% × 29 years = $28,420

DEFINED CONTRIBUTION PLAN

WHAT IS IT?

Golfer gab

Par—the ideal number of strokes to complete a hole, allowing for two putts
Birdie—one under par
Eagle—two under par
Bogey—one over par
Double bogey—two over par

A defined contribution pension plan, also known as a money purchase plan, provides a pension based on funds accumulated over the course of your employment. The amount of pension you will receive at retirement is based on how much is set aside and how well the invested money performs. Investment choices could be made solely by your employer or, as an employee, you may be able to participate in these investment choices.

Under this plan, you and your employer contribute a fixed percentage based on your annual earnings. Generally, you contribute a certain amount and your employer will match it.

WHAT IS THE BENEFIT?

You can calculate a rough estimate of what you can expect as retirement income based on total contributions and assuming a constant contribution rate, the investment return over a specified period of time, and the annuity interest rates.

ARE THERE OTHER CONSIDERATIONS?

Because your ultimate pension amount is significantly affected by how well your money is invested, find out as much as you can about where your money is being invested. Review the status of your pension fund regularly.

OTHER KINDS OF COMPANY PLANS

There may also be other company plans that are not registered pensions but are geared to help you save for your retirement. Two such plans include:

- **Group RRSP.** A Group RRSP is a collection of individual RRSP accounts administered through your employer. You decide how much you want to contribute and how those contributions should be invested. Your contributions are taken directly from your salary, thus reducing your gross income at the source. In effect, you get the RRSP tax deduction without having to wait until you file your tax return.
- **Deferred Profit Sharing Plan (DPSP).** A DPSP is a registered savings plan that holds contributions from your employer based on corporate profits. Contributions can only be made by the employer. At retirement you have several options:
  - take the money in a fully taxable lump-sum;
  - take the money in periodic instalments over 10 years;
  - buy an annuity;
  - continue enjoying tax-free growth by transferring the funds to an RRSP or RRIF.

Personal Savings

One of the most important sources of potential retirement income is that generated by personal investments. Since government benefits may pay a minimal income, and company pensions may not provide enough to live on and are not available to everyone, your personal savings, including registered and non-registered investments, should be a larger component of your retirement plan. That means you have to maximize your investment in order to provide an adequate retirement cash flow. Your registered investments, such as your Registered Retirement Savings Plan (RRSP), will be a primary source of retirement income.

WHAT IS A REGISTERED RETIREMENT SAVINGS PLAN (RRSP)?

An RRSP is a savings plan that is registered with Revenue Canada. It is not a specific product. We illustrate an RRSP as an umbrella because it can cover several different investments. Besides helping you put money aside for your future, RRSPs also provide three major benefits:

- Money invested in an RRSP grows on a tax-deferred basis, so that all of your investment dollars go to work for you. Tax is deferred until the money is withdrawn.
- The amount you invest in your RRSP directly reduces your taxable income, which means you get a tax deduction today.
- When you withdraw money from the plan, it is treated as regular income and taxed for that year. If you wait until you retire, your income may be lower and you will likely pay less tax.

You can open and contribute to an RRSP through a bank, trust company, life insurance company, investment dealer, mutual fund company, financial planner, or broker. RRSP-eligible products can be purchased with a lump sum investment or through regular contributions, that is, contributions made weekly, biweekly, monthly, or quarterly. There is no limit to the number of RRSPs you can own. For a given tax year you have until 60 days into the next year to make your contributions.

HOW MUCH CAN I CONTRIBUTE?

Your maximum contribution must not exceed 18% of your previous year's "earned income," as defined by Revenue Canada, to a maximum of $13,500, minus any pension adjustment (if you are, for example, a member of a company pension plan). This maximum contribution amount is set until the year 2003. Check your Notice of Assessment for your limit, issued by Revenue Canada with your previous year's tax return.

If you contribute less than your maximum allowable amount to an RRSP in any given year, the unused contribution room can be carried forward indefinitely. We recommend, however, you attempt to maximize your contributions on a yearly basis, since the government can change this at anytime.

As well, you are allowed a $2,000 lifetime over-contribution. This excess amount cannot be used to reduce your gross income for tax purposes. The over-contribution will need to be, at some time in the future, claimed against income. If you exceed the $2,000 over-contribution limit, the excess amount is taxed at 1% a month.

Did you know?

Currently, Revenue Canada allows you to invest up to 20% of the book value (original cost) of each RRSP account in eligible foreign investments. Investing outside Canada means greater opportunity for investment growth.

Because Jessie belongs to the hospital pension plan (a defined benefit plan), her RRSP contribution limit takes into consideration the amount of her pension adjustment. Last year she earned $50,000 and her pension adjustment (PA) was $5,750, as calculated by her pension administrator. For Jessie to be a *Woman In The Know*, we recommend that she take full advantage of the benefits of an RRSP and make her maximum RRSP contribution.

RRSP Limit Calculation:	$50,000 × 18% = $9,000
Less Pension Adjustment:	− $5,750
Maximum RRSP Contribution:	$3,250

Golfer gab

Slice—when a right-handed golfer hits the ball to the right (left-handed to the left) *Hook*—when a right-handed golfer hits the ball to the left (left-handed to the right) *In the rough*—refers to the position of the ball off the groomed part of the hole

WHAT ARE THE TYPES OF RRSPs?

- A **personal RRSP** is a plan registered in your name to which you contribute.
- A **Spousal RRSP** allows a couple to create a retirement fund for both spouses and can be an effective income-splitting tool. A taxpayer may choose to contribute to an RRSP in his or her spouse's name while claiming the contribution as a deduction on his or her own tax return. Although typically the spouse in the higher tax bracket contributes to a Spousal RRSP to benefit from the deduction, it is important when establishing a Spousal RRSP to consider the *anticipated* income level of each spouse at retirement.

A Spousal RRSP spreads the income at retirement between both individuals, which could have the effect of reducing taxes when the funds are withdrawn. Any funds contributed to a Spousal RRSP are considered the property of the spouse in whose name the RRSP is registered and is taxable in his or her hands when withdrawn. The only time this would not be the case is if the funds are withdrawn within three years of any contribution; then the funds withdrawn would be taxed in the hands of the contributing spouse (this is called the Three Year Attribution Rule).

To be deductible, the total of all amounts the spouse contributes to both an individual RRSP and the Spousal RRSP may not exceed his or her own RRSP contribution limit.

Marie earned $30,000 last year. She and her husband have both fully maximized their RRSP contribution room and neither contributes to a company pension. According to Revenue Canada's Notice of Assessment, Marie can make an RRSP contribution of $5,400 (calculated by $30,000 "earned income" × 18%). Marie's husband, John, earned $60,000 last year, and Revenue Canada calculates his contribution room at $10,800 (calculated by $60,000 "earned income" × 18%). For Marie to be a *Woman In The Know*, we recommend that:

i) she continues maximizing her RRSP contributions annually, and

ii) she discusses the benefits of a Spousal RRSP with her husband. If John opens a Spousal RRSP (in Marie's name), he can contribute on her behalf and still receive the tax deduction against his income. At retirement, when money is withdrawn from their RRSPs for income, this will help to balance the amounts they each receive, creating a lower combined tax liability.

- **Locked-in RRSPs**, or Locked-in Retirement Accounts (LIRA), are created to transfer-in vested pension funds that you take with you if you leave an employer prior to retirement. In most provinces locked-in registered funds cannot be converted into retirement income until you reach age 55 unless the pension plan provides for conversion at an earlier age. Accumulated savings in a Locked-in RRSP or Locked-in Retirement Account (LIRA) cannot be transferred to a regular RRIF or withdrawn as a lump sum. Instead, they must be transferred to a Life Income Fund (LIF), a Locked in Retirement Fund (LRIF), or a Life Annuity no later than the end of the year in which you turn 69.

Determining Your Income Sources

Golfer gab

Handicap—your average number of strokes (in your best 10 of your last 20 games) over the Canadian Professional Golf Association "course rating"

Scratch handicap—an expert golfer who usually shoots par or under is referred to as having a scratch handicap

Mulligan—the chance to take your shot again. Not an official term, but handy when you're just starting out. Reserve this for practice rounds away from diehard golfers

CALCULATING YOUR MONTHLY RETIREMENT SAVINGS GOAL

In Step 1, you determined where you are today and where you want to be in the future, financially. We have discussed the various sources of retirement income available to help you achieve your goals. For many of us, there may be a "gap" between where we are today and where we want to be in the future, which cannot be filled by the retirement income available. To fill this "gap", a saving strategy needs to be determined.

The Retirement Planner will help you determine this strategy. By completing the worksheet, you will be able to project more accurately what you will need to save on a monthly basis to meet your retirement goals.

RETIREMENT PLANNER

STEP 1   Determine Your Annual Retirement Income

	Example	You
1. Refer to your Projected Annual Retirement Cash Outflow Worksheet, found on pages 24–26. This is where you calculated your Estimated Retirement Cash Outflow (line E), based on your lifestyle requirements at retirement. This figure represents an estimate of your annual retirement income needs. Insert this amount on line (A).	$30,000	_____ (A)

If you have not completed your Projected Annual Retirement Cash Outflow Worksheet, base your estimate for line (A) on 60 to 80% of your current gross annual income, to maintain your standard of living at retirement.

2. You will need to adjust your annual retirement income needs for future inflation. From the table below, select the number of years until you retire. Enter the corresponding inflation factor on line (B).   **1.27**   _____ (B)

Years to Retirement	2	4	6	8	10	12
Inflation Factor*	1.06	1.13	1.19	1.27	1.34	1.43

*assumes 3% inflation

3. Multiply line (A) by line (B). This is your annual retirement income needs adjusted for inflation.   **$38,100**   _____ (C)
($30,000 × 1.27)

STEP 2   Determine Your Sources of Retirement Income

	Example	You
1. Estimate the annual amount of income you expect to receive from sources other than your personal savings. Examples include income from a company pension plan, government benefits (such as CPP/QPP and OAS), or rental income.	$11,430 (30% × $38,100)	_____ (D)

As an estimate, if you have a company pension plan, multiply line (C) by 60%. If you do not have a company pension plan, multiply line (C) by 30%. Use an even lower percentage if you are uncertain about the future availability of government benefits.

2. Subtract line (D) from line (C). This is the amount of annual retirement income you will need to fund from your personal savings, such as your RRSP.   **$26,670**   _____ (E)
($38,100 − $11,430)

STEP 3   Determine Your Personal Savings Goal

	Example	You

1. From the table below, select the number of years you expect your retirement income to last and enter the corresponding factor on line (F).

   Example: 15.44   You: _____ (F)

# of Years Income Is Needed	15	20	25	30	35
Factor*		12.36	15.44	18.10	20.40	22.40

   *assumes a 6% pre-tax annual rate of return, 3% annual inflation, and that the funds will be depleted by the end of the period selected.

2. Multiply line (E) by line (F). This is the amount you need to save prior to retirement in order to produce your annual retirement income.

   Example: $411,785 ($26,670 × 15.44)   You: _____ (G)

3. Enter the total amount you have already saved in RRSPs.

   Example: $200,000   You: _____ (H)

4. From the table below, select the number of years until you retire and match it with the return you expect your savings to earn. Enter the corresponding factor on line (I).

   Example: 1.59   You: _____ (I)

Years to Retirement	2	4	6	8	10	12
Annual Rate of Return						
4%	1.08	1.17	1.27	1.37	1.48	1.60
6%	1.12	1.26	1.42	1.59	1.79	2.01
8%	1.17	1.36	1.59	1.85	2.16	2.52
10%	1.21	1.46	1.77	2.14	2.59	3.14

5. Multiply line (H) by line (I). This is the amount your current RRSPs will be worth at retirement.

   Example: $318,000 ($200,000 × 1.59)   You: _____ (J)

6. Subtract line (J) from line (G). This is the additional amount you must save by the time you retire in order meet your retirement income goal.

   Example: $93,785 ($411,785 − $318,000)   You: _____ (K)

   If this number is less than zero, you're ahead of your retirement savings goal! Consider other goals you may have and put a strategy in place to achieve them.

STEP 4   Determine Your Monthly Savings Goal

	Example	You
1. From the table below, select the number of years until you retire and match it with the return you expect your savings to earn in the meantime. Enter the corresponding factor on line (L).	122.00	_____ (L)

Years to Retirement	2	4	6	8	10	12
Annual Rate of Return						
4%	24.93	51.89	81.04	112.58	146.70	183.59
6%	25.39	53.92	85.98	122.00	162.47	207.95
8%	25.86	56.03	91.21	132.25	180.12	235.96
10%	26.34	58.20	96.76	143.41	199.86	268.17

2. Divide line (K) by line (L). This is how much you need to save each month to achieve your retirement savings goal.

$769
($93,785 ÷ 122.00)

_____

LEARNING TO INVEST WISELY

The goal of retirement planning is to effectively plan to access your income from all available sources. In our discussion of retirement income sources in the last section, we determined that income generated from government or company pension plans form a fixed base to your retirement income; you have little control over the amounts you'll receive. However, with your personal savings, you have ultimate control over how much you save, how you invest, and how much you receive as income at retirement. In this section we discuss:

- how investments earn income,
- the financial markets, and
- types of investments.

How Investments Earn Income

Investments can generate three types of income:

- **Interest.** A financial institution, company, or government pays you interest in exchange for the use of your money. You lend the money for a specified period of time at a specified rate of interest.
- **Dividends.** When a company needs money, it seeks investors to purchase shares of the company. When you purchase a share, you are eligible to receive a portion of the company's profits, which are paid out in dividends.
- **Capital Gains.** When you realize a profit from the sale of an asset, such as an investment or real estate, you earn a capital gain—the difference between the purchase price and the sale price of the asset. When you realize a loss on the sale, this is deemed a capital loss.

ENHANCING INVESTMENT GROWTH

The key to maximizing your income from investments is letting the income you earn grow over time. Instead of taking the immediate income from your investment, allow income to accumulate, thereby earning income on your income. This is known as compounding. The two most important factors of compounding are time and rate of return:

- **Time.** The more time your money has to compound, the more you will accumulate. As you approach and enter your retirement, you'll want to take advantage of compounding and also continue to make some long-term investments.
- **Rate of return.** Rate of return is represented as a percentage and is based on the amount of income that is earned on an investment. If your money compounds at a higher rate of return, you will end up with more money.

THE FINANCIAL MARKETS

All investments are offered through two financial markets—the debt market or equity market. And when you invest you are either a lender or an owner.

- **Debt Security.** You are a lender whenever you buy an investment that pays interest. Debt securities are issued by a government or company when it needs to raise money, usually in the form of treasury bills (T-bills), commercial paper, or bonds. You lend your money to the government or company and it in turn agrees to repay your principal on a certain date, plus a fixed amount of interest. Short-term debt securities (up to one year) are called *money market securities*; long-term debt (one to 30 years) securities are called *fixed income securities*.

Tip

Double your investment— consider the "Rule of 72." Divide the number 72 by the interest rate earned on your investment. The answer will give you the number of years it will take for your original investment to double. For example, $1,000 invested at 8% will take nine years to become $2,000. (72 ÷ 8% = 9).

- **Equity Security.** You are an owner whenever you buy an investment that has the potential to increase in value. Equity securities are issued by a company to raise money, but you actually purchase stock in the company in exchange for a share of potential profits. Profits can be paid out in the form of dividends or are reinvested into the company. Equity securities are also called *growth securities*.

ASSET CLASSES

Investments are often classified according to three asset classes. Each of these asset classes contain investments with similar characteristics.

- **Safety Assets** (money market securities) are short-term debt securities. They are bought and sold in money markets, which link investors who want to earn competitive rates on their surplus cash with governments and companies needing short-term financing.
- **Income Assets** (fixed income securities) are longer-term debt securities. They are bought and sold in fixed income markets, which link investors who want to invest for more than one year with governments and companies needing longer-term financing.
- **Growth Assets** (growth securities) are equity securities, such as company stocks. They are bought and sold in equity markets through exchanges such as the Toronto Stock Exchange (TSE) or the New York Stock Exchange (NYSE).

THE RISK/RETURN TRADE-OFF

Each asset class has a different level of risk and expected return associated with it. Investments that have the potential for the highest returns usually have the highest risk. Conversely, lower-risk investments usually offer lower returns. This fundamental principle of investing is called the "risk/return trade-off."

Types of Risk

Investments are vulnerable to several types of risk:

- **Market risk.** All economies move in cycles of expansion and contraction. As an economy moves through each stage of its cycle, some investments will perform better than others.
- **Interest rate risk.** The market value of an investment will change as interest rates change.
- **Purchasing power or inflation risk.** Inflation refers to how much more money you need to spend in the future to buy the same goods today. For example, the cost of a loaf of bread a decade ago was far less than today. Inflation has a direct impact on the return of an investment. To keep your purchasing power intact and growing, you need to earn an investment return above the rate of inflation.
- **Foreign exchange risk.** When you invest globally, you are investing in an asset denominated in a foreign currency. Your investment will fluctuate depending on how the Canadian dollar is trading against that foreign currency.
- **Default risk.** When buying debt securities issued by a government or company, your investment return is dependent on the issuer's financial ability to pay its obligation to you. Issuers with higher default risk will compensate investors by offering a higher return.
- **Liquidity risk.** Liquidity risk refers to your ability to easily convert an investment into cash without suffering a loss or penalty.

INVESTING TO REDUCE RISK

Good day, ladies
Some private golf clubs still reserve special ladies' days and/or tee-off times for women. Some courses also require Bermuda shorts and socks to be a minimum length and even ban sleeveless shirts. Check the course rules and regulations for play before heading out.

Although there are hundreds of investments to choose from, each will fall into one of the three asset classes: *safety*, *income*, or *growth*. The following graph shows the growth of one dollar invested in the three asset classes over 20 years.

The graph clearly shows that growth investments have performed the best over this time. So why not invest all your money in growth investments? The answer is *risk*. Just when you need your money, the markets could be down. Alternatively, if you invest only in income investments, you are vulnerable to falling interest rates by the time your investments mature. The solution? Aim for a mix of the asset classes in your investment portfolio to reduce your overall risk, while improving your investment return.

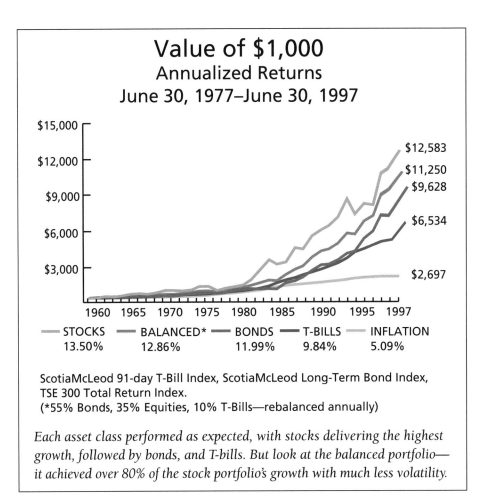

Value of $1,000
Annualized Returns
June 30, 1977–June 30, 1997

ScotiaMcLeod 91-day T-Bill Index, ScotiaMcLeod Long-Term Bond Index,
TSE 300 Total Return Index.
(*55% Bonds, 35% Equities, 10% T-Bills—rebalanced annually)

Each asset class performed as expected, with stocks delivering the highest growth, followed by bonds, and T-bills. But look at the balanced portfolio— it achieved over 80% of the stock portfolio's growth with much less volatility.

HOW DO I PICK THE MOST SUITABLE ASSET MIX?

As an economy expands and contracts, some investments will perform better than others. No matter where we are in the economic cycle, at least one asset class will be performing better than the others. Instead of trying to time the cycle, a sensible solution is to diversify your investments among the options in each asset class.

For instance, a recovering economy will create healthy company profits and rising stock prices in growth investments. A corresponding rise in interest rates will put a damper on bond prices in fixed income investments. We will elaborate on this concept when we discuss investments sold in the fixed income market. Higher interest rates benefit safety investments, but the inflation that often accompanies a recovery could offset returns. This is known as "purchasing power risk."

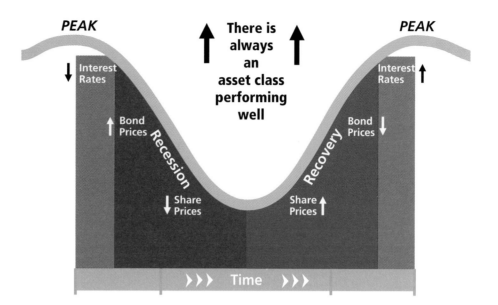

Types of Investments

As mentioned, there are several investment options within each asset class. In this section we look at the main features and benefits of specific products to assist you in making informed investment decisions.

You can purchase an individual investment or a mutual fund. A mutual fund pools the money of many people in order to purchase a number of investments. Professional managers use their expertise to decide which investment to purchase, according to specific objectives.

Depending on the investment or mutual fund you are buying, you can purchase them just about anywhere—through banks, trust companies, financial planners, stockbrokers, insurance companies, or directly from the mutual fund company.

SAFETY ASSET INVESTMENTS

WHAT ARE SAFETY ASSET INVESTMENTS?

The safety class consists of bank accounts, short-term GICs, term deposits, and money market investments. Although available in Canadian dollars, most are also available in U.S. dollars. Minimum investments will apply and they depend on the institution where you purchase them. Safety investments are short-term debt securities (maturing in up to one year) issued by governments, banks, and major companies on the money market. They include federal and provincial government treasury bills, bankers' acceptances, and commercial paper. Compared to stocks and bonds of the same issuer, they carry the lowest risk. However, in exchange for this higher degree of safety, they usually have the lowest return potential.

WHY SHOULD I HAVE SAFETY INVESTMENTS?

Safety investments should be included as part of a well-balanced portfolio. They add stability and liquidity, and help reduce overall risk. They are also ideal for building an emergency fund or saving for short-term goals. Safety investments are considered cash equivalents because they are highly liquid and have very low risk.

Safety investments offer:

- a fixed rate of return
- interest income
- high liquidity
- little risk to your initial investment
- little opportunity for growth
- RRSP- and RRIF-eligibility

HOW DO SAFETY INVESTMENTS WORK?

Unlike GICs or term deposits, other investments available in the money market are normally sold at a discount—less than face value—and mature at face value. The difference between the purchase price and the face value is your interest income. Instead of regular interest payments, you receive all your interest at maturity. For example, you decide to buy a three-month Government of Canada T-bill with a face value of $10,000. You pay the discounted price of $9,942.40. At the end of the three months, you receive the face value of $10,000. The difference—$57.60—is your interest income, which equates to a 2.3% annual yield.

Yield and Price

The yield on a money market investment is quoted as a percentage and is usually slightly higher than interest rates on GICs and term deposits of similar terms. Current interest rates, term to maturity, and credit quality of the issuer all influence yield and market price.

Yields on money market investments will move in tandem with general market interest rates. Corporate investments usually offer higher yields than government investments to compensate investors for the higher possibility of default. Likewise, longer-term investments usually have higher yields than shorter-term investments because there is a longer period during which market prices may fluctuate. (All things being equal, the higher the yield, the lower the market price.)

WHAT KINDS OF MONEY MARKET INVESTMENTS CAN I BUY?

Treasury Bill

A treasury bill is a short-term (less than one year) obligation of the federal or provincial government. Since treasury bills are government-backed, they are considered virtually risk-free if held to maturity. The minimum purchase will vary but is generally $5,000 face value.

Put on your dancin' shoes

Ballroom dancing is enjoying a resurgence. It is a fun way to get fit, meet people, and have a romantic evening out. One hour of ballroom dancing roughly equals walking 27 kilometres.

Bankers' Acceptance

A bankers' acceptance is a short-term (less than one year) obligation of a major corporation that is unconditionally guaranteed ("accepted") by a major chartered bank. The risk is considered to be the same as that of the accepting bank, not that of the original issuing corporation. The minimum purchase is $100,000 face value.

Commercial Paper

Commercial paper is a short-term (less than one year) obligation of a major corporation and is only backed by the financial strength of the issuing corporation. It usually offers the highest yields in the money market. Risk will vary with the issuing corporation. The minimum purchase is $100,000 face value.

Money Market Mutual Funds

Money market funds are a pool of individual safety investments such as T-bills, bankers' acceptance, and commercial paper. Professional managers make the investment decisions and manage the maturities of the investments on your behalf, with an average term to maturity of up to 180 days for the entire portfolio.

In Canada money market funds are managed to maintain a fixed unit price of either $10.00 or $1.00. Interest accrues daily and is normally paid monthly. Yields and interest income are not guaranteed, but vary with current short-term interest rates. Although the mutual fund itself is not guaranteed by the Canada Deposit Insurance Corporation (CDIC) or the Régie de l'assurance-dépots du Québec, the underlying investments may be guaranteed by the issuer. This will depend on the mutual fund and the investments contained in the fund.

Money market funds are highly liquid—they can be bought or sold on any business day.

Ruth is a conservative investor. Her portfolio is invested in low-risk and low-yield investments including: treasury bills, Canada Savings Bonds, and savings accounts. With low interest rates, Ruth is at risk of depleting her capital and outliving her money. For Ruth to be a *Woman In The Know*, we recommend she think about diversifying her investments among all three asset classes so she is protected against market and inflation risk and has the potential to earn higher returns.

FIXED INCOME INVESTMENTS

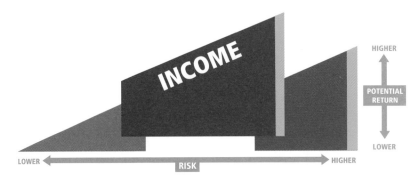

WHAT ARE INCOME INVESTMENTS?

Income investments are sold in fixed income markets and include mortgage-backed securities and government and corporate bonds. Minimum investments typically begin at $5,000 face value for bonds and mortgage-backed securities.

WHY SHOULD I HAVE INCOME INVESTMENTS?

Fixed income investments should be included as part of a well-balanced portfolio. Most offer a regular stream of income over the lifetime of the investment and all have the potential to generate capital gains whenever interest rates move lower (or capital losses when interest rates move higher). They also help reduce overall risk.

> ### Fixed-income investments offer:
>
> - fixed level of interest income
> - terms from one to 30 years
> - higher yields than safety investments
> - low to moderate risk if held to maturity
> - potential for capital gains or losses if sold prior to maturity
> - RRSP- and RRIF-eligibility

HOW DO FIXED INCOME INVESTMENTS WORK?

Fixed income investments are really nothing more than formal IOUs from the issuer, either governments or corporations. In exchange for the use of your money, the issuer promises to return the face value of your investment by a certain date and pay you regular interest, usually semi-annually but sometimes monthly.

Many fixed income investments are issued and mature at face value, but are bought and sold at current market value. The amount of interest you receive is simply the interest ("coupon") rate times the face value of your bond. For example, a $10,000 face-value bond with a coupon rate of 7% pays $700 a year in interest.

Between the issue date and the maturity date, the market price of the investment can fluctuate. If you are planning to hold your investment to maturity, price changes don't matter—you are likely interested in receiving the regular interest income. Price changes only matter if you decide to sell your investment before it matures. Since market prices can change, you could realize a capital gain or loss if you sell your investment before maturity. (Remember, a capital gain or loss is simply the difference between the price you pay for an investment and the price at which you sell it.)

Fixed income investments will carry more risk than money market investments from the same issuer because your money is on loan for a longer period. However, they will normally also offer higher returns.

WHY DO PRICES CHANGE?

The current market price reflects:

- current interest rates
- term to maturity
- credit quality of the issuer

A fixed income investment may sell for more than its face value (at a premium) or less than its face value (at a discount).

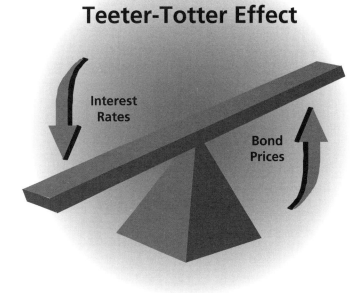

Teeter-Totter Effect

Current Interest Rates

The value of a fixed income investment will rise and fall in the opposite direction of current interest rates. Think of it as a teeter-totter, with prices at one end and interest rates at the other. When interest rates rise, prices fall. When interest rates fall, prices rise. For example, a bond purchased a year ago paying 7% interest is less attractive to investors if current interest rates are 9%. To attract buyers the bond will have to fall in price. If you sell the bond prior to maturity, you will receive less than you paid for it. However, if current interest rates fall to 5%, your bond paying 7% is that much more valuable. If you sell it before maturity, you will receive more than you paid. Remember, though, if you hold your bond to maturity, you will always receive the face value.

Term to Maturity

The prices of fixed income investments don't move up and down in lock step with interest rates. Price is also linked to the maturity date. Picture the teeter-totter again, this time with long-term bonds at one end, short-term bonds near the middle, and interest rates at the other end.

For a given movement in interest rates, prices of longer-term investments will tend to fluctuate more than prices of shorter-term investments. Again, this is the result of a longer period during which prices may fluctuate. However, to compensate investors, longer-term investments will normally offer higher returns.

Credit Quality of the Issuer

Prices are also influenced by the financial strength and stability of the issuer. Will the issuer be able to pay interest on schedule and return the principal as promised? Or is there a chance of default? Investments issued by the federal government have virtually no credit risk, since the Canadian treasury is unlikely to default on a loan. For corporations, however, insolvency is not inconceivable.

As a rule, corporate investments offer higher yields than government investments because of the possibility of default. Credit ratings among corporations can vary widely. Independent agencies like the Dominion Bond Rating Service (DBRS) and Canada Bond Rating Service (CBRS) regularly review corporate debt issues and rate their risk, providing valuable assistance to investors. When purchasing the investment be sure to ask what kind of rating has been given to the corporate or government investment.

WHAT KINDS OF FIXED INCOME MARKET INVESTMENTS CAN I BUY?

A wide variety of fixed income investments are available. Here we highlight some common ones that appeal to new and experienced investors alike.

Government Bonds
Government of Canada Bonds

Government of Canada bonds are fully guaranteed by the federal government for terms of one to 30 years. They are considered to be the safest Canadian fixed income investment with a term over one year you can buy—even safer than GICs or term deposits. Because they offer such a high degree of security and liquidity, Government of Canada bonds often have lower yields than other bonds. They generally pay interest semi-annually until maturity, when the face value is repaid. The minimum investment is usually $5,000 face value.

Provincial and Municipal Bonds

Provincial and municipal bonds are fully guaranteed by the issuing provincial government or municipality for terms of one to 30 years. Credit quality varies by the issuer, but in some cases the risk is considered only marginally higher than Government of Canada bonds. They generally pay interest semi-annually until maturity, when the face value is repaid. The minimum investment is $5,000 face value.

Did you know?

Canada Savings Bonds (CSBs) and provincial savings bonds are really savings certificates that have characteristics more like GICs than bonds. Currently sold each fall, CSBs are issued by the federal government and pay a fixed rate of interest. The initial price (market price) never changes, and you receive that same amount (face value) at maturity. Maturities vary by series and currently range from 10 to 12 years. They are also RRSP- and RRIF-eligible.

CSBs are redeemable at any time, but no interest is paid if you cash them within the first three months. Since interest is paid only at month end, try to cash them at the beginning of a month.

There are two types of CSBs: regular interest and compound interest. Regular interest CSBs pay interest annually by cheque or direct deposit to your bank account. Compound interest CSBs don't provide annual interest payments. Instead, interest accumulates until the bond is cashed or matures.

If you hold compound CSBs outside a registered account, you must report the accrued interest each year, even though you don't actually receive the interest until maturity.

GICs and Term Deposits

Unlike bonds, you always purchase GICs and term deposits at face value. Although GICs and term deposits are considered fixed income investments, you can't resell them to another investor. Therefore, you do not have the potential to generate capital gains and, conversely, are immune to any capital losses.

Term deposits usually have a lower interest rate than GICs because you can cash them in before maturity. Most GICs, on the other hand, are locked in for the full term. If you want to cash in a GIC early, you may have to pay a penalty or sell it back to your financial institution at current market value or up to face value, which could be less than what you paid. For this reason GICs should be "buy and hold" investments.

Strips

A bond has two components: the principal, which is repaid at maturity, and the interest coupons, which represent your right to receive fixed interest payments. Strips are created when the individual interest coupons are separated from the principal ("residual"). The coupons and the residual are then sold as separate investments.

Strips are commonly created from federal and provincial government bonds. They are always sold at a discount to mature at face value. The longer the term to maturity, the deeper the discount. The difference between the discounted purchase price and the face value is your interest income. The usual minimum investment for a stripped bond is $5,000 at maturity.

With strips you don't receive regular fixed interest payments the way you do with ordinary bonds. This is because the interest is compounding and isn't paid until maturity. Strips usually have higher yields than regular bonds with similar terms and credit quality. Their prices, however, are more sensitive to interest rate movements.

You can buy strips in various denominations and maturity dates, which allows you to structure your portfolio to suit your needs. They are ideal for registered retirement plans since the interest income earned remains tax-sheltered until withdrawn. If you hold strips outside of a registered plan, interest must be reported annually and tax paid at your marginal tax rate even though you don't receive the interest until maturity.

Mortgage-Backed Securities

Mortgage-backed securities (MBSs) represent a proportionate share in a pool of mortgages insured by the Canada Mortgage and Housing Corporation (CMHC). Unlike most government bonds, which pay semi-annual interest, MBSs provide monthly payments that are a blend of the principal and interest accruing from the pool of mortgages. These investments also require a minimum $5,000 investment, face value.

Although the amount you receive at maturity is reduced by the interim principal payments, your monthly income is that much higher. For instance, in addition to monthly payments, you can normally expect to receive 94% to 98% of the face value at maturity because of these interim principal payments.

Income Mutual Funds

Income funds invest in a pool of fixed income securities. Rather than deciding which investment to buy and what term to select, you can choose a single fund that matches your financial goals and risk tolerance. Choices range from mortgage funds and government bond funds for more conservative investors to corporate or global bond funds for more aggressive investors.

For the birds

Whether you do it from your kitchen window or on day-long hikes, bird-watching—or "birding" as true enthusiasts call it—is a fun way to get back to nature and relax. You can encourage bird activity in your own backyard by setting out some water and seed.

Income funds usually pay interest monthly or quarterly, which is advantageous to retirees interested in receiving income more often than just once or twice a year. The income will vary according to the amount of interest paid by the investments in the portfolio. Unlike individual investments, income funds don't offer a fixed rate of return and don't have a maturity date. Instead, the fund managers buy and sell fixed income investments to maintain an average term to maturity in the portfolio.

It's important to recognize that although some or all of the investments held in an income fund may be guaranteed by the federal government, the mutual fund itself is *not* guaranteed. This is because you hold units of the fund, not the investments themselves.

Like the underlying securities, the value of an income fund will fluctuate with interest rates. Although rising interest rates will cause unit prices to fall, they also increase the potential for higher income as individual investments mature and are reinvested at the higher rates.

GROWTH INVESTMENTS

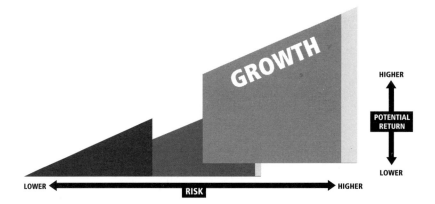

WHAT ARE GROWTH INVESTMENTS?

Growth investments are company stocks purchased in the equity markets. When a company initially issues stock, the investors supply the company with money to finance operations by buying this initial offering. These investors become part owners of the company or shareholders. In this section we introduce you to the stock market and how it works.

WHY SHOULD I HAVE GROWTH INVESTMENTS?

Growth investments should be included as part of a well-balanced portfolio because they add the potential for higher returns. This growth potential helps you build wealth faster and protects your portfolio against a loss of purchasing power caused by inflation. However, to achieve higher returns, you will have to accept more risk.

By the book

More and more women are discovering the joys of book-reading clubs. They're a great way to become well read, discuss literature, and socialize with friends old and new. Many bookstores offer step-by-step start-up instructions; some even host their own clubs.

> **Growth investments offer:**
>
> - high potential for capital growth
> - higher risk than other assets
> - moderate income in the form of dividends
> - a hedge against inflation
> - RRSP- and RRIF-eligibility

HOW DO GROWTH INVESTMENTS WORK?

There are two types of companies: public and private. The shares, or stock, of public companies trade on regulated stock exchanges; the financial results of these companies are available to the public. The shares of private companies don't trade on an exchange and are held by a small group of investors. Our focus will be on shares of public companies.

Once the shares of a public company are issued, they trade freely at prices dictated by supply and demand. Although a company gets no money for the shares beyond the initial offering, open trading can create greater awareness of the company and enhance its credibility.

A share issue provides a company with necessary cash, but management gives up a certain amount of control by allowing shareholders a say in how the company is run. For example, each common share is generally entitled to one vote in the election of company directors at annual meetings and on special issues such as mergers.

Why Buy Stock?

People buy stock for two reasons: higher return potential and preferential tax treatment of capital gains and dividends. Few investments have greater potential for appreciation than stocks. (Remember, a capital gain or loss is simply the difference between the price you pay for an investment and the price at which you sell it.) Dividends are paid out of company profits.

Since investors don't like uncertainty, they prefer companies with steady earnings growth and consistent or rising dividends over the years. This is viewed as a sign of a financially sound company able to weather economic downturns. As well as the potential for above-average returns, shareholders enjoy the added benefit of favourable tax treatment for capital gains and dividend income.

Historically, stocks have provided a greater potential for capital gains over the long term than any other investments. Because of their high returns, stocks are an excellent hedge against inflation over time. However, they also experience more ups and downs along the way.

Buying and Selling Stocks

Buying and selling stocks works much like an auction. When there is a limited number of sellers, buyers try to outbid one another until the shares are sold to the highest bidder. This is basically how share prices rise. When the same process works in reverse, share prices fall. The price of a stock is ultimately based on what buyers and sellers think it's worth at a given time.

The *bid price* is the price a buyer is willing to pay for a stock, while the *ask price* is the price the seller wants for it. Stocks are usually traded in *board lots*. A board lot of shares priced between $1 and $100 is 100 shares. For a stock trading at $10, you will pay $1,000 plus commission to buy a board lot. Shares not sold in board lots are called *odd lots*. You should avoid odd lots because commissions are generally higher and they can be harder to sell.

To buy and sell stock you will need to open an account with a broker. To place orders, you call your broker with instructions on how many shares of which stock to buy or sell and at what price. Your broker receives a commission for every order you complete. The commission is usually based on the size of the order. You receive a confirmation when your order is completed.

Marie has a bit more disposable income now that she's back at work. She has been thinking about getting into the stock market, but was wondering what type of brokerage firm would best suit her needs. Marie has the option of dealing with a discount broker, where Marie will make her own investment decisions and pay less commission. Or she can deal with a full-service broker, who will give her advice on which stocks to purchase but will charge a higher commission. Marie needs to assess how comfortable she is with making her own investment decisions before she can determine which type of broker is best suited for her.

Are your shoes made for walking?

Walking is one of the best fitness activities—it's low impact and can be aerobic if you quicken the pace. To participate, all you need is a good pair of walking shoes. Opt for treaded rubber-soled shoes that will absorb the impact as you walk and protect you from slipping.

WHAT KINDS OF EQUITY MARKET INVESTMENTS CAN I BUY?

There are two basic types of stock: common and preferred.

Common Stock

Common stock represents part ownership in a company. Common shareholders have voting rights but rank behind creditors, bondholders, and preferred shareholders for payment should the company fail.

Dividends are paid at the discretion of the company's board of directors. The board may decide to reinvest some or all of the profits in the company. It may decide not to pay any dividends at all if the company is not performing well, or it may raise or lower dividends as it sees fit.

Types of Common Stock

Common stock is often classified according to the characteristics of the underlying company.

Blue Chip Stocks

Blue chips are stocks of large reputable companies with a long history of profitability and regular dividend payments. Examples are chartered banks and utilities. For these reasons blue chips often form the foundation of a stock portfolio and are often used by retired investors seeking a regular income.

Growth Stocks

Growth stocks have above-average potential for growth and are expected to sustain this growth over a relatively long period. They offer greater capital gains potential, but pay little or no dividends because earnings are usually put back into operations.

Value Stocks

These are stocks of fundamentally strong companies, whose value is considered to be underestimated by the stock market. Value companies may be currently out of favour and selling at bargain prices, but are thought to have good potential to increase in value over time. However, they may be considered more volatile than blue chip or growth stocks.

Small-, Mid-, and Large-Cap Stocks

A company's market capitalization is the number of shares outstanding multiplied by the share price. In the Canadian market a small-capitalization, or "small cap," company has a market capitalization of less than $400 million. Mid-cap companies have a market capitalization of $400 million to $1 billion, while large-cap companies have a market capitalization greater than $1 billion. Smaller companies offer high growth potential but are somewhat riskier than larger companies because they are not as well established and have less capital to draw on.

Preferred Stock

Like common shareholders, preferred shareholders are part owners of a company. However, preferred shareholders rank ahead of common shareholders when it comes to dividend payments and claims on the company's assets. Preferred shares have a fixed dividend, which may be presented as a dollar amount or a percentage of the face value of the share. This makes preferred shares a popular choice among retirees, because they can take advantage of the regular dividend payments and maximize their after-tax income through the dividend tax credit. The trade-off is that dividends paid to preferred shareholders generally don't rise when the company prospers, and preferred shareholders usually don't have voting rights.

Where do I buy stocks?

Stocks are bought and sold on either a physical exchange or via the electronic over-the-counter market. Stock exchanges are private non-profit organizations made up of "member firms," or brokerage houses. The two most common stock exchanges to Canadian investors are the Toronto Stock Exchange (TSE) and the New York Stock Exchange (NYSE).

Indexes

An index is a broad representation of a market and is considered the benchmark for the performance of that market. Well-known stock market indexes include:

TSE 300 Total Return Index
The TSE 300 is the bellwether index for the Canadian stock market. It consists of 300 representative Canadian companies listed on the TSE.

Dow Jones Industrial Average
The world's best-known stock index is the Dow Jones Industrial Average. It is a weighted average of 30 industrial stocks that trade on the NYSE.

Standard & Poor's (S&P) 500 Stock Price Index
The S&P 500 consists of 400 industrial stocks and 100 utility, financial, and transportation stocks, most of which trade on the NYSE.

Equity Mutual Funds

Equity mutual funds are also referred to as growth or stock funds because they invest in a pool of stocks. Depending on its objective, an equity mutual fund might invest in many industries or regions, or focus on a single industry or country. Some are designed to mirror a benchmark index like the TSE 300 Total Return Index. The prices of these growth funds fluctuate with the stock market and general economic conditions.

MORE ABOUT MUTUAL FUNDS

We've already briefly discussed mutual funds in terms of the three asset classes. Given the significant growth of the number of mutual funds in the past decade and because of the benefits they provide you as an investment choice, we will go into greater detail about

- how they work,
- the benefits,
- what to buy,
- how to choose one, and
- associated costs.

HOW DO MUTUAL FUNDS WORK?

When you buy units of a mutual fund, you become a part owner of all the investments held in that fund. You receive your proportionate share of any interest, dividends, capital gains, and foreign income the fund earns. In addition, by claiming foreign tax credits, you may also be eligible to recover your proportionate share of any foreign taxes paid by the fund. Units of a mutual fund can be bought and sold on any business day at the current market price, or "net asset value". The net asset value is calculated at the end of each business day. Fund expenses are deducted from the closing market value of all the investments in the portfolio. The result is then divided by the number of units outstanding. Except for money market funds, which have a fixed unit price, the unit price will fluctuate daily according to changes in the value of the individual investments.

Retired and Wired

If you have a home computer, all you need to do is buy a modem to get connected to the Internet. Many seniors find e-mail an excellent way to keep in touch with old friends from work, and it's much cheaper to post e-mail messages than to talk long-distance.

NET ASSET VALUE CALCULATION

Closing market value of fund assets	$1,000,000
Less: Fund expenses	$20,000
	$980,000
Divided by: Number of units outstanding	100,000
Equals: Net Asset Value	$9.80

WHAT ARE THE BENEFITS OF MUTUAL FUNDS?

- **Convenience.** Buying and selling mutual funds can be as easy as speaking with a registered mutual fund representative at your local bank branch or calling your financial planner or broker. Regular account statements and reports simplify your record-keeping.
- **Professional Management.** Few people have the time or resources to stay on top of financial trends and evaluate individual stocks and bonds. Professional money managers make the investment decision to ensure that the fund achieves its objectives.
- **Affordability.** Minimum investments can be as low as $25 per fund if you make regular purchases through a pre-authorized chequing plan. The amount you select is transferred directly from your bank account at regular intervals—weekly, monthly, every payday, etc.—and is invested in your selected mutual fund(s). For retirees who are budgeting for certain goals, this is an excellent strategy.
- **Flexibility.** Most funds are part of a group, or "family", of funds and, as such, give you the flexibility to move some or all of your money from one fund to another as your needs change or new opportunities arise.

- **Diversification.** A basic principle of sound investing is to spread your portfolio over a range of investments. This risk-reduction technique reduces the impact that one poor choice can have on your portfolio. Mutual funds typically hold around 50 to 100 different securities. Most investors would find it difficult and expensive to assemble a portfolio of that size.
- **RRSP- or RRIF-eligibility.** Mutual funds are an excellent way to take advantage of the benefits of tax-deferred investing through RRSPs. Most domestic funds are 100% RRSP- or RRIF-eligible, while most global funds are eligible for the 20% foreign content limit.
- **Regular Income.** Income from bonds is generally paid semi-annually; dividends from stocks are generally distributed quarterly. When these investments are held in a mutual fund, which comprises such a diversified portfolio, the income can be distributed monthly or quarterly, providing a more regular stream of income.

Marie and her husband, John, are setting up a regular savings program to help their children finance future weddings and accumulate downpayments for their first homes. As this is still several years away, Marie and John could consider a well-diversified mutual fund portfolio for their savings program. Mutual funds will give Marie and John the diversification and growth potential for their savings to accumulate over time. By establishing a pre-authorized purchase plan, they will benefit from dollar-cost averaging. A little forward thinking and investment in mutual funds will go a long way towards assisting their children's future needs.

WHAT KINDS OF MUTUAL FUNDS CAN I BUY?

Money Market Mutual Funds are funds with investments in money market securities (safety asset class), such as T-bills, commercial paper, and bankers' acceptance. They offer security to retirees who want a solid investment base.

Income Mutual Funds invest in fixed income market securities (income asset class), such as government bonds or mortgage-backed securities. They offer a regular income stream to retirees.

Growth Mutual Funds invest in stock (growth asset class). They offer high growth potential and help retirees protect their income from inflation.

Surf the Web

There are several websites that deal specifically with seniors' concerns, such as the Canadian Association of Retired Persons (CARP) (http://www.fifty-plus.net). Try your neighbourhood library or your local high school for Internet orientation sessions.

Some mutual funds are not purely defined by their asset class. They include:

- **balanced funds**, which invest in a mix of stocks, bonds, and money market investments. Fund managers adjust the asset mix according to market and economic conditions. This one-stop-shopping approach to investing is ideal for retirees who don't have time to oversee their portfolio mix.
- **global funds**, which invest in the money markets, bonds, or stocks of foreign countries. Funds can be invested in one country or region, or a group of countries. These offer both higher growth and risk potential, particularly in emerging markets such as Southeast Asia and Latin America. Global funds keep your portfolio diversified beyond the borders of Canada.

HOW DO I CHOOSE?

There are so many funds and fund companies competing for your investment dollar that deciding between them can be challenging. In mutual fund investing, performance and volatility will depend on market trends, the nature of the investments held by the fund, and the management style. Except for money market funds, which have a fixed unit price, the net asset value of a mutual fund will fluctuate according to market conditions. Consider the following when deciding which mutual funds to buy:

Track Record. All funds are subject to short-term market risk and can fluctuate from month to month or year to year. Go back at least three to five years and look at the average percentage return, then compare it with those of other similar funds. A good-quality fund, under the direction of a skilled fund manager, should have competitive performance returns when compared with its peers, regardless of the market fluctuation. But remember, while this gives you an idea of a fund's success, it's not a surefire guarantee of the fund's future performance.

Prospectus. A prospectus is a formal legal document that provides key information you should read before purchasing a mutual fund. The fund's objectives, fees, and performance history can all be found in the prospectus.

WHAT ARE THE ASSOCIATED COSTS OF MUTUAL FUNDS?

Equally important as fund performance are the associated costs of investing. The two main types of expenses are fund expenses and sales commissions, and these may figure prominently in your decision.

- **Fund expenses** include management fees and other operating costs that are paid directly from a fund's assets. All mutual funds pay a management fee to their fund managers. This fee is calculated daily as a percentage of net assets and can often vary between 0.25% and 3.5%. In general, the more complex the fund, the higher the management fee. Money market funds tend to have the lowest management fees, while global funds tend to have the highest. The management fees, together with the fund's operating expenses—legal, auditing, and administration fees—make up the management expense ratio (MER). The MER is the best measure of total costs when you are comparing funds.

  In addition, it is important to remember that management expenses are paid directly by the fund before the average percentage return is calculated.

- **Sales commissions**, or "loads", are what investors pay the mutual fund company when they purchase or sell their mutual fund units. This commission, or load, is used to compensate the salesperson, often an independent broker or financial planner, for assisting the investor with their investment decisions. If the commission is collected when you purchase the units of the fund, it is referred to as "front-end load". If collected when you sell the units, it is referred to as "back-end load". Another type of load, fairly new to the mutual fund industry, is the "level load." With a level load no sales fee is charged at the time of purchase or redemption. Instead, the sales charge is applied on a daily basis in the same way as a management fee. You can also buy a mutual fund and pay no sales commission. These funds are called "no-load" funds. Most no-load funds are sold through banks and trust companies, although a few independent firms sell them, as well.

How Loads Work

Because there are so many variations, you should always review the fund's prospectus and ask the fund company or your mutual fund sales representative to explain your options before you invest.

No load. With no-load funds, you do not pay a sales charge to buy, sell, or own the fund. A $1,000 investment goes to work right away with the entire $1,000. In addition, at the time of redemption no sales charge is applied.

Front-end load. Say you put $1,000 in a fund and pay a front-end load of 4%; then $40 goes to the salesperson and $960 is invested in the fund.

Back-end load/Deferred sales charge. With a back-end load fund all your money is invested when you buy the fund, but you are charged a redemption fee if you sell your units within a certain time period (often six to eight years). Depending on the fund family, the fee is either based on the market value of your redemption or calculated according to the cost (or book value) of your original investment on a declining percentage basis, depending on the number of years you have owned the fund.

Level Load. If you invested $1,000 in a level load fund with a sales charge of 1%, then $0.03/day or $10/year goes to the salesperson for as long as you continue to hold the fund. For further details on a particular fund's deferred sales charges, check the fund's prospectus.

ASSESSING YOUR POST-RETIREMENT INCOME SOURCES

Throughout your career you have probably accumulated retirement funds in the three previously mentioned sources: government benefits, company pension, and personal savings. If you've made your career working at home and you are married, you will probably be sharing some of your spouse's retirement funds. In either case, as you approach and enter retirement, managing these funds requires a new level of understanding and involvement. Regarding your government benefits, you need to determine if you are eligible to receive these benefits, and when you should elect to receive them, taking into account how the timing fits into your overall income needs. Your company pension will be received according to the rules of your particular plan; however, knowing when and how much you will receive is critical to effective retirement income planning. Lastly, the most active role you will play is in managing your personal savings, with an emphasis on maximizing the benefits of your Registered Retirement Savings Plan (RRSP).

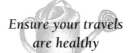

Ensure your travels are healthy

A big factor in your decision to travel or live abroad in retirement will be the cost of travel health insurance. Premiums go up as you get older, and it is likely you will no longer have an employee benefits package to cover insurance. If you're travelling with a pre-existing condition, make sure you're up front about it with your insurance broker.

On retirement you may discover you do not need your RRSP funds immediately to pay your bills. In that case you can leave your plan intact and continue to allow your funds to accumulate tax-deferred until the end of the calendar year in which you turn 69. You may also discover that your RRSP will be a valuable source of income to fill the gap or shortfall that exists between your income needs and your available income sources. We will review some important strategies in the next section that will help you maximize all sources of your retirement income.

Regardless of your situation, by the end of the calendar year in which you turn 69, you are required to convert your RRSP funds into one or more retirement income options. There are three ways to do this:

- transfer your RRSP to a Registered Retirement Income Fund (RRIF);
- buy an annuity; or
- withdraw the lump sum from your RRSP (subject to withholding tax).

In this section we will explore the features and facts of your post-retirement income options.

Registered Retirement Income Fund

WHAT IS IT?

A Registered Retirement Income Fund (RRIF) is a natural extension of an RRSP and is governed by similar investment rules. A RRIF is a plan that converts the investments held in your RRSP into an income stream. You will be required to withdraw a minimum amount of money from the plan each year. There is no maximum amount. Because it is registered, your investments continue to grow tax-deferred. However, the money you withdraw from the fund must be reported as income and is taxed at your marginal tax rate. There is no withholding tax deducted on the minimum mandatory withdrawal, but amounts withdrawn from a RRIF in excess of the minimum amount are subject to withholding tax based on the same rates that are applicable to RRSP lump sum withdrawals.

Withholding tax rates (as at 1997)		
Withdrawal	**All provinces (except Que.)**	**Quebec***
up to $5,000	10%	21%
over $5,000 and up to $15,000	20%	30%
over $15,000	30%	35%

*The 1997 Quebec budget proposes that these rates increase, effective January 1, 1998, to 25%, 33%, and 38% respectively.

WHAT IS THE MINIMUM PAYMENT?

The annual minimum withdrawal is set by the federal government according to your age. It is based on a percentage of the market value of your RRIF at the beginning of the calendar year. The percentage for each year is determined by your age as of January 1 of that year, and increases as you get older. RRIF payments must start by the end of the year after you open the RRIF.

From the table below you can determine your RRIF annual minimum payment for the upcoming year, multiply the value of your RRIF plan at the beginning of the calendar year by the appropriate percentage that corresponds to your age as of January 1 of that year.

RRIF Annual Minimum Payment (AMP)	
Age (as of Jan 1)	**RRIF opened in 1993 and after**
	Percentage of market value
under 68	$1/(90 - \text{age})$
68	4.55%
69	4.76
70	5.00
71	7.38
72	7.48
73	7.59
74	7.71
75	7.85
76	7.99
77	8.15
78	8.33
79	8.53
80	8.75
81	8.99
82	9.27
83	9.58
84	9.93
85	10.33
86	10.79
87	11.33
88	11.96
89	12.71
90	13.62
91	14.73
92	16.12
93	17.92
94+	20.00

Ruth would like to convert her personal RRSP into a retirement income option. If she goes the route of a RRIF, she wonders what the annual minimum withdrawal payment would be when she's 69. At that age she estimates her RRIF would be worth about $100,000.

Her annual minimum payment would be: $100,000 x 4.76% = $4,760.

She could arrange to have this amount paid directly to her bank account monthly, quarterly, semi-annually, etc., according to her specific needs.

WHAT ARE THE FEATURES OF A RRIF?

RRIFs offer flexibility. You can withdraw as much income as you need as long as you meet the required annual minimum payment. You decide how often you receive this income (monthly, quarterly, semi-annually, or annually) and it can be automatically deposited into your bank account. You can change this schedule, withdraw extra amounts at any time (subject to the terms of the investments you choose), or withdraw all your funds and close your RRIF at any time.

Depending on where your plan is held, RRIFs also offer a wide variety of investment opportunities that fall within the three asset classes. This flexibility allows you to continue to diversify your portfolio, rebalancing your investments between the safety, income, and growth asset classes. And just like in your RRSP, you should continue to take advantage of the 20% foreign content rule.

WHAT IS A MANAGED RRIF?

By the time your retirement approaches, you may have accumulated a substantial amount of money in retirement savings. Managing these savings effectively to meet your goals can sometimes be a complex, time-consuming experience. You might want to seek the services of a professional to either help you manage your portfolio or manage it entirely for you. Some financial institutions are providing this service for an annual fee, usually 1%, based on a percentage of your total portfolio. They may also prepare a tax-reporting package and might even pay your bills if you go on an extended holiday.

WHAT IF I HAVE A SPOUSAL RRSP?

If your spouse has been contributing to an RRSP in your name, or vice versa, the RRSP must be transferred to a spousal RRIF when the planholder turns 69. With respect to the minimum RRIF withdrawal amounts, a spousal RRIF is governed by the same rules as a personal RRIF.

On your mark ... get set ... relax!
If you've been constantly on the go, adjusting your pace may be a challenge. Learning to relax comes more easily to some than others. Deep-breathing exercises are an easy technique to help you slow down, as they deliberately slow your heart rate.

WHAT ARE THE ADDITIONAL TAX IMPLICATIONS OF A SPOUSAL RRIF?

Minimum spousal RRIF payments will always be taxed in the hands of the planholder. Withdrawals made over the minimum amount will be taxed in the planholder's hands except when contributions made to the spousal RRSP were made within the previous three years. In this case the amount above the minimum RRIF payment will be taxed in the *contributor's* hands. This is known as Revenue Canada's "Three-Year Attribution Rule".

WHAT IF I HAVE A LOCKED-IN RRSP?

As we've mentioned previously, you may have a locked-in RRSP if you transferred vested company pension proceeds when leaving an employer prior to retirement. These funds cannot be accessed until you reach a certain age, depending on your provincial or federal pension legislation. Ask your former employer or consult your pension agreement for details of the age requirement. We will highlight some of your options here, but for further details contact your provincial or federal pension regulator.

Money invested in a Locked-In RRSP, also known as a Locked-In Retirement Account (LIRA), can only be converted to a Life Income Fund (LIF), Locked-In Retirement Income Fund (LRIF), or a Life Annuity. This decision must be made by the end of the year in which you turn 69.

LIFE INCOME FUND (LIF)

A LIF is similar to a RRIF in that you have flexibility in selecting either individual investments or mutual funds from the three asset classes. The annual minimum payment is calculated exactly the same as the RRIF annual minimum payment. The remaining funds continue to be tax-deferred as long as they remain in the plan. However, unlike a RRIF, there is a maximum payment amount. The maximum yearly payment is in place to ensure that sufficient funds remain to purchase a life annuity with the remaining proceeds when you reach 80. A LIF must be converted to a life annuity at that time.

LOCKED-IN RETIREMENT INCOME FUND (LRIF)

The LRIF is available only in Alberta and Saskatchewan, and it is similar to a LIF with one exception: there is no requirement to convert the LRIF to a life annuity at age 80.

Annuities

WHAT IS AN ANNUITY?

An annuity is a contract between you and a financial institution wherein you (the annuity holder) will receive a stream of fixed amount payments in exchange for the payment of a sum of money. You can elect to receive the payments either monthly or annually for the rest of your life or for a specified term. There are three main types of annuities:

- A **Fixed Term Annuity**, which can be registered or non-registered, provides you with a guaranteed income for a specified number of years, and in the case of registered plans, not exceeding the age of 90. If you die before the term of your contract, your estate will receive the unpaid balance.
- A **Straight Life Annuity** provides you with income for the rest of your life and can only be purchased through a life insurance company. This type of annuity provides the most income per dollar purchased. However, no further payments are made to your estate or beneficiaries after you die. This type of annuity is more common among single people. If you are married and want to purchase this type of annuity, you must sign a waiver with the life insurance company.
- A **Joint and Last Survivor Annuity**, another insurance product, continues to provide payments after the death of the first spouse and stops on the death of the second, with no funds paid to the second person's estate. This type of annuity is for married couples.

Ruth's husband died last year. Fortunately, her husband (who was a professor) was a member of a pension plan and Ruth receives a survivor's benefit. Now that she is retired, without an incoming salary, she needs an additional source of retirement income. Ruth was a beneficiary of her husband's life insurance policy and upon his death received a $200,000 lump sum payment. For Ruth to be a *Woman In The Know*, she should consider purchasing an annuity with the proceeds of the insurance benefits to provide her with a regular stream of retirement income. The type of annuity selected will determine the amount of income received during her lifetime, and will also depend on whether or not she wants to leave any balance of the annuity to her estate or beneficiaries.

WHAT IS THE MINIMUM PAYMENT?

Revenue Canada does not regulate minimum or maximum withdrawals. However, your contract with the financial institution will determine the size and frequency of payments, based on the amount you pay for the contract, current interest rates, and the term of the annuity. For life annuities, age and sex are also factors, as mortality rates are used.

WHAT ARE THE FEATURES OF AN ANNUITY?

Once you've purchased an annuity, there are no ongoing decisions to make. You receive a regular stream of income for the term of the annuity (or for life). But it's important to be aware that annuities are less flexible than RRIFs. Once an annuity is purchased, it's irreversible. You give your payment in exchange for a contract that gives you specified periodic income payments. The size of the payments will be set based on the type of annuity purchased and interest rate at the time of purchase. Inflation levels will affect the purchasing power of your guaranteed income, and you will no longer have a fund of money to access in the event of an emergency.

Get a physical

On retirement, resolve to see your health care provider. A full assessment will establish a baseline for your health status. Also, it may help identify any other risk factors of which you were unaware, such as your lifestyle and history of diseases in your family.

How do I choose between a RRIF and an annuity?

You've read all about RRIFs and annuities. Now how do you choose between the two? Look at the checklist below and tick off points that apply to you. If you have checkmarks in both lists, you may find a combination of the two options best suits your needs.

RRIF Checklist:
- I am not concerned solely with having a guaranteed payment and am willing to take some risk to achieve some investment growth.
- My income needs may vary, so I want the flexibility to change my payment schedule and make extra withdrawals as needed.
- I want to stay involved in the investment decisions for my savings.
- I'm concerned about what inflation will do to my income.
- I want to defer taxes on my retirement assets for as long as possible.
- I want to ensure any unused retirement funds will go to my estate.

Annuity Checklist:
- I want a fixed income that's guaranteed for the rest of my life (or a specific term).
- I want to eliminate investments and interest risk, and lock in my investment at current interest rates.
- I don't want to make investment decisions or manage my investments.
- I'm not very concerned about leaving unused retirement funds to my estate.
- I am prepared to purchase a guaranteed income with my retirement funds, knowing that I will only be entitled to receive the income described in the contract.

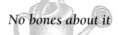

No bones about it

As we age, we may be prone to a loss of bone density, a condition known as osteoporosis. Research shows that weight-bearing exercise like walking, low-impact aerobics, and dancing can have a positive effect on bone loss by slowing down the rate of depletion.

Did you know?

An elderly woman who lived in a desirable apartment in France signed over the lease to a man who would pay her an annuity of about $10,000 a year until her death, at which time he would get the apartment. The man died at the age of 77, after paying the woman more than $180,000, double the apartment's market value. His family was legally obliged to continue payments after his death until the woman died one year later—at the age of 122. Talk about a successful retirement plan!

Collapse Your RRSP

When you collapse your RRSP and withdraw the proceeds in cash, you pay tax on the full amount at your marginal tax rate, and withholding taxes will apply when funds are withdrawn. If you then invest the proceeds, you will have to pay tax on any income you earn. For this reason this is the least-favoured alternative, because you must report the redeemed amount as income at tax-filing time and the amount will be fully taxable. If you don't need the money right away, consider a RRIF or an annuity.

STRATEGIES TO MAXIMIZE YOUR RETIREMENT INCOME

As you tend to your retirement garden, there are several strategies you can adopt before and during your retirement to make your garden as beautiful as possible, whether it's a tiny container garden or your entire backyard. The same goes for retirement investing. Now that you have an understanding of how investing works and your options for creating a post-retirement income stream, you're ready to combine these two key aspects of your retirement plan. The goal is to fund the retirement lifestyle of your dreams by maximizing your retirement income. Here are some strategies:

- Minimize your taxes.
- Diversify your assets.
- Take advantage of dollar-cost averaging.
- Build an investment ladder.
- Create income through dividends.
- Buy and hold.
- Consolidate your investments.
- Use non-registered assets first.

Minimize Your Taxes

You pay taxes based on your *marginal tax rate*, which is the rate of tax you pay on your last, or "highest," dollar of income. Our tax system is called a progressive tax system because, as your income rises, so does your tax rate. Therefore, you pay more tax on your last dollar of earnings than on your first. By reducing your taxable income, you can lower your marginal tax rate and save on taxes. Federal tax rates are the same across the country, but provincial tax rates vary widely. High-income earners are charged federal and provincial surtaxes in addition to the basic taxes.

PLAN YOUR INVESTMENTS ACCORDING TO THE TAX CONSEQUENCES

As noted earlier, investment income earned through interest, dividends, or capital gains will affect your taxable income. It is important to learn how each type of income is taxed in order to apply effective tax planning strategies to maximize income.

HOW IS MY INVESTMENT INCOME TAXED?

If you invest your money in a *registered retirement savings plan* such as an RRSP or RRIF, you don't pay any tax on the interest, dividends, or capital gains within the plan, because it is tax-deferred. As you withdraw funds from your registered plans, they will be taxed as earned income.

   Non-registered investment income is taxed according to the type of income received and is generally taxed in the year it's earned, regardless of when it's received:

- **Interest** is fully taxable at your top marginal tax rate.
- **Dividends** from Canadian corporations qualify for the dividend tax credit, meaning you pay less tax on dividend income.

How the Dividend Tax Credit Works

To calculate the dividend tax credit, you include in your income 1.25 times the actual amount of the dividend you receive. This is your "grossed-up" dividend. Your federal tax credit is equal to 13⅓% of the grossed-up dividend.

- **Capital Gains** are only 75% taxable. This means that if you earn $100 in capital gains, you will pay tax on $75 of the gain. (Capital losses realized in the year are only 75% available to offset the taxable portion of capital gains realized in the current year, or the three previous years. In very special circumstances, a carry-forward may be applied indefinitely in the future.)

- **Foreign Income** is fully taxed as earned income, regardless of the source of investment return. Taxes paid on this income, however, could qualify for the foreign tax credit or be deductible from your income.

The chart following illustrates the after-tax return of the three different types of income—interest, dividends, and capital gains. When investing outside your RRSP, consider the tax consequences. Dividends are the preferred source of income, producing the highest after-tax return, followed by capital gains and interest. Bear this in mind when you're balancing your portfolio. For example, if all of your investments are earning interest income, you will pay a higher rate of tax than if you have a percentage of your portfolio earning dividends or capital gains.

After-Tax Returns

You've just made $1000 ... or have you?

- Assumption —51.64% marginal tax rate (1997—highest marginal tax rate in Ontario)
  —Inflation not taken into consideration
- Actual tax rates will vary according to income and province of residence

USE THE THREE Ds OF TAX PLANNING

Governments continue to tighten income tax rules. Still, there are ways to ease your tax burden, especially if you're retired. Use the "three Ds" of tax planning—deduct, defer, and divide.

DEDUCT

Reduce your taxable income by using all of the tax credits and tax deductions you are allowed when you file your income tax return.

What are tax credits?

Tax credits are a direct reduction to your total tax owing. We will highlight some of the most commonly available tax credits, but rules and percentages are subject to change. Make sure you take advantage of the following tax credits if they are applicable to you:

Age credit. When you turn 65 you become eligible for a federal tax credit. However, that credit decreases by a set amount for every dollar you earn over a specified maximum. In 1997 pensioners earning more than $49,134 are ineligible for the age credit.

Pension credit. If you are receiving pension income outside of government sources, you are entitled to a federal tax credit of 17% of that income, not to exceed $1,000.

Medical Expense Credits. If you are no longer covered by company benefits or are even partially covered, you can still qualify for medical expense tax credits for scores of services not covered by provincial medicare, among them:

- all prescription drugs
- dental services
- hospital bills
- wheelchair
- glasses
- pacemaker
- the cost of building a wheelchair ramp and other necessary renovations.

You are allowed a federal credit of 17% of the amount by which eligible medical expenses exceed the lesser of $1,614 or 3% of net income. You can also pool expenses with your spouse, but the lower income earner should claim the credit because his or her 3% threshold will be lower.

Charitable donations credits. This is a tiered credit. You are eligible to receive a 17% federal tax credit for the first $200 donation, and 29% for any additional charitable donations. Instead of claiming small amounts every year, save your receipts for up to five years to make the most of this tax credit. You can also pool your donations with your spouse so that the higher earner can claim all the tax credit.

Jessie is interested in making the most of available tax credits. She makes regular contributions of $50 a year to three charities. For Jessie to be a *Woman In The Know*, we suggest she defer claiming her donation each year and combine them for at least two years. This way she will have accumulated more than $200 of donations, putting her in the higher-tiered federal tax credit range of 29%, thus increasing her refund.

Milk that calcium for all it's worth

Many women give up milk early in life because of its high fat content and because they lose the taste for it. But you can drink skim milk or choose low-fat milk products and still satisfy your daily calcium requirements.

Tip

Check with your accountant or a tax-planning guide for a complete list of tax credits and tax deductions that may be applicable to you.

What are tax deductions?

Tax deductions reduce your total income, on which your federal taxes are calculated. They include RRSP contributions, alimony or maintenance payments, and interest paid on money borrowed for investment purposes.

DEFER

Earn money this year and delay the tax you pay until sometime in the future when it's more advantageous for you. The most common method of deferring taxes is with an RRSP or company pension. When you retire and start to withdraw the money, your tax rate will likely be lower than it is during your peak earning years. Here are the ways to maximize tax deferrals:

- Try to contribute the maximum you're allowed to your RRSP every year.
- Delay converting your RRSP to a RRIF for as long as possible.
- Calculate your annual minimum RRIF payment based on the age of the younger spouse.
- Try to withdraw only the minimum from your RRIF every year.
- Make the withdrawal from your RRIF as close to the end of the year as possible.

DIVIDE

Dividing is also referred to as income-splitting. To reduce your family's overall tax burden, utilize opportunities to split income with your spouse or other family members if they are in a lower tax bracket. One way is to set up a spousal RRIF and share Canada Pension Plan benefits, as mentioned previously in the **Determining Your Retirement Income Sources** section.

Diversify Your Assets

While the chant of real estate agents has long been "location, location, location," financial planners advise you to "diversify, diversify, diversify." Diversifying means spreading your investments around to reduce overall risk. Therefore, consider diversifying:

- among the three asset classes to reduce the risk of buying an investment at the wrong time. In addition, you will also benefit from receiving various types of investment income, which is subject to different tax treatment.
- within the asset classes to reduce the risk of one poor-performing investment pulling down your overall return. This applies to diversifying the maturities of your investments so that you will never have all of your funds coming due in the same year when rates may be unusually low, or miss opportunities to invest when rates are higher because your money is tied up.

- among countries, subject to the 20% foreign content limit for registered assets, to reduce foreign currency risk or the risk of one economy performing poorly, and to capitalize on burgeoning foreign markets.

When diversifying for retirement, consider your retirement lifestyle goals—how much time you have until you need the money and how much you have to invest. Remember, your retirement could last as long as 30 or 40 years. Don't make the common mistake of being too conservative in your investing. Transferring all your holdings to safety investments significantly reduces your ability to generate income and keep up with inflation. It is important to build a retirement portfolio that is balanced with the right mix of investments from the three asset classes.

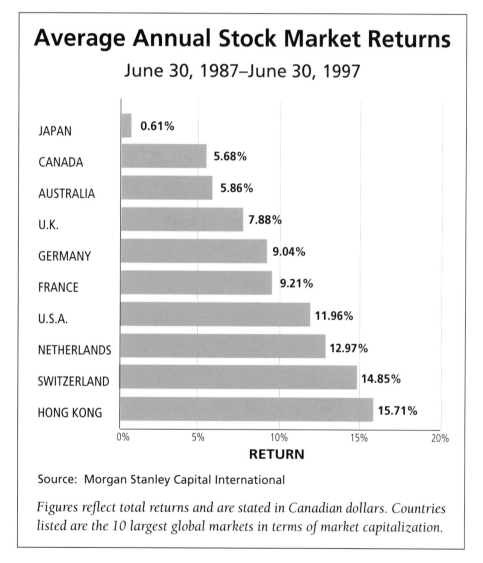

Average Annual Stock Market Returns
June 30, 1987–June 30, 1997

Country	Return
JAPAN	0.61%
CANADA	5.68%
AUSTRALIA	5.86%
U.K.	7.88%
GERMANY	9.04%
FRANCE	9.21%
U.S.A.	11.96%
NETHERLANDS	12.97%
SWITZERLAND	14.85%
HONG KONG	15.71%

RETURN

Source: Morgan Stanley Capital International

Figures reflect total returns and are stated in Canadian dollars. Countries listed are the 10 largest global markets in terms of market capitalization.

BALANCING YOUR PORTFOLIO

Experts estimate that asset mix accounts for more than 80% of a portfolio's return in the long run. Investment class, therefore, is far more important than how well an individual investment might perform. The goal is to obtain the highest expected return for a given level of risk. This is especially important for women, since women tend to be more conservative than men in their investing, yet must make the money last longer. Depending on your years until retirement and the amount invested, if you lose money by investing unwisely, you are not likely to have time to recover the loss.

The following steps and worksheet will help you develop a personalized investment portfolio designed to address your retirement goals and personal needs.

- **Step 1: Determine your investor profile.** Answer the eight questions on the next page to determine your investor profile and enter the corresponding points in each box.
- **Step 2: Your asset mix.** Match your point score from Step 1 to determine the appropriate investor profile and suggested asset mix.
- **Step 3: Choosing your investments.** As we've said, it's wise to diversify within each asset class. Try to aim for four to eight investments in your portfolio. This will provide sufficient diversification without becoming unmanageable. Incorporate your existing investments into your new asset mix. This is known as rebalancing your portfolio. Remember to include some global investments for growth potential outside of Canada.

By completing this worksheet, you have now determined your **investor profile**. This profile will help you determine how you should invest your money among the three asset classes according to your personal situation. Build your investment portfolio or reallocate funds in your existing portfolio, keeping this profile in mind.

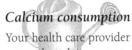

Calcium consumption
Your health care provider may also advise you to keep up your calcium consumption as you get older. Nutritionists recommend two servings of dairy product a day. One serving is equal to:
- one 8-oz cup of milk
- one cup of plain yogurt
- two one-inch cubes of cheese

Marie has completed the worksheet and answered the eight questions to determine her investor profile. With a point score of 25, Marie falls in the "Income and Moderate Growth" investor profile. For Marie to be a *Woman In The Know*, we recommend that her RRSP portfolio be invested among the three asset classes as indicated by her profile:

5% Safety, 55% Income, and 40% Growth

YOUR INVESTMENT PORTFOLIO WORKSHEET

STEP 1:   *Determine Your Investor Profile*

If you are not in a position to accept any risk to your investment(s), it is recommended that you do not continue with this questionnaire and that you consider investing in GICs, or money market investments, such as T-bills or Money Market Funds.

1) The statement that most clearly defines my investment objective(s) is:

RRSP   Non-RRSP

- I want to ensure my capital is safe and I do not need income at this time.   *0 Points*
- I require a steady stream of income from my investments.   *1 Point*
- I have some need of income, but am also interested in capital growth.   *2 Points*
- I would like long-term growth and I am less concerned about income at this time.   *5 Points*
- I'm only interested in growth over the long run.   *6 Points*

2) I plan to start withdrawing money from my investment in:

RRSP   Non-RRSP

- Under 2 years (short term)   *1 Point*
- 2 - 5 years (mid term)   *2 Points*
- 6 - 10 years (mid to long term)   *5 Points*
- Over 10 years (long term)   *9 Points*

3) My current investments are best described as follows:

RRSP   Non-RRSP

- I have little or no investment experience.   *0 Points*
- Mostly T-bills, GICs or Term Deposits.   *0 Points*
- Mostly bonds, strips or income mutual funds.   *2 Points*
- A mix of money market, bond, and stock investments and/or mutual funds.   *3 Points*
- Mostly stock or stock mutual funds.   *4 Points*

4) Assume that you have $10,000 to invest for a four-year period. You are considering four investments options. Each will have a different range of potential end values. Knowing that investments with higher possible returns typically involve greater risk, which investment would you be most likely to choose?

RRSP   Non-RRSP

Investment	Potential Value after 4 yrs High	Low	
A	$ 13,156	$ 10,125	*1 Point*
B	29,635	9,465	*4 Points*
C	42,510	6,250	*6 Points*
D	81,316	4,375	*8 Points*

5) I respond to fluctuations in my investments in the following manner:

RRSP   Non-RRSP

- I will sell quickly any time my investment loses value or money.   *1 Point*
- Day-to-day market movements make me uncomfortable. If an investment loses value over a 3- to 6- month period, I am likely to sell it and look for a better alternative.   *2 Points*
- I realize that markets may rise and fall randomly. I usually watch my investment for at least a year before making changes.   *4 Points*
- I believe that a long-term investment strategy will maximize potential returns. Even if poor market conditions resulted in sizeable losses in a given year, I stay invested.   *6 Points*

Although the following questions are more personal in nature, they are an essential part of determining the best mix of investments for you.

6) The current value of my RRSP and non-RRSP investment portfolio, including investments held at other institutions (e.g., mutual funds, stocks, bonds, GICs, money market investments, savings/chequing accounts), but excluding real estate is:

RRSP   Non-RRSP

- Under $25,000   *1 Point*
- $25,000 - $49,999   *2 Points*
- $50,000 - $99,999   *3 Points*
- $100,000 - $250,000   *4 Points*
- Over $250,000   *5 Points*

7) My current age is:

RRSP   Non-RRSP

- Under 30 years   *4 Points*
- 30 - 45 years   *5 Points*
- 46 - 55 years   *3 Points*
- 56 - 65 years   *1 Point*
- Over 65 years   *1 Point*

8) My personal income is in the following range:

RRSP   Non-RRSP

- Under $25,000   *1 Point*
- $25,000 - $49,999   *2 Points*
- $50,000 - $74,999   *3 Points*
- $75,000 - $125,000   *4 Points*
- Over $125,000   *5 Points*

RRSP   Non-RRSP

TOTALS

STEP 2:   *Your Asset Mix*

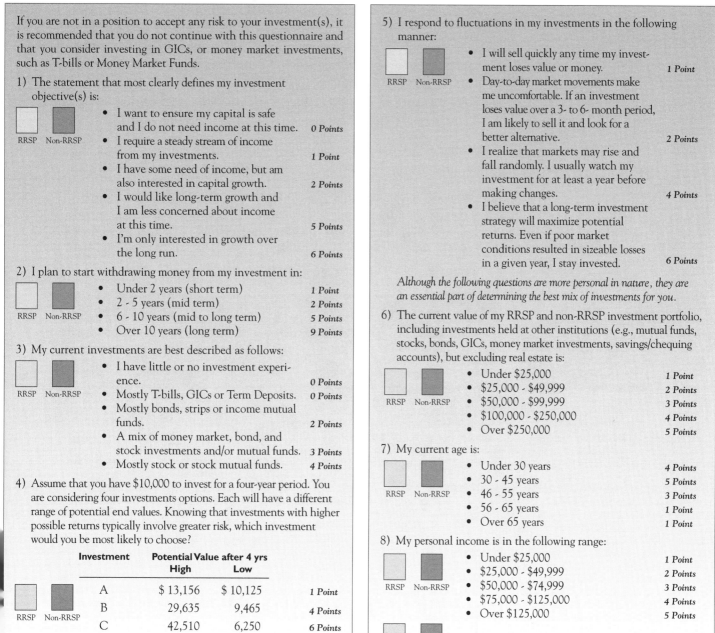

Point score ▶ Investor Profile ▶	6 - 12 Safety of Principal	13 - 19 Income	20 - 26 Income and Moderate Growth	27 - 34 Balanced Growth	35 - 42 Aggressive Growth	43 - 48 Maximum Equity Growth
Asset Mix ▶	Money Market 75% / Income 25%	Growth 20% / Money Market 10% / Income 70%	Growth 40% / Money Market 5% / Income 55%	Money Market 5% / Growth 60% / Income 35%	Money Market 5% / Growth 80% / Income 15%	Growth 95% / Money Market 5%

REBALANCING YOUR PORTFOLIO

It's a good idea to review your investments at least once a year or when faced with goal and lifestyle changes. This will help you maintain a portfolio that fits your specific objectives and tolerance for risk. To remind yourself to review your portfolio annually, you may want to tie this into a special date, for example, your birthday or wedding anniversary.

You may find that your portfolio needs to be rebalanced or adjusted back to your target asset mix. There are two reasons this need may arise:

- investments have variable rates of growth, and
- your investment objectives or personal circumstances have changed.

Rebalancing can be accomplished by transferring money from one asset class to another or by making additional contributions to the classes that are underrepresented. Rebalancing is an investment strategy designed to react to—not anticipate—changing market trends. It's an effective way to ensure you stay on the road to your retirement goals.

Marie has $55,000 in her RRSP, which currently comprises $5,000 in a registered savings account and $50,000 in a term deposit maturing at the end of the year. For Marie to be a *Woman In The Know*, we recommend she reallocate the investments in her existing RRSP portfolio according to the suggested asset mix for her investor profile:

	Current Portfolio			Recommended Portfolio	
	$ 5,000	9%	SAFETY	5%	$ 2,750
	$50,000	91%	INCOME	55%	$30,250
	$ 0	0%	GROWTH	40%	$22,000
Total	$55,000	100%		100%	$55,000

Take Advantage of Dollar-Cost Averaging

Dollar-cost averaging is like stocking up on coffee when it's on sale. Let's say you spend the same amount of grocery money on coffee each week. When coffee's on sale you may stock up on it because the price is lower. However, when the sale is over you will go back to purchasing the same amount as before.

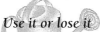

Use it or lose it

In all our efforts to keep our bodies fit, we sometimes forget to keep our minds active too. Brainteasers like crossword puzzles or enrolling in a general interest course are great ways to exercise your brain to decrease such side-effects of aging as memory loss. New activities every day will help stimulate your brain.

Dollar-cost averaging can be applied two ways:

1) Investing in Mutual Funds

By investing a fixed amount of money at regular intervals, e.g., monthly, you automatically buy more units of the fund when prices are low, and fewer when prices are high. This doesn't guarantee you will make a profit or won't take a loss, but it does usually result in a lower average cost over time. A pre-authorized chequing plan or pre-authorized purchase plan will automatically buy more units with money from a designated bank account.

2) Systematic Withdrawals

When creating your retirement income stream, you have a choice of how often you would like to receive payments, depending on the type of investment. Instead of one or two larger payments a year, consider smaller, more regular payments. Again, you will be able to take advantage of market swings. You will also be leaving more money in your account to grow and compound over the course of the year. This same strategy would apply to your RRIF.

Build an Investment Ladder

Laddering, or staggering, the maturities of your fixed income investments is an effective way to reduce risk and maximize returns. This will ensure that all your money doesn't come due at the same time, when interest rates may be low. Let's assume you have $25,000 to invest for five years. Rather than purchasing one $25,000 bond that matures five years from now, you could buy five different bonds, with terms of one to five years—the longer terms will likely pay a higher rate of interest. This means you'll never be "locked in" when rates are high, nor will all your investments come due when rates are low.

How to Construct an Investment Ladder

- Choose the term, depending on the length of time you require a predictable income. Most investors pick five- to eight-year terms.

- Determine the number of steps on your ladder. The more rungs you build, the shorter the period between each maturity date. This allows you to be less vulnerable to changing interest rates. But too many rungs make reinvestment more difficult. Ideally, you should have about five to seven rungs, which results in your investments being about one year apart.

- Formulate a reinvestment strategy. As each investment matures, reinvest it at the longest acceptable maturity.

Fixed-income bonds with low to moderate risk, such as federal or provincial government bonds, are ideal for laddering. If you don't require a regular income from your investments between maturities, you can use strip bonds. *(Don't forget, when holding strip bonds outside of a registered plan, the interest earned must be reported annually on your tax return.)*

Jessie has a $25,000 GIC maturing this year. She is surprised at how much interest rates have fallen since purchasing the investment five years ago. Jessie may want to consider some alternative investment choices for her GIC maturity. She is still interested in safe or low-risk investments, and two appropriate options may be:

1) individual fixed income investments, such as Government of Canada bonds or high-quality corporate bonds that have the potential to offer higher rates of interest than GICs.

AND/OR

2) construct a "ladder" of fixed income investments, with each bond maturing one year apart. With the $25,000 Jessie could select a combination of five $5,000 bonds and build a ladder like the one below:

$5,000 Province of Ontario 6% coupon maturing August 1998

$5,000 Government of Canada 6.25% coupon maturing November 1999

$5,000 Province of Nova Scotia 7% coupon maturing March 2000

$5,000 Province of Alberta 7% coupon maturing July 2001

$5,000 Government of Canada 7.25% coupon maturing August 2002

Create an Income through Dividends

For those seeking a regular stream of income at a more favourable tax rate, dividend-paying shares should be considered part of the income component of a diversified portfolio. Generally, preferred shares carry a higher dividend yield than common shares. With preferred shares your returns come from the dividend, with some potential for capital gain when the shares are sold.

Dividends on stocks are paid to shareholders every quarter, either by direct deposit into a brokerage account or by cheque. Since the dividend yield is usually set when the corporation issues the stock, the amount will remain the same. When reporting the income on your tax return, dividends receive preferential tax treatment and are eligible for the Dividend Tax Credit. In other words, you as an investor retain more after-tax income from Canadian-source dividends than from interest-bearing investments.

Buy and Hold

Buy an investment and *hold* it for as long as you can. This simple principle of investing allows you to ride out short-term market fluctuations and hold for the long term, in anticipation of a market recovery. Although these fluctuations can be unsettling, remember why you're investing in the first place—to finance your retirement lifestyle. Regardless of market conditions, selling your investment for less than you paid for it constitutes a "real loss". If the value decreases and you don't sell, the loss is a "paper loss". Leaving your investment intact despite a paper loss gives it the opportunity to gain in value once again. By selling you lose that chance forever.

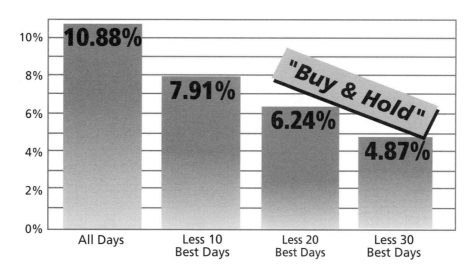

Timing Isn't Everything
Annualized Returns
June 30, 1982–June 30, 1997

From June 30, 1982, to June 30, 1997, the TSE returned an average of 10.88% a year. By trying to time the market and missing just the 10 best trading days in those 15 years, your return would have dropped to 7.91%. By missing the 20 best days, your return would have been 6.24%. If you had missed the 30 best days, your return would have fallen to 4.87%. Even though staying invested includes all the bad days, a "buy-and-hold" strategy works better in the long run.

Consolidate Your Investments

As you approach retirement, you've probably opened a number of registered and non-registered investment plans. Keeping track of them all can be a chore, especially when you're busy fulfilling your retirement dreams. Consolidating these plans into two accounts—one registered, one non-registered—has several advantages:

- You receive just one monthly/quarterly statement per account to update you on the progress of all your investments.
- You can easily monitor your asset allocation, which saves you time and money.
- You can maximize your foreign investments in registered plans to the allowable 20%.
- Your investments are conveniently in one place when you transfer your RRSP into a RRIF.
- You can easily manage income withdrawal.

Use Non-registered Assets First

Don't forget your booster

Be sure to have your tetanus booster shot every ten years. This is especially important for outdoorsy and active retirees who may cut themselves in the garden or on a hike, for example.

Since investments held in your registered plans are tax-sheltered, in most instances it is advisable to use your non-registered investments first to meet your retirement income needs. This allows you to leave investments in your registered plans longer to grow on a tax-deferred basis. In addition, whenever possible you should keep your interest-paying investments in your registered plans to accumulate tax-free, and your capital-gain and dividend-paying investments held outside your registered plans, since this income is taxed at a lower rate.

Another Unique Option— Reverse Mortgage

Many seniors have built up considerable equity in their homes and/or vacation properties. You may want to consider tapping into that equity to supplement your retirement income.

If you don't want to leave your family home or community, you can access that equity through a **reverse mortgage** or home equity plan. This option is becoming more popular with seniors living in certain provinces and is offered through a variety of agents or brokers. Reverse mortgages allow you to tap into your home's value, essentially taking either a lump sum or monthly income without making any monthly repayments. As the interest accruing on the mortgage is tax-deductible as an investment loan, this amount will offset the taxable portion of the monthly payment annuity, effectively creating a "tax-free" income for the homeowner.

This can be arranged for the life of the homeowner or a fixed term. Several restrictions may apply, such as minimum ages and maximum available equity percentages. If you don't need the extra money, you can use it to help your children buy homes or continue their education. Basically, you're giving them part of their inheritance early.

A reverse mortgage is an ingenious way to get at your money, but it has its drawbacks. Due to the complexity and associated costs of reverse mortgages, a lawyer should be consulted before pursuing this option. In addition, as interest is ultimately charged and compounded by the product administrator, it is a relatively expensive product.

PROTECTING YOUR ASSETS THROUGH ESTATE PLANNING

You work hard all your life to finance a secure retirement. You've carefully planned the amount of money needed and when, and you've invested your savings wisely to meet those needs. But there's another related step to consider—estate planning.

Estate planning may sound like the domain of the rich, but nothing is further from the truth. In fact, it may be even more important to make sure all your expenses are covered if you have limited resources and want to preserve as much as you can for your surviving family.

What Is Estate Planning?

Estate planning is the process of organizing your personal assets to minimize taxes and simplify the settling of your estate for your family. You will need an up-to-date list of what you own in order to decide how your assets will be distributed. You've listed your personal assets on your **net worth statement**, found earlier in the book. Assets such as:

- RRSPs, RRIFs, annuities
- savings and investments
- valuables and collectibles (artwork, jewellery)
- life insurance policies
- real estate

The total value of these assets is based on the current market or resale value.

In this section we will address:

- Why plan your estate?
- Preparing a will.
- Minimizing your estate.
- Buying life insurance.

Why Plan Your Estate?

Your death sets into motion a number of expenses that can't be avoided but can be minimized by effective estate planning.

PROBATE FEES

Many wills in Canada go through what's known as probate, a legal process wherein the courts validate the will and confirm the appointment of the executor. Probate fees are usually based on the size of the estate. These fees generally apply to the total value of the assets of the estate, excluding outstanding debts on real property. For example, Ontario levies the highest probate fees, starting at $5 per $1,000 on the first $50,000, and $15 per $1,000 on the remainder. Fees are usually attached to the process of probate, including lawyers, accountants, and executors.

Probate Fee Schedule

Province	Fee Schedule
Alberta	Progressive schedule ranging from $25 for the first $10,000 to a total maximum of $6,000 for estates greater than $1 million
British Columbia	$0 for estates less than $10,000; $200 fee for estates between $10,000-$25,000; $6 per $1,000 of assets thereafter; no maximum.
Manitoba	$5 per $1,000 of assets; no maximum
New Brunswick	$5 per $1,000 of assets; no maximum
Newfoundland	$50 for the first $1,000; $4 per $1,000 of assets thereafter; no maximum.
Nova Scotia	Progressive schedule ranging from $75 for the first $10,000; $500 for estates worth $200,000; $3 per $1,000 of assets thereafter; no maximum.
Ontario	$5 per $1,000 for the first $50,000; $15 per $1,000 thereafter; no maximum.
Prince Edward Island	Progressive schedule ranging from $50 for the first $10,000; $400 for estates worth $100,000; $4 per $1,000 thereafter; no maximum.
Quebec	No probate for notarial wills; request for will verification: $800 for holograph or witnessed wills
Saskatchewan	$12 for the first $1,000; $6 per $1,000 thereafter; no maximum.

Source: Institute of Canadian Bankers

INCOME TAX

Even after you die, you still don't get out of paying income tax! Your executor must file your final income tax return within six months after your death or by April 30 of the following year, whichever is later.

1. **Registered Plans.** Unless you've named a spouse or dependent child or grandchild as beneficiary on your RRSP or RRIF, assets from these plans will be treated as though they've been cashed in immediately before your death and taxed as income.

Stave off influenza

Our Canadian winters can be especially brutal on seniors. Ask your doctor about getting vaccinated against influenza. You may still get the flu, but a much milder case.

2. **Non-registered assets, such as stocks, mutual funds, and vacation homes.** These investments (excluding your principal home) are subject to the "deemed disposition rule"—that is, they are treated as though you sold them immediately before your death at a fair market price. The difference between the fair market value of the assets and the amount they originally cost when you purchased them may then be subject to a capital gains tax.

3. **Foreign Tax.** If you have property or a business located outside Canada or if you were a resident or citizen of another country when you died, your estate may be subject to foreign estate taxes and succession duties. A winter home in Florida, for example, could mean your estate will pay capital gains tax in *both* countries, as well as U.S. estate tax on the deemed disposition of that property.

FINAL PERSONAL EXPENSES
(INCLUDING OUTSTANDING DEBT PAYMENTS AND FUNERAL COSTS)

By the time you retire, you will likely have minimal personal debts from mortgages or car loans. But you may have some outstanding credit card payments, a line of credit, or some other personal loan that must be paid. As well, traditional funeral costs are $4,000 and up.

IT'S YOUR FUNERAL

Planning your own funeral or memorial service relieves your family of the burden and stress of making major decisions quickly at a time of great emotional stress. It also ensures you make your exit the way you want to.

- **Preplanning a Funeral.** If you plan your funeral with a funeral home, cemetery, and/or crematorium, the executor of your will is responsible for ensuring your wishes are met. Tell your family and executor what kind of funeral you want, providing them with either general instructions, such as "keep it simple," or with specific details outlined in a letter of wishes.

- **Prepaying a Funeral.** You can also go so far as to prepay for your funeral, but be sure to let your executor and family know so that they don't end up paying twice. The arrangements are written in a contract with a funeral home, cemetery, or crematorium and paid for in advance by placing the amount in a plan trust that earns interest until the funds are used for the funeral (which also means there will be additional income, in excess of contributions to the plan, to claim on your final-year income tax return). Depending on your province of residence, the contracts can include two key points: (i) a clause that says the funeral home will cover any additional costs if the details of the funeral for which you prepaid end up costing more at the time of your death, and (ii) a description of how the funds will be returned to your estate if the trust builds more money than is needed to cover costs.

Preparing a Will

Retirement planning puts you in touch with your financial situation. Drawing up a will is an extension of that planning. A will is really a sort of love letter to your family. It is a legal document that ensures that, even after your death, you are distributing your assets the way you want.

Although it is one of the most important aspects of estate planning, many people delay making a will. As a result, many people die without one, which is known as "intestate". If you die intestate, the court will appoint an administrator to dispose of your assets according to a rigid statutory formula. Your loved ones, including your spouse, are powerless to direct your affairs because the provincial law decides who gets what with no regard to your wishes or the needs of your dependents.

You should review your will whenever your family circumstances change, such as marriage, divorce, birth, death of your beneficiaries, or a significant change in your assets.

As you approach retirement, you probably already have a will, but now is the time to review it. If you don't have a will, now is the time to make one. A basic will costs as little as $100, depending on the complexity of your estate.

The three most common types of will

- **Conventional or Formal Will.** This is a standard will and is valid in all provinces. A lawyer will draw up the will, which you have handwritten or typed, and it must be signed by you and two witnesses, both of whom must be with you at the same time. The witnesses cannot be beneficiaries or spouses of beneficiaries under the will.

- **Notarial Will.** This type is valid only in Quebec. A notary must read the will to you in the presence of two other notaries, or one notary and two witnesses. You and the witnesses then sign the will. The notary keeps the original will.

- **Holograph Will.** This type of will is accepted in only some provinces, as long as it is signed, wholly written in your handwriting, and dated. It can, however, often inadvertently be ambiguous. Legal action may be required to clarify your wishes.

What Is a Codicil?

If you wish to revoke any old clauses or add new clauses to your will, you can do so by adding an amendment, or codicil, rather than redoing the entire will. A codicil must be executed and validated like a will.

CHOOSING YOUR EXECUTOR

One of the most important aspects of preparing your will is choosing an executor. An executor, or estate trustee, is a person or institution you name in your will to look after your assets and settle your estate. An executor's duties can include filing a number of different tax returns, paying debts and taxes, and in some cases completing funeral arrangements.

Think carefully when determining who your executor will be. Your spouse or adult child is probably the easiest choice, particularly if your estate is fairly uncomplicated. But remember, your spouse and children will be in mourning. They may be too overwrought to carry out such an important duty. You could also choose your lawyer, an accountant, or a friend. When making your choice, it is also prudent to consider any potential family conflicts arising from your selection of your executor. An alternative executor should also be named in the event that your first choice is unable to do it. In any case, your executor should

- live in the same vicinity as you,
- be around the same age or younger than you,
- be aware and capable of handling the responsibility,
- be aware of the time commitment involved,
- be willing to do the job.

If you have a large estate, your spouse may be able to handle it alone, but may appreciate the help of a professional executor, such as a trust company. This provision must be specified in the will.

Executors are entitled to payment for their services unless otherwise stipulated in the will. These fees should be negotiated before your death; otherwise the courts will refer to a rate schedule of accepted fees.

For your eyes only
Every woman will experience varying degrees of far-sightedness as she ages (inability to see objects in close range). After age 50, you should have your eyes checked every year or two to measure changes in vision.

Jessie has been meaning to update her will. The last time it was updated was seven years ago when she was going through her divorce. She is considering making her daughter the executor of her estate because she feels Sandy is mature enough to take on this responsibility. For Jessie to be a *Woman In The Know*, we recommend that she first discuss the matter with her daughter to see if she understands the role of an executor and to see if she is willing to take on the responsibility. If her daughter agrees and Jessie feels comfortable with the decision, she should review (with Sandy) the contents of her will.

Did you know?

Executors can be held personally liable if anyone successfully contests the manner in which they have performed their duties.

POWER OF ATTORNEY

No doubt you don't like to think about becoming incapacitated to the point that you are unable to deal with your affairs, but it could happen. A power of attorney is a legal document giving someone the authority to make decisions for you when you can't because of illness, accident, or absence. In this context, attorney doesn't necessarily mean lawyer—a friend, spouse, or adult child can act as your power of attorney, as long as they are willing to act on your behalf and are trustworthy. You may even prefer to select an impartial power of attorney from a trust company.

Without a power of attorney, no one can sign legal documents or cheques for you. This means bills are left unpaid, and your dependents may go on indefinitely without the benefit of your financial support. It's up to you how much power to give your attorney. It could be unlimited power or could be restricted to a period of time, type of property, or specific conditions.

Although you don't need a lawyer to prepare a power of attorney, it's a good idea to have one review it in case you've missed something. Power of attorney laws vary from province to province; in fact, some provinces allow you to appoint a "Power of Attorney for Personal Care". Personal care decisions include deciding on your health care measures, choosing a place for you to live, and daily decisions affecting your safety and well-being. Be aware, however, that a power of attorney is void upon your death.

Did you know?

A **living will** (also known as an Advance Health Care Directive) is like a personal care power of attorney. This document outlines your wishes in regard to medical care should you become physically or mentally incapacitated.

Strategies for Minimizing Your Estate Costs

There are a number of estate planning strategies that will help reduce the size of your probatable assets and/or minimize taxes. Following are the most commonly used estate planning strategies. We encourage you to seek professional advice for a more in-depth review of strategies that would best benefit you.

Designate beneficiaries on RRSPs, RRIFs, and life insurance policies.
At death registered proceeds go directly to the beneficiaries named in the plan. If there are no named beneficiaries, the proceeds become part of your "estate", or total personal assets. RRIF or RRSP proceeds willed to a surviving spouse may be transferred into his or her RRIF or RRSP tax-free. This is known as a "Refund of Premium to Spouse". If RRIF or RRSP proceeds are left to anyone other than a surviving spouse or dependent child or grandchild, they are fully taxable in the year of death.

Life insurance benefits are generally payable to one or more specified beneficiaries of the insured, and therefore do not generally constitute part of the estate. Since proceeds paid to the beneficiary are paid outside of your estate, they are exempt from probate fees and are not subject to income tax.

Designating someone such as a spouse or child as beneficiary on your life insurance policies, RRSPs, and RRIFs, means that on your death, these assets are passed on to beneficiaries outside of the estate, thus reducing the value of the estate and minimizing probate fees owed.

Block the sun

For many women, retiring means spending more time in the sun. But too much sun is a health hazard. You should continue to use a sunscreen with maximum protection and always wear a hat to protect your face and scalp from the sun.

Hold property and other assets as joint tenants.
When planning to leave property or assets to a loved one or business partner, for example, consider registering the property in both names as "joint tenants". On your death, the assets automatically pass to the surviving joint tenant without being lumped into your estate; this way you avoid probate fees charged on those assets. However, there are legal and tax issues that arise when you transfer assets into joint registration, so be sure to ask for professional advice before making any changes to your property.

Share your assets by making cash gifts and charitable donations.
Provided your retirement income is ample, the most cost-effective way to lower estate costs is to bequest, redirect, or transfer to adult family members a gift of cash while you are living. Even though tax attribution rules state you must report any income (except taxable capital gains) earned on money you give to your spouse or children under the age of 18; adult children who receive a cash gift are responsible for paying the tax on any income earned on the gift.

Donating to community charities, including hospitals and universities, enables you to give back to the community while receiving a tax benefit at the same time. Charitable donations can provide significant tax deductions during your lifetime and even up to 100% of your total income for your estate upon death. Further details can be obtained from the planned-giving office of your favourite charity.

Utilize any unused RRSP contribution room.

If you die leaving unused RRSP contribution room for that year, your estate can still receive the tax benefit by contributing to a Spousal RRSP. Leave instructions with your executor to do this.

Freeze your estate.

Individuals can freeze their estate at its present value by transferring the assets to their heirs, who then enjoy any subsequent gains and pay any resulting income taxes. Such transfers usually trigger immediate capital gains tax since transfers between family members are deemed to have taken place at fair market value. In most cases estate freezing is implemented by transferring assets to a trust or by transferring shares of a corporation, rather than a direct transfer of physical assets.

In some circumstances a $500,000 capital gains exemption exists for certain small business corporations and family-owned farm properties. Estate freezes are generally quite complex and can trigger various forms of tax consequences, so you should seek professional tax advice when considering this option.

Set up a trust.

Setting up a trust involves giving your assets to a trustee, who manages the assets on behalf of a third party, your beneficiary. These assets are not included in the total value of your estate, thereby potentially reducing probate fees and taxes. A trust is treated as a separate entity and can be set up while you are alive, which is called an *inter vivos trust*; or it can be set up in your will to take effect after your death, which is called a *testamentary trust*.

While both types of trusts have similar motivations, they face different tax treatments. Undistributed income left in an inter vivos trust is taxed at the highest personal marginal tax rate, while testamentary trusts face the progressive schedule of marginal tax rates that apply to individuals. Despite the imposition of high marginal tax rates, inter vivos trusts may be effectively used in a case where the owner wishes to retain control of the assets.

A specific type of trust often used in estate planning is a *spousal trust*. A spousal trust is one option that can satisfy a need or desire to provide income to a surviving spouse for the rest of his or her life, and at the same time ensure the eventual delivery of the trust assets to other persons who are designated when establishing the trust. This is a trust where all the income generated by the asset(s) included in the trust is attributable to the originating spouse. Additionally, prior to the death of the originating spouse, no one else is entitled to the asset except the recipient spouse.

Establishing a trust is a complex process that must be set up by a lawyer. Assets in a trust can be distributed immediately at the time of death, or they can be invested and earn income to provide a beneficiary with long-term income.

Seek professional services.
Estate planning to minimize costs can be a complex procedure. By hiring a professional, such as a lawyer, accountant, or trust company representative, you will ensure you have considered all the strategies.

One of Ruth's biggest concerns is how to deal with the use, ownership, and ongoing maintenance costs of the much-loved family cottage. Her oldest son clearly uses the cottage the most and does the majority of the maintenance work, but the other three children don't have the time. They do, however, love visiting the cottage and would like to spend more time there. For Ruth to be a *Woman In The Know*, we encourage her to have a family discussion about the use of the cottage after her death. She should consider providing instructions regarding the use of the cottage and division of maintenance costs among her four children in an updated will. If Ruth has an interest in providing for some of the expenses, she could consider a testamentary trust to provide enough money to cover any ongoing maintenance costs. Most important, Ruth must determine the ownership rights of the cottage among her children in the event of her death.

Buying Life Insurance

Life insurance pays a benefit to your beneficiaries after your death in exchange for premiums you paid while you were alive.

WHY BUY LIFE INSURANCE?

While you raise your family, you buy life insurance to replace your income and ensure your family can maintain their lifestyle if you die. In retirement you probably have different needs and responsibilities, but you will still want to consider having some life insurance to help your spouse and family cover your final expenses and any debts you may have. Life insurance can also play an important role in estate planning, including:

- **Donating to charity.** If you have an interest in donating to a charity, consider life insurance to fulfil this wish. You will receive a charitable tax credit for the value of any life insurance assigned to the charity and any premiums paid by you. Alternatively, if you wish, your estate can receive a tax credit by donating the proceeds of the policy to the charity after your death.
- **Protecting business interests.** If you're involved in the ownership of a business, it is important to recognize the implications your death will have on the ongoing operation of the business and the potential tax owing. There are a variety of uses for insurance as a method to protect not only the survival of the business but also the overall costs to your estate.
- **Estate preservation.** Although life insurance is normally used to create an estate for your heirs, it can also be used to pay the taxes on your estate and settle any other debts. Life insurance benefits are generally payable to one or more specific individuals and therefore do not generally constitute a part of the estate, thereby reducing probate, legal, and executor fees. However, a life insurance policy may also specify the estate as the beneficiary. This allows the executor to distribute the proceeds as needed.

Heart of the matter

The incidence of heart disease continues to increase in women. Despite this, the significance of chest pain in women as a symptom of heart attack is often underestimated. Any unexplained pain, particularly associated with exertion or activity, should be reported to your doctor.

Tip

If you named a beneficiary, the death benefit of your life insurance policy will not be subject to tax and usually will be distributed within 30 days of submitting a death certificate or other proof of death to the insurance company.

Types of life insurance

Term Insurance

Term insurance pays a specific death benefit for a period of time. For plans that renew at set periods, e.g., 10 years, the premium may increase with each renewal and you may be required to requalify. "Term to 100" is term insurance that guarantees premiums remain the same every year until a specified age—in this case, 100.

Permanent Insurance

Permanent, or "whole life," insurance combines lifetime coverage with a savings component, or "cash value." The cash value is designed to keep the premium level, and in some instances may allow you to stop paying premiums after a specified age or number of years. The cash value accumulated in the early years is used to meet the premium requirements in the later years. If you elect to withdraw the cash value, these proceeds will become taxable.

Universal Life

Universal life offers lifetime coverage but has the added flexibility of allowing you later on to choose the premium amount, change the premium amount, and even the payment period. Universal life policies also have a tax-deferred investment option. This is especially useful if you have already used up all your RRSP contribution room.

HOW MUCH LIFE INSURANCE DO I NEED?

LIFE INSURANCE WORKSHEET

Your life insurance needs will vary as your responsibilities, values, and circumstances change over time. The following worksheet will help you determine your current life insurance needs.

Step 1 How much do you need to pay off your debts and cover ongoing expenses?

Life insurance makes sense if you have major financial commitments and obligations, such as children and significant household expenses, including a mortgage or rent. It also makes sense if an extended-family member will be dependent on your future income.

Consider how much your family will need to pay for major debts or expenditures, and to maintain ongoing expenses:

1. **Outstanding balance on your mortgage.** $_____ +

2. **Current bills.** $_____ +
     (i.e., credit cards, utility bills, and other short-term bills)

3. **Outstanding balance on loans and other debt.** $_____ +
     (i.e., auto loan, line of credit, etc.)

4. **Child's education** $_____ +

     *As an estimate use $4,000 per year per child if children will live at home
     while attending university/college, and $10,000 per year if they will live
     away from home.*

5. **Expenses upon death** (i.e., funeral costs, probate fees, lawyer fees, etc.) $_____ +

     If unsure, use an estimate of $20,000 (funeral costs start at $4,000).

6. **Emergency Fund** (i.e., equivalent of 3 to 6 months' expenses) $_____ =

Amount needed to pay off debts and cover ongoing expenses?
(Add lines 1 to 6) $_____ (A)

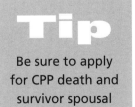

Be sure to apply for CPP death and survivor spousal benefits.

Step 2 How much income would your family need?

Life insurance can provide a source of ongoing income to support your family. A lump-sum amount is provided upon death, which in turn is typically invested to provide an ongoing income to the family.

1. **Annual income.** $_____(B)

   As an estimate, use 70% of your current annual income as some
   expenses will be reduced with one less family member.

2. **From the table below, select the factor that corresponds to the**
   number of years you wish to provide an income for your family. $_____(C)

# of Years Income Is Needed	10	15	20	25	30	35	40
Factor*	8.47	11.64	14.26	16.43	18.22	19.70	20.92

   *assumes 7% rate of return, 3% annual inflation, and that funds will be depleted by the
    end of the period.

3. **Multiply Line (B) by Line (C). This is the amount required to provide an**
   income for your family for the number of years selected. $_____(D)

Step 3 Total amount needed to pay off debt and provide an income.

1. **Add Lines (A) and (D). This is the total amount your family will require**
   to pay off outstanding debts and maintain their standard of living. $_____(E)

Step 4 Determine the value of your existing assets and life insurance coverage.

Life insurance need not be, and often is not, the only source of ongoing income for survivors. Other sources of income can include savings, real estate, investments, and government pension plans.

1. **Group Life Insurance** $_____+
   If you are a member of an employer-sponsored or professional
   association life insurance plan, enter the amount of coverage.

2. **Personal Life Insurance** $_____+
   Enter the total amount of any existing life insurance coverage.
   This includes all term, whole life, and universal policies.

3. **Mortage Insurance** $_____+
   If your mortgage is currently life insured, enter the current
   outstanding balance on your mortgage.

4. Liquid Assets (Non-RRSP) $_____ +

*Enter the total amount you have invested in Guaranteed
Investment Certificates, Canada Savings Bonds, treasury bills,
money market mutual funds, and bank accounts.*

5. Long-Term Assets $_____ +

*Enter the total amount you have invested in stocks, bonds, real estate,
and non-money market mutual funds.*

6. Current value of RRSPs $_____ =

Many people prefer to leave the value of their RRSPs out of the calculation
of life insurance needs. This way, the funds can be left to grow and form part
of a spouse's retirement income. If you include the value of RRSP assets, reduce
the current value by 40% to allow for the fact that these funds are fully taxable
on withdrawal.

Total funds available from existing assets (adds lines 1 through 6 above) $_____(F)

Step 5 Determine how much insurance you need?

**1. Subtract Line (F) from Line (E). This is the amount of life insurance
required to meet your needs.** $_____

HOW DO I BUY LIFE INSURANCE?

Like any major purchase you should shop around for the best deal. Ask
friends or family for referrals of life insurance agents with whom they have
dealt. Make sure you feel comfortable with the person you choose and that he
or she is qualified to do the job.

Jessie, Marie, and Ruth are attending their Wednesday-night choir rehearsal. During a break they strike up a conversation about retirement. Because Jessie and Marie are just starting to think about and plan their retirements, they are very interested in what Ruth has to say about what it's like to be retired. How did she find the transition from work to retirement? What does she do to fill her time? What about income? During the conversation they realize that although they have different retirement goals, they all agree that each of them should be taking certain steps to ensure they can meet these goals.

It could be exploring retirement income options, learning about investments, minimizing taxes, or planning their estate. With the assistance of a qualified professional to guide them, Jessie, Marie, and Ruth can feel in control of their goals. Ruth sums up her own situation this way: "My financial security, combined with good health, has allowed me the freedom to pursue my own interests, as well as spend time with family and friends." Her advice to Jessie and Marie is simple: "What you need to do is envision what you want in your retirement and start planning ahead of time."

STEP 3
IMPLEMENTING YOUR RETIREMENT ACTION PLAN

A garden doesn't become beautiful on its own. It takes will and determination—and lots of nurturing! The same is true for your retirement plan. You start by setting your retirement goals, then acquiring the knowledge to determine the alternatives available to successfully reach your retirement dreams. Finally, you put the necessary plans in place to make sure you will have the kind of retirement you want. For many, this third step is the

hardest to implement. Perhaps you've procrastinated in starting to develop a retirement plan because you thought it was too complicated or time-consuming. But you now know that's not the case. And just as the rewards of a well-planned garden are plenty, so too are the benefits of a well-planned retirement.

Up to this point we've guided you through planning for your retirement and exploring your retirement alternatives. In this last step of your retirement plan we'll help you integrate your goals and your new-found knowledge into developing a successful **Retirement Action Plan**.

DEVELOPING YOUR RETIREMENT ACTION PLAN

The purpose of an action plan is to get you closer to your retirement dreams. The Retirement Action Plan will help you take your retirement goals and decide what you need to do to make them happen.

Life after death

Because women usually outlive men, many women have to make the difficult adjustment of living alone for part of their retirement. Bereavement counsellors generally advise that you resist making any major changes in your life for at least one year after the death of a spouse.

Our action plan summarizes the topics we've covered in the previous sections of the book. Under each of these sections we've itemized elements of your retirement plan that you should review each year. Each yearly review item provides:

- a **Date Reviewed** column to indicate when you've completed the task;
- an **Action Notes** column to remind you of things you need to do, e.g., make an appointment with a lawyer or financial advisor;
- a **Date Completed** column to record the date you will have completed the items in your **Action Notes** column.

We've also addressed other questions that you don't need to review every year, but that you should consider as you approach retirement. Some questions may not pertain to your individual circumstance, but if they do, mark the **Yes** column and complete the **Actions Notes** and **Date Completed** columns, as indicated above.

1. RETIREMENT GOALS

Ensure you have completed your retirement goals.

Yearly review	Date Reviewed	Action Notes	Date Completed
Have you defined your personal retirement goals?			
Have you defined what your financial retirement goals will cost you?			
Annually: Have you reviewed your retirement goals to assess your progress and redefine if necessary?			

2. NET WORTH/CASH IN/OUTFLOW

Staying on top of your current financial situation as it changes is vital to a successful retirement plan. Chart your progress towards financial independence.

Yearly review	Date Reviewed	Action Notes	Date Completed
Have you completed your Net Worth Statement?			
Annually: Have you updated your Net Worth Statement?			
Have you completed your Cash In/Outflow Worksheet?			

Yearly review	Date Reviewed	Action Notes	Date Completed
Annually: Have you updated your Cash In/Outflow Worksheet?			
Have you completed your Projected Annual Retirement Cash Outflow Worksheet?			
Annually: Have you updated your retirement cash flow?			
Have you reviewed your Retirement Planner to ensure you are saving enough?			
Annually: Have you updated your Retirement Planner?			

Other Considerations	No	Yes	Action Notes	Date Completed
Do you have enough money in your emergency fund?				
If you have debts, are you • paying the one with the highest interest rate first? • planning to be debt-free at retirement?				
Have you had your home(s) reassessed for its current market value?				

3. RETIREMENT INCOME SOURCES

It is important to know how much money you can expect to receive from the three main sources of retirement income: government benefits, company pension plans, and your own personal savings. Monitor these sources on a regular basis so you can determine how any changes will affect the fulfilment of your retirement goals.

Yearly review	Date Reviewed	Action Notes	Date Completed
Have you determined the value of retirement income you are going to receive from the three main sources? • government benefits (e.g., CPP, OAS) • company pension plans • personal savings			

Yearly review	Date Reviewed	Action Notes	Date Completed
Annually: Monitor the level of retirement income to be received from the three main sources.			

Other Considerations	No	Yes	Action Notes	Date Completed
Have you confirmed when you want to start drawing CPP?				
Have you contacted the Income Security Programs division of Human Resources Development Canada to verify your estimated government pension amounts?				
Have you marked on your calendar when you will apply for OAS (six months in advance)?				

4. POST-RETIREMENT INCOME SOURCES

You will probably create your retirement income stream through a combination of payments from RRIFs, annuities, and pensions.

Yearly review	Date Reviewed	Action Notes	Date Completed
Have you selected a retirement income option (e.g., annuity, RRIF) for: • your RRSP? • your locked-in RRSP?			
If you currently have a RRIF, you are determined your annual minimum withdrawal payment?			
If you currently have a LIF, have you determined your annual minimum and maximum withdrawal payment?			

Other Considerations	No	Yes	Action Notes	Date Completed
Do you have any special needs for large cash purchases, which may increase your withdrawal requirements?				
Have you considered setting up a spousal RRIF or splitting a pension to minimize your household income taxes?				

5. INVESTING STRATEGIES

Maintain a balanced portfolio and monitor it on a regular basis to assist you in reaching your retirement goals.

Yearly review	Date Reviewed	Action Notes	Date Completed
Have you reviewed the Investment Portfolio Worksheet to determine that your current mix is in line with your current investor profile?			
Have you rebalanced your portfolio to the appropriate asset allocation mix?			

Other Considerations	No	Yes	Action Notes	Date Completed
Have you started a systematic withdrawal program for your income needs or savings program for your goals?				
Have you determined if an investment ladder would help you meet your income needs?				
Is income through dividends a consideration for you to increase income and reduce taxes?				
Have you consolidated your RRSP/RRIF holdings?				
Is a reverse mortgage a consideration for your situation?				
Are you using all your allowable tax credit and deductions?				

6. ESTATE PLANNING

The final element of your retirement plan falls under Estate Planning—the effective arrangement of your personal assets to preserve enough capital in your estate to cover any debts or taxes or to provide an inheritance.

Yearly review	Date Reviewed	Action Notes	Date Completed
Is your will up-to-date?			
Is your power of attorney up-to-date?			
Have you reviewed your estate planning strategies?			
Have you reviewed your Life Insurance Worksheet to make sure your estate is adequately covered?			

Other Considerations	No	Yes	Action Notes	Date Completed
Have you named beneficiaries for your • RRIF? • RRSP? • Life insurance? • Annuities? • Pension Plan? • Deferred Profit Sharing Plan?				
Have you informed family members where your financial records are kept, including income tax returns, insurance policies, safety deposit box keys, and bank account statements?				
Have you informed your executor where to find your will and your instructions for funeral arrangements, if any?				

ENJOY YOUR GARDEN!

Knowledge is the key to mastering any pursuit, whether it's gardening or planning for your retirement. As you sit back in your lounge chair with brilliant blooms abounding, we hope you've gained an added sense of security about your retirement. But don't stop now. We encourage you to keep reading and learning about retirement planning. The key to success in your retirement planning is to avoid procrastination and maintain a winning attitude as you apply the steps and strategies discussed in this book. A motto to live by is **Knowledge Is Power**. You are exercising your power by taking an active role in your retirement planning.

Whether you dream of a windowbox of petunias or a greenhouse full of orchids, each lovingly tended flower will bring a smile to your face—the satisfaction of a job well done.

APPENDIX
WANT TO LEARN MORE?

We hope this book has inspired you to learn more about planning for your retirement. You can get more information by attending education seminars, utilizing investor services, or joining an investment club. In addition there are a number of experts who can provide you with a wealth of information and assist you in making your financial decisions.

EDUCATIONAL SEMINARS

Many financial institutions, investment dealers, and mutual fund companies offer seminars or information sessions on retirement planning. Check your local newspaper and radio stations for notices of sessions near you.

TD's Women In The Know© program is a perfect example of a seminar series designed to educate women and encourage them to take control of their finances. For a list of seminars near you visit any TD Bank branch and ask for a copy of our *Investment Opportunities* bulletin or call our toll-free Investment Centre.

INVESTOR SERVICES

Many financial institutions offer toll-free telephone services you can call for information on investing, financial markets, and specific company products. TD Asset Management Inc. is no exception, offering investors toll-free access to Investment Specialists who are licensed to provide investment guidance and advice, as well as sell mutual funds and fixed income investments.

Most financial institutions also offer a wealth of information through their Internet sites. Many sites have interactive tools to help you reach your retirement goals. For example, the Mutual Fund Centre on TD's website has tools to help you structure your personal portfolio, develop a savings plan, and calculate how much you need to save for retirement.

INVESTMENT CLUBS

You may be motivated to share your knowledge and interest in investing with fellow soon-to-be retirees. An investment club is a perfect way to learn from others' experiences and test new investment waters.

An investment club is a group of people who have a common interest in investing and want to pool their money to invest in a portfolio of stocks, bonds, and/or mutual funds. Members meet regularly to talk about potential investments and determine if they're right for the club. Each member makes regular monetary contributions to the pool, and everyone votes on the investment decisions.

These clubs are a great way for people with small amounts of money to participate in larger investments, usually saving money on commission. By investing as a group, you decrease your individual exposure to risk.

For more information about investment clubs, contact: Investors Association of Canada, 380–26 Soho Street, Toronto, Ontario M5T 1Z7

FINANCIAL ADVISORS

Financial advisors can help you make sound financial decisions. They may be bank or trust company employees, independent financial planners, insurance agents, or full-service stockbrokers. The best financial advisor for you will depend on the amount of money you have to invest and the type of service you require.

HOW DO I CHOOSE MY FINANCIAL ADVISOR?

Choose your financial advisor as you would your doctor or lawyer. Ask your friends for the names of their financial advisors (if they're satisfied customers!) and set up a meeting to find out if their recommendation is someone with whom you feel comfortable. Remember, you are going to be revealing a lot of personal information to this person. Make sure you can trust him or her to keep everything confidential.

Treat your potential advisors as if they're applying for a job. Here's a list of sample questions to ask in your "job interview":

- How long have you been a financial advisor?
- What are your qualifications?
- Can you provide two or three references from satisfied clients?
- How many clients do you have?
- How are your fees structured?
- Who handles *your* finances?
- How do you distinguish between good and bad investments? (Trick question. There really are no good or bad investments—the secret is matching the right investment with the right investor.)

STAY IN TOUCH

Retirement Strategies for Women: Turning Dreams into Reality is the second of the *Women In The Know* books, and it has been written to supply you with more knowledge and new insight into setting and meeting your retirement goals. Our hope is that this book has provided you with a greater sense of purpose and direction on your road to financial independence and a successful retirement.

As you read and refer to this book before and after your retirement, we'd appreciate any comments you may have. Please feel free to let us know if the book has been helpful. You can contact us at:

Women In The Know
c/o TD Asset Management Inc.
Toronto Dominion Bank Tower
P.O. Box 100
Toronto-Dominion Centre
Toronto, Ontario
M5K 1G8

Toll-Free Investment Centre 1-800-268-8166

Internet site: http://www.tdbank.ca/mutualfund

E-mail address: funderman@tdbank.ca

ACKNOWLEDGEMENTS

A project of this magnitude always requires total commitment and dedication to ensure final satisfaction. As we embarked on this journey, we spent endless hours pouring over research and discussing what we believed would benefit our readers most. The fact that we are all female enabled us to empathize with and understand the issues women encountered before us and helped us envision what we ourselves might face in retirement.

Equally important to our research was the tremendous experience we have gained by speaking to women across the country through our Women In The Know seminar series. Of the 40,000 women we have met, many confirmed the need for ongoing education emphasizing the importance of managing one's finances to gain control of one's financial destiny. The women who participate in our seminar program are truly our inspiration. They encourage our team to educate and motivate all women to take charge of their financial futures.

As we formulated our strategy for this book, we quickly discovered that our knowledge and expertise would be complete only by relying on the outstanding resources we are fortunate enough to encounter in our daily working lives. The dedication and commitment of a number of people in assisting us in our endeavour is greatly appreciated. In particular, a special thanks is owed to J. Mark Wettlaufer, President, TD Asset Management Inc., for encouraging our efforts and pushing us to strive to be the best. In addition, we appreciate the involvement and sincere commitment to the women's program of the Bank's executive: Charlie Baillie, Allen Bell, Arthur English, Duncan Gibson, Bob Kelly, and Bud McMorran. Also to our co-workers, who invested many hours of their own time and who exhibit a true sense of team spirit: Miranda Koffski, Laura Steele-Gunter, Michelle Collis, Anna Gaetano, and Jennifer Rose. Special thanks to our colleagues at TD Asset Management, who are always willing to provide assistance and guidance: Tom Hill, Angell Kasparian, Andrew Trimble, Alice Fang, Cindy Denwood, Karl Schulz, John Ciampaglia, Steve Geist, Garry Goss, Derek Allister, Angela Dickens, and Hilari D'Aguiar.

Our gratitude is further extended to everyone at the Toronto-Dominion Bank who provided insightful suggestions: Nicholas Chan, Edna Chu, Jane Stubbington, Karen Young, Bill Bennett, Judith Baird, Bonnie Matchen, Walter Kobzar, Pearl Moffat, Anne Fiorita, Tim Watson, Anne Marie Cerio, Roseanne Peel, Catherine Taylor, Don Lacey, Kelly Gray-Harley, Stephen Stewart, and Barry Gollom. We also appreciate the efforts of Robert Murray and his associates at Price Waterhouse, for reviewing the book in its entirety, and David Holmes and Katherine Holmes of Holmes Communication, whose creative talent and support we know we can always rely on.

And finally, special recognition is extended to Jeannette Mann, Carol Mizgala, Carolyn Rose, and Elaine Steele, who represent the women we hope will read and learn from this book. The feedback and guidance they provided to ensure we were addressing the issues most critical to their own experiences contributed immensely to the book.

In closing, it is with great pleasure that we have formed a partnership with Genesis, a charitable research foundation that continues to play a key role in improving the quality of life for women. Their strong commitment to the advancement of health care through research represents hope for many women and their families. With pride, we donate all proceeds generated from the sale of this book to this organization.

On a personal note, we owe our greatest appreciation to our families, who provided support and encouragement throughout the writing of this book.

Sandy Cimoroni,
Beth Grudzinski,
Patricia Lovett-Reid

INDEX

Outdoors in Arizona
A Guide to Hiking and Backpacking

ARIZONA
HIGHWAYS BOOK

Author
John Annerino
Additional text and editing by
Peter Kresan and **James E. Cook**
Illustrations by
W. Randall Irvine
Photography by
Arizona Highways Contributors

Friends hike in Madera Canyon, a choice area for bird-watching, en route to the top of Mt. Wrightson. (See page 100.) Peter Kresan

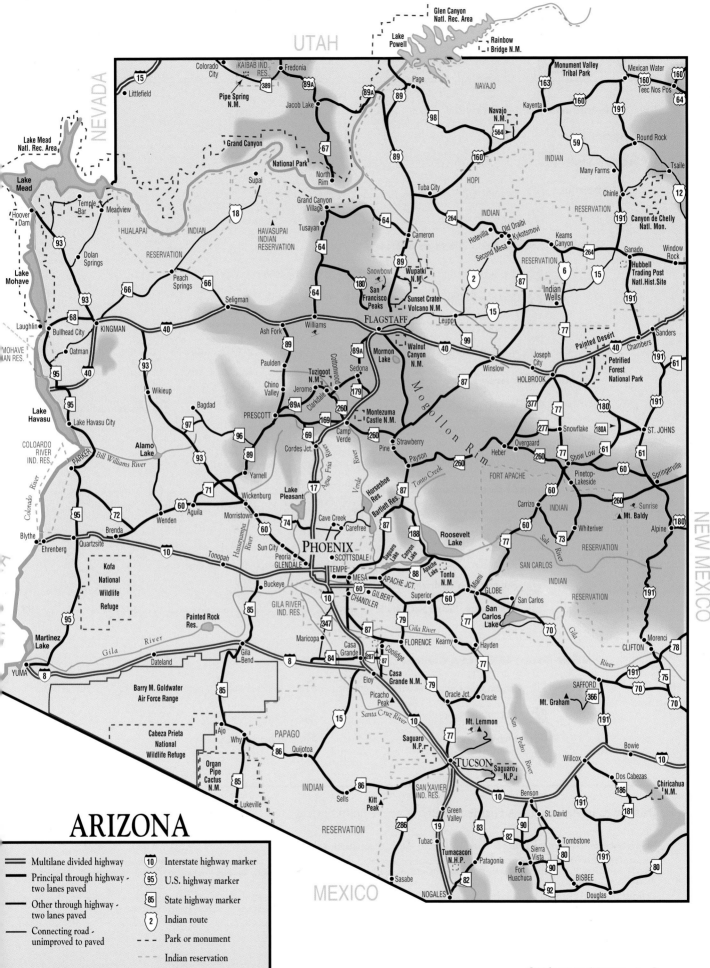

ARIZONA

Legend	
═══ Multilane divided highway	🛡10 Interstate highway marker
━━━ Principal through highway - two lanes paved	⬡95 U.S. highway marker
━━ Other through highway - two lanes paved	⬭85 State highway marker
─── Connecting road - unimproved to paved	② Indian route
	- - - Park or monument
	∙∙∙∙∙ Indian reservation

Contents

Outdoors in Arizona — A Guide to Hiking and Backpacking

Wesley Holden — Book Editor; **James E. Cook** — Associate Editor; **W. Randall Irvine** — Design

Prepared by the Books Division of *Arizona Highways* magazine, a monthly publication of the Arizona Department of Transportation.
Nina M. La France, Publisher; Bob Albano, Managing Editor; Robert J. Farrell, Associate Editor; Cindy Mackey, Production Director; Ellen Straine, Production Assistant, third printing.

Library of Congress Catalog Number 86-70969
ISBN 0-916179-50-8

ARIZONA

1 Principal Hikes

6 Hikes At A Glance

10 Interstate Highways

160 U.S. Highways

UTAH

NEVADA

CALIFORNIA

NEW MEXICO

MEXICO

Page
Kingman
Flagstaff
Holbrook
Prescott
Show Low
Phoenix
Ehrenberg
Globe
Yuma
Casa Grande
Safford
Tucson
Benson
Nogales

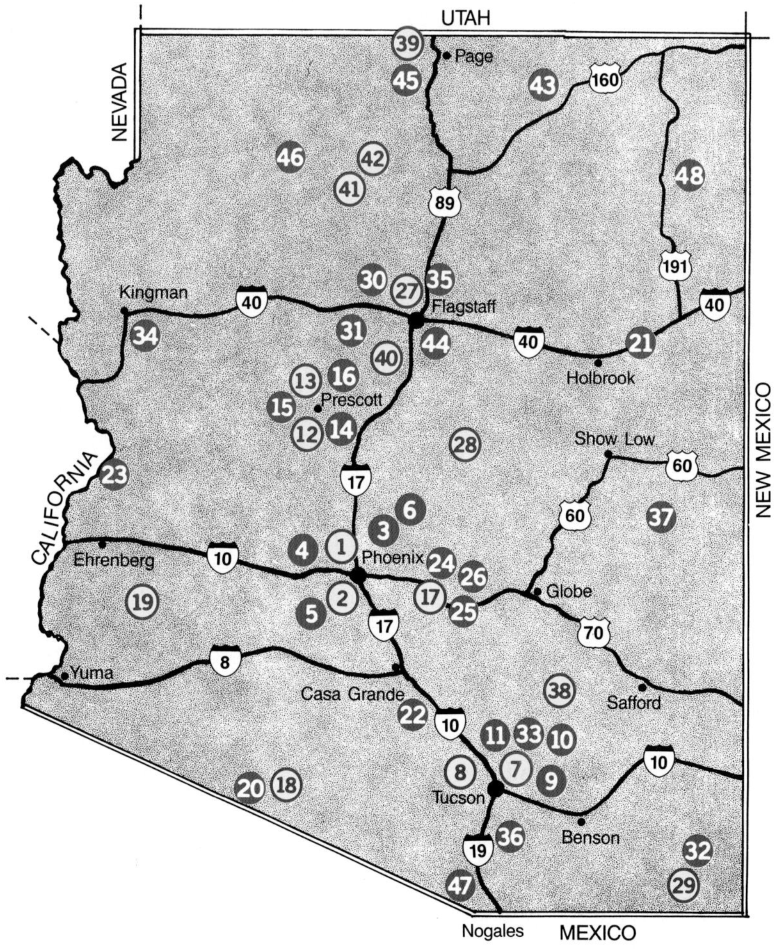

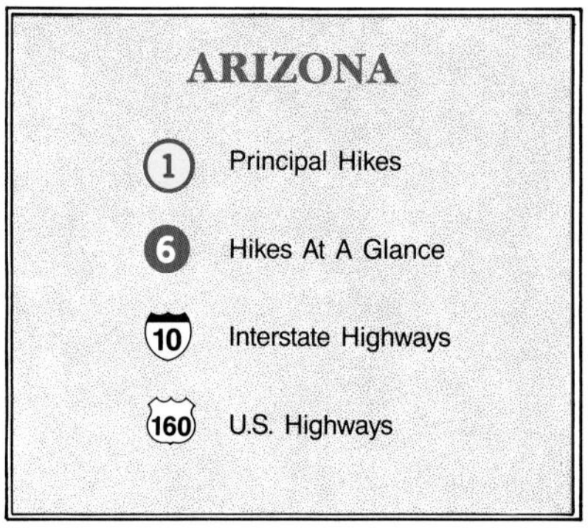

Introduction
by Stewart L. Udall

"Always...the rhythmic, body-honing, soul-cleansing act of walking."
—Colin Fletcher
The Man Who Walked Through Time

There is a simple reason why Arizona is a hiker's paradise. It is space—the state's generous endowment of lands held in trust by the federal and state governments. There is ample room to roam and to explore because more than half of Arizona's land mass is owned by all of us, and we are free to enjoy it without being challenged as trespassers.

The essence of the well-publicized Arizona life-style is the incredible array of outdoor recreation options offered by the spacious people-to-land ratio available to us. Every time I ponder that three million Arizonans share the same number of square miles as fifty-two million West Germans—and remember that states such as Texas and Iowa have only a few sparse acres of public lands—I glory in the wide-ranging outdoor recreation opportunities we have in the Southwest.

Among the most respected—and oldest—of such opportunities is trail hiking. This book is a splendid sampler for anyone interested in hiking Arizona's trails. Its principal author, John Annerino, elected to explore the whole range of options walkers and back-packers have. The text in this guidebook begins in the backyards of our big cities, ranges over stretches of our singular desert terrain, leads us across some of our scenic mountains, and concludes with a guided tour of a select few of Arizona's canyons—with a climax walk into the Grand Canyon itself.

The diversity of Arizona's outdoor estate makes it a walkers' wonderland:

■ to savor in winter. Our state has some of the most interesting desert environments in the United States —including two of the largest low-desert wildlife refuges (Kofa and Cabeza Prieta) in America.

■ to enjoy in all seasons. Arizona has a belt of pine-clad mountains which encompass the world's largest ponderosa pine forest and embrace unusual mountain "islands" rearing their refreshing ramparts in the southern part of the state.

■ to wander over anytime. There are remote wilderness areas in places such as the Gila Box and the Arizona Strip, where hikers seeking solitude can find untrammeled patches of beautiful land.

■ an astonishing array of canyons to explore. Arizona calls itself "The Grand Canyon State," but rugged walkers quickly discover that the hundreds of large and small canyons crisscrossing every part of the state are its most dominant geographical feature.

Moreover, as the author reminds us, the Arizona earth is a "book" which contains special chapters for those with ecological interests. The Grand Canyon itself is, of course, *the* incomparable classroom for

Grand Canyon hikers. George McCullough

geologists. Birders who want to study one of the widest arrays of birdlife in the United States congregate in southern Arizona. Botanists can have a field day almost anywhere in the state, and our region has long been a mecca for amateur archeologists and anthropologists interested in the cultures of the American Indian.

Outdoor enthusiasts should also be made aware that some of Arizona's finest—and most inaccessible—wild and scenic lands are owned by Indian tribes. Arizona has within its borders a higher proportion (27 percent) of Indian-owned land than any other state in the union. Fortunately, most tribes make part of their land available for outdoor recreation to non-Indians willing to pay appropriate fees and observe tribal and conservation regulations.

Among the most valuable tips in this primer about Arizona hiking are the descriptions of the day hikes available to the residents of our largest cities. To me, nothing adds more to the Arizona life-style than the opportunity offered to metropolitan parents to get their kids on nearby nature trails at young ages.

In this respect, Tucson has an unexcelled outdoor environment. It is the only large U. S. city bordered on two sides by a national monument (Saguaro National Monument) and on the other two sides by areas that are part of our national system of wilderness lands. Venturesome Tucson youngsters can take a lunch,

leave their homes on foot, spend the day in some of the nation's choice wild lands, and return at nightfall.

To me, walking is the best pastime there is. It is free, and it induces us to burn up our own calories, not irreplaceable hydrocarbons. It is, medical experts tell us, the best exercise in which we can engage. And it also is a form of recreation in which each person can set his or her own pace. And, besides, if we open our senses to nature's sights and sounds, such excursions offer each of us precious tranquil moments when our home, that we call the earth, can whisper wisdom in our ears.

Stewart L. Udall

Born in the small town of St. Johns, Arizona, to pioneer parents, attorney Stewart L. Udall has long been a conservationist and outspoken advocate for America's wild and natural lands— as congressman, Secretary of the Interior, and private citizen.

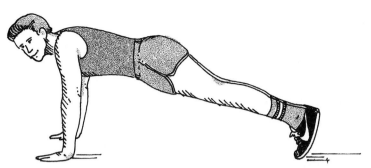

"When I was about six years old, my father said, 'Do not sleep after sunrise; wake as soon as daylight appears. Run toward the dawn. You should do this everyday. Run out as far as you can.'"

Sinyella, Supai Indian circa 1900

1. Conditioning

In another era, it was commonplace for Native Americans to cross vast tracts of uncharted wilderness on foot, most often running, because in one way or another their lives depended on it. The Tarahumara Indians of Chihuahua, Mexico, are noted for their legendary, 48-hour, 200-mile kickball races through an immense canyon called Barranca del Cobre. They could also run a deer to death easier than most modern Americans can run down a pasture horse and bridle it.

The Mojave Indians of southeastern California ran up to 100 miles a day across the Mojave Desert to trade with coastal tribes. As early as 1774, Fray Francisco Garces—a prodigious hoofer who trekked some 2000 miles throughout the Southwest in quest of souls—had a chance encounter with several Mojave runners. "Here [somewhere in the Mojave desert], I met four Indians, who had come from Santa Clara to traffic in shell beads. They are carrying no food supply, nor even bows for hunting."

Here in Arizona the Tohono O'Odham made a spiritual pilgrimage to the Gulf of California for salt, and the Hopi would run 40 miles to tend their small fields of corn.

Hunter-gatherers by nature, we have for the past few millenia moved steadily away from our natural inclination to explore the wilderness. Fortunately, the backpacking and running booms of the 1970s did much to bring us back in touch with this important part of our past and future.

Modern people have no reason to run a hundred miles. But what we can learn from these first Americans is how best to prepare and travel through Arizona's wild lands, be it a day hike or a weeklong backpack trip.

☐ **Physical:** Let's say you've got your sights set on hiking up 4808-foot Mt. Ajo in Organ Pipe Cactus National Monument in the early spring. You should do some shorter desert hikes to condition your body

for both the physical and environmental demands that will be placed on it. On the other hand, if you're out to hike the 12,000-foot-plus summits of the Kachina Peaks Wilderness, you should do some shorter, high-altitude hikes, say on Kendrick Peak, to train for it. One key to a successful and enjoyable hike is to duplicate the environmental conditions of your proposed hike in your training. (See *Backyard* chapter.) Just as you wouldn't train for a hike up 12,670-foot Humphreys Peak by jogging a few miles in the desert a few days a week, you shouldn't train for a hike through the length of Paria Canyon—a desert—by limiting your hiking to the forests of northern Arizona. Try to plan your first couple of day hikes, and overnight backpacking trips, in an environment your body is already physiologically adapted to, and one your mind is psychologically comfortable with.

In addition to simulating distance, elevation loss and gain, and environmental conditions, your training should be well-rounded enough to deal with unexpected situations that sometimes occur during a backpack. Be physically trained to hop from boulder to boulder, or to crawl under, or climb over, fallen trees; for creek or stream crossings; and for the possibility of getting "turned around" and having to double your mileage to get back to your car. Even the best hikers get disoriented. As Daniel Boone once said, "I ain't never been lost before, but I've been in some mighty strange country for three or four days."

You also have to remember that, unlike the great Native American runners who traveled light and fast, you will probably be carrying a 30- to 40-pound backpack. You may want to supplement your training hikes with some upper-body conditioning exercises that will help strengthen your back and shoulders. In combination with these, you should have a regular aerobic program that includes either brisk walking, running, cycling, and/or swimming.

What works best for somebody else may not be what works best for you. You may prefer a weekly program of ballet, modern dance, yoga, or the martial arts. The most important thing to remember is the only way to really get in shape to backpack Arizona's deserts, mountains, and canyons is to hike deserts, mountains, and canyons.

(Left) Wherever you plan on hiking, conditioning begins at home. And running is one of the most popular ways to get fit. Ken Akers.

□ **Mental Preparation:** This, without question, rivals the importance of being in good physical condition. If you head into the boonies with the attitude that nature is out to get you, or that you're going to "conquer" nature, you're going to have a fight on your hands and there's no question who's going to get whipped. So take a little time, a few weeks, before your first overnighter and read everything you can about the area you're going to hike. Try pre-visualizing what the area is going to be like. Once you're out in the middle of Yahoo Holler, you will already have laid important psychological groundwork to deal with both real and imagined problem situations.

Prepare yourself for the entire trip, but deal with today today, and tomorrow tomorrow. If you're embarking on what to you is a long backpack, and you start thinking about the entire hike, the scope of it just may overwhelm you. Take it a manageable piece at a time, until you reach the next spring or ridgetop; soon you will have put a series of those intermediate goals together.

What if you're bored with a particular stretch of trail, or what if climbing a series of switchbacks is just plain hard work? Disassociate yourself from the physical act of backpacking by daydreaming the same way you do on a long car drive. But what about the flip side, when you're hiking a narrow and precipitous trail? Obviously, you want to relax yet *concentrate* on every step you take, the lifting, carrying, and placing of each footstep, until the scary part is over.

And lastly, plan your trip for good conditions, but be prepared psychologically for a worst-case scenario. We all enjoy a sunny, carefree hike, but conditions in the wilderness can change suddenly and drastically. Your responses to those changes should be flexible and mature. Go as a student and learn what nature has to teach you. You may experience what naturalist John Muir felt when he wrote: "Nature's peace will flow into you as sunshine flows into trees. The winds will blow their own freshness into you, and the storms their energy, while cares drop off like autumn leaves."

2. What to Bring

For overnight hiking, you have two basic options: (a) You can labor under a Volkswagen-size backpack with all the amenities of home, or (b) you can travel lighter and faster. I prefer the latter.

□ **Clothing:** For desert hiking, there are two schools of thought on how many, and which, garments you should wear. The bushmen of Africa's Kalahari desert wear little except for a loin cloth. The nomadic Bedouin of Syria and North Africa, on the other hand, cover their heads and bodies with a long, flowing garment of cotton and wool called a *bernoose*.

You'll probably find the middle ground works best: a well-broken-in pair of lightweight hiking shoes, with good traction; cotton or light wool athletic socks; light colored, loose-fitting cotton pants (shorts if your legs are already conditioned to the sun and brambles); a cotton t-shirt, or long-sleeved cotton shirt; a cotton hat, or a headband if hats give you a

headache, as they do me; and a good pair of sunglasses.

If you're going to make an overnighter of it, and the season warrants it, you'll want a good wool watch cap, a warm jacket, and perhaps a change of socks. Again, how much you bring depends on how much you want to carry. Watch the ounces, and the pounds will take care of themselves.

For a canyon hike like Aravaipa or Paria, you should keep a dry change of shoes and clothes in your pack. They'll make evenings much more comfortable.

For mountain hiking, depending on the season, you may need warm, snowproofed boots; a pair of thick wool socks, lined with thin nylon socks to draw the moisture away from your feet; loose-fitting wool pants and shirt; wool sweater; wool gloves or mittens, and a wool hat; a down or fiberfill coat; dependable rainwear; a change of wool/blend or poly-pro underwear; and additional warm clothes carried in your pack.

□ **Equipment:** You can get as elaborate and high-tech as you want, but I'm going to suggest you keep it simple. Remember, *you* have to carry it.

□ **General:** The basics, whether you're doing a desert day hike or an extended mountain backpack, include: a good knife, pocket or sheath; "strike anywhere" matches in a metal match container; a small butane lighter (or a flint and steel if you know how to use it); a roll of surgical adhesive tape, and a comb; a tweezer as a bare minimum first aid kit; a small flashlight; a small container of iodine for dressing wounds and water purification; Moleskin to pad sore spots and blisters on your feet; aspirin for minor aches and pains; topographical maps folded and sealed in a ziplock baggie, along with a pen; plastic water bottles; and, for day hiking, a small day pack to put this gear in along with your lunch or a snack.

For overnight backpacking, you need the following as a bare minimum:

□ **Desert:** Take a pack large enough for a lightweight sleeping bag, or if it's mid-summer, a wool blanket or cotton sheet; an ensolite pad; a *minimum* of four quarts of water; food; a change of clothes if you desire; and whatever other personal items you think you need to carry. (I didn't mention a tent, because in most desert areas you can usually find a rock overhang to shelter yourself from seasonal rain. You might consider a tube tent, but practice using one before you try it out on the desert for the first time.)

☐ **Mountain:** For mountain backpacking, you would do well to add a tube tent or mountain tent, depending on the weather; a dependable stove; clothes, food, and other gear you may need for inclement weather.

☐ **Canyon:** This is where you should seriously consider using a "soft" frameless or internal-framed pack versus an external framed pack. In exposed canyon and peak hiking situations you can ill afford to be thrown off balance. External framed packs do not conform to your body the way soft packs do, making scrambling awkward and difficult. An external frame pack acts like a kite in high winds, and has more of a tendency to catch on tree branches and rock outcrops.

The other basic piece of gear you need for hiking canyons like Buckskin/Paria and the upper end of the West Fork, where plunge pools are the norm, is either an army surplus river bag to stuff all your things in for the swim across (large double-stretch, double-layered garbage bags will work in a pinch), or an air mattress. I prefer the river bag hands-down.

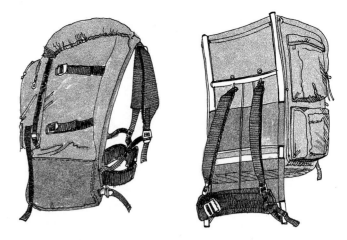

☐ **How to Pack:** There are opposite poles of thought on whether the weight of a pack should be high or low. I prefer the latter for several reasons. Packing your heavy gear like water, stove, fuel, food, etc. on the bottom of your pack keeps the center of gravity lower, which makes the weight far more manageable for general hiking as well as scrambling. I line the inside of the pack with my ensolite pad, which serves as an additional cushion between my back and whatever's inside the pack; put my sleeping bag on top of the gallon water jug; and put clothes, food, and a one-quart water bottle atop the sleeping bag for easy access.

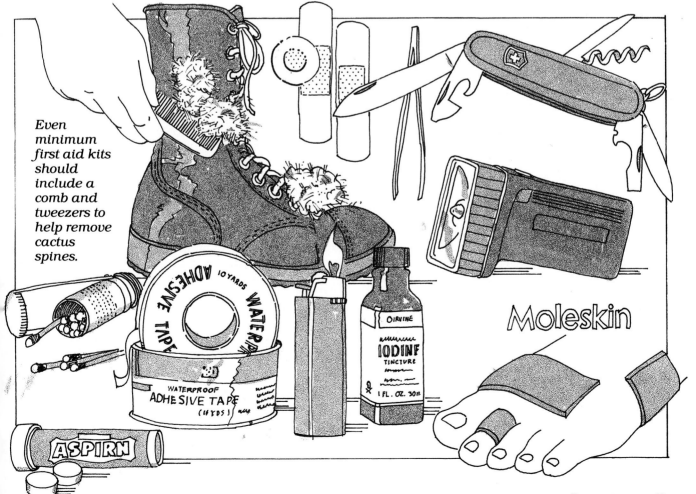

Even minimum first aid kits should include a comb and tweezers to help remove cactus spines.

(Above) A compass, a ballpoint pen, and topographical maps sealed in a ziplock plastic bag will help the modern explorer navigate Arizona's wild lands. W. Randall Irvine

☐ **Maps:** As a minimum, you should carry the topographical maps listed at the end of each major hike described in this book. They're available at many outdoor equipment shops, or by writing Branch Distribution, U.S. Geological Survey, Federal Center, Denver, CO 80255, (303) 236-7477. If you write the U.S. Geological Survey for some of the maps mentioned in this book, ask for a price list and index. It is an overlay of Arizona with the names and locations of individual quadrangle maps highlighted on it so you can see which maps you might need for other hikes not described in this guide or for other outdoor activities. You also should request a copy of the booklet on how to read a topographical map.

If you have not used topographical maps before, you will quickly learn how valuable they are simply because their contour lines tell you the shape of the terrain. Most USGS maps are now 7½-minute maps: each map or "quadrangle" covers 7½-minutes of the earth's surface, approximately 4 miles. (There are 60 minutes to one degree of longitude or latitude.)

The chart on the margin of each map shows its "contour interval" — the difference in elevation between the irregular red lines that follow the earth's contours on the map. Contour lines 80 feet apart, for example, will be few and far between on the flat desert, but crowded close together on steep mountainsides. On a road map, of course, either area would appear "flat." USGS topographical maps also show "section lines," straight survey lines at one-mile intervals, man-made structures, such as buildings,

which occur as tiny black squares. Other symbols are used to represent springs, windmills, ranches, cemeteries, and other features.

If I'm hiking in a National Forest roadless or wilderness area, I'll also carry Forest Service recreation maps for each particular area. While these maps do not have contour lines, they do have trail and road numbers, as well as more recent information on available and reliable water sources. For this book the editors have added information on the maps that is pertinent to the specific hikes.

3. Method of Travel

Let the season be the indicator. If you're doing a desert backpack in the spring, you should start your hike at daybreak and hike until mid-morning, take a siesta in the shade during the warmest part of the day, and resume your hiking mid-afternoon. However, if you're doing a winter, mountain hike, you'll probably want to sleep in and start your hike when things warm up; stop for lunch, hike through the afternoon, and make camp long before the sun goes down.

☐ **When to Go:** You probably wouldn't enjoy your first hike up 12,670-foot Humphreys Peak in midwinter; it obviously would be more enjoyable in the summer or early fall. However, summer, specifically during July/August monsoon season, is not necessarily the ideal time to hike the peak because of the danger from lightning.

On the other hand, you probably wouldn't enjoy hiking Aravaipa Canyon during late fall or winter, because the days are short and the air is cool. That makes wading back-and-forth across the creek unpleasantly cold and even dangerous. Better to go late spring or early fall. There are exceptions to these general guidelines. Weigh environmental factors against your experience and physical capabilities before you decide when to do a particular hike.

☐ **Waterhole-to-Waterhole:** One of your biggest considerations while hiking in a region as diverse as Arizona is water. It seems there is either too much or not enough. Most often the case will be not enough water. That means you should plan your hike from one reliable or perennial water source to the next. Otherwise, you must carry a *minimum* of a gallon of water a day, at eight pounds a gallon, for mountain or desert hiking. If you hit a spring heat wave in the desert, you'll need two to three gallons a day just to replace the massive fluid deprivation. Obviously, the requirements for water, and its sources, should figure into all your hiking plans.

☐ **Hiking Techniques:** You might think hiking is just putting one foot in front of the other, and for the most part it is. However, there are two techniques you'll find helpful. Going uphill you want to use what is called the "reststep." Basically, you take a short step with one leg, lock your knee, and take the next step, lock your knee, and so on. Locking your knee enables you to rest on the skeleton of one leg while the other takes the next step.

The second technique, called the "shuffle," is used for hiking downhill. Most beginning hikers have a tendency to break each and every downhill step. That not only puts an incredible amount of torque on your ankle, knee, and hip joints, but it can make hiking exhausting and dangerous if you're walking along an exposed trail. The key to the shuffle is to relax your body and your leg muscles, so the shock of each step downhill is absorbed by your leg muscles. It also gives you a better feel for the trail. If you do start to slide on a ball-bearing type surface, you can control your descent easier. Both of these techniques require a little practice before they're perfected, but they'll make your hike easier.

4. Outdoor Skills

You need to practice several outdoor skills until they are second nature. First is how to build a fire. While campfires are not permitted in national parks and monuments, they can save your life if you need warmth or to signal for help. Before building a fire, ask yourself whether you really need one, and if there is any danger to the environment. If a fire is necessary, keep it small and use an existing fire ring if available. Avoid volcanic rocks, which contain gases, and streambed rocks which might hold moisture; heat can explode either kind, sending dangerous fragments through the air. As you break camp, be sure the fire is dead out, completely covered, and that the area is returned to its natural state.

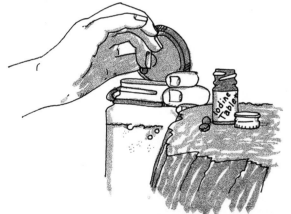

☐ **Water Purification:** Unless you obtain water directly from a spring, you should purify it. There are half a dozen methods. Although some people prefer chlorine treatment, especially to process water for large parties, iodine in tablet form is more dependable. Iodine forms a shell around a nasty little amoeba called ghiardia so it can pass through your system without wreaking havoc.

Given time and proper equipment, boiling water is the surest means of purifying it. Five to 10 minutes at 212 degrees Fahrenheit will kill both bacteria and viruses.

If you do use iodine or chlorine, remember that large doses can be toxic; that potency generally decreases with age; that effectiveness of the chemical depends on water temperature and amount of organic material suspended in the water; and that the chemical should be thoroughly dissolved in the water, which should then sit for at least thirty minutes before use.

As far as a water purification tube or "straw" is concerned: They work great sucking out of a water glass in your kitchen, but when you are in the bush, thirsty, and trying to replenish a two-quart fluid deficit, they are agonizingly slow.

☐ **Equipment Related:** There are several equipment-related techniques you should perfect before you head into the bush. The two most common are how to use, maintain, and repair (in the field) a camp stove; and how to erect a tent. Okay, so you know how to operate your stove and set up your tent, but can you do it in a rain squall or snowstorm *before* you start suffering from exposure? If there is any possibility you are likely to encounter those kinds of inclement conditions, make sure you have practiced these techniques until they are instinctive.

5. Emergencies and Hazards

☐ **Desert:** The greatest hazards of hiking in the desert are heat-related. Make sure your physiology is acclimated to a hot and dry environment. You can do this by living and exercising in a desert environment, or by simulating the conditions in your training. Thirst is a poor indicator of fluid requirements. Pre-hydrate yourself with enough water before the start of your hike so that your urine is clear. Carry, and continue drinking, enough water throughout the duration of the hike to maintain clear urine. If it starts to turn yellow, you need to drink more water; if it is dark yellow, you need to stop exercising and replenish lost fluids with water until it is clear again.

Cover sensitive skin from the sun, either with cotton garments and/or sun screen-type ointments.

Loose, volcanic rock is typical of desert hiking. Watch your step and wear shoes with ankle support. If you don't put your hands and feet into places you can't see, you probably won't be bitten by a snake or other poisonous reptile. Be careful how you step over a log or rock which might shelter a rattlesnake. If you do get bitten, *stay as calm and still as possible.* Accelerated heartbeat from anxiety or exertion will pump the venom faster. Chemically activated cold packs, available at drug stores, can slow down the rate at which venom travels.

There are several methods of dealing with snakebite and little agreement among physicians about which is best. Be familiar with the various methods—cut-and-suck, ligature/cryotherapy (cold packs), antivenin or hydracortizone injections—and decide which you would use. If possible, get to a hospital quickly. At least, send someone for competent help.

Perhaps the most common injury of all in the desert environment is a brush with cactus, so be sure your first aid kit has a comb and tweezers—the comb to remove large (anteriorally-barbed) cactus spines and the tweezers to pluck out the clusters of hairlike spines called glochidia.

Mine shafts and tunnels should also be avoided for obvious reasons.

☐ **Mountain:** The biggest hazards in the mountains will be cold-related. Hypothermia is called the "killer of the unprepared," and what I consider to be far and away the most insidious and dangerous of physiological hazards. Hypothermia is more commonly called "exposure." You don't have to go high to get hypothermia. It's a hazard that runs through sea, desert, wilderness, and mountain survival. You can be in excellent physical condition, and the temperature doesn't have to be below freezing. In fact, hypothermia most often occurs in 30-50 degree air temperatures.

All it takes is inadequate or damp clothing and a cool breeze for the body to begin the process of losing heat faster than it can be replaced. Add to that wet clothing from snow or cold water immersion, and you go from the wind chill factor to the wet chill factor, which is even more dangerous. Your body temperature only needs to drop a degree or two before your judgment and reaction time are impaired. Add the effects of exhaustion, and people start doing very foolish things.

Your body's built-in system for treating hypothermia is through shivering, and obviously you shouldn't let things get that far. If they do for some reason beyond your control, such as cold water immersion, rewarm yourself by getting out of your damp clothes and into dry ones, drinking hot fluids, and covering yourself with a sleeping bag.

However, if you, or someone else, goes into the second stage of hypothermia, there is little chance of the body being able to rewarm itself—no matter how much clothing or how many sleeping bags you use—unless heat is applied internally with hot liquids and externally with additional clothing, fire, or a car heater, and, if that's what it takes, another body. You prevent hypothermia by knowing the symptoms, staying dry

Arizona's numerous high mountains rise abruptly from the surrounding lowlands and offer a radical change in life zones — from warm desert to alpine woodlands. One of the greatest hazards for mountain hikers is hypothermia, or exposure.
Fred Griffin

and out of the wind, wearing enough of the right clothing, and wearing that wool hat.

Mountain or altitude sickness comes from going too high too fast, so make sure you have done enough training hikes to acclimate yourself to the thin air you'll encounter on most of the mountain hikes.

Stay off ridgetops and open meadows during lightning storms.

Unless you're an experienced mountaineer, avoid the higher mountain peaks during heavy snows and winter storm warnings.

☐ **Canyon:** The most likely threat in any canyon hike is from flash floods. Avoid canyon-bottom hiking during peak spring runoff, the summer monsoons, and any other time there's the slightest possibility a canyon will "flash."

☐ **General:** Know basic first aid and how to treat blisters, cuts, sprains; how to do cardiopulmonary resuscitation (CPR); how to remove cactus spines, and what should be carried in an individual or group first aid kit.

☐ **Escape Routes and Self-Rescue:** Above all, don't go into the bush thinking that if you get into trouble, somebody's going to be able to rescue you with a helicopter. You not only should be self-reliant, but you should realize there are some areas in Arizona, and certain weather conditions, where an expeditious rescue is next to impossible. Know your escape routes before you embark on a hike, and don't burn any bridges if you have any doubts about your capabilities or the trail ahead.

6. Survival

"Mile after mile the journey stretches through this land of 'silence, solitude, and sunshine,' with little to distract the eye from the awful surrounding and desolation dreariness except bleaching skeletons..."

Report of the Boundary Commission upon the Survey and Remarking of the Boundary between the United States and Mexico west of the Rio Grande.

Pioneered by Father Kino in the late 1600s, Arizona's *Camino del Diablo*, Highway of the Devil, claimed the lives of many—some say more than 400—enroute to the California goldfields in the 1850s. Like the pioneers who headed west along the Gila, Santa Fe, and Oregon trails, those who traveled the Devil's Highway were a hardy lot. But sheer hardiness and courage didn't always compensate for poor planning and the hazards of trekking over 150 miles of waterless desert. In those days, you learned about survival first hand, often the hard way.

Today there are two ways to learn about survival, the difficult way or the "easier" way. As the word itself suggests, survival is not fun, nor is it particularly easy, though some survival texts now tell us how to chuckle through all but the most dire survival situations if we use their elaborate techniques.

But let's be realistic. When was the last time any of us caught a three course brunch in a snare, trap, or deadfall? How many of us could start a fire with a crudely made bow drill? And when was the last time you found any potable water in someplace as dry as the lower Sonoran desert in midsummer? Hopefully, none of us will ever have to find out. But as the headlines every year point out, a large number of people are thrust back into survival situations, whether the cause is a plane wreck, flat tire, or poor planning. And unless you have actually practiced the survival techniques that took primitive man years to master, the odds are against you making them work when you're already suffering from heat exhaustion, hunger, and exposure.

So here are some practical tips that will help you avoid hard-core, primitive survival situations:

☐ Carry more water than you think you'll need.
☐ Don't hike in the heat of the day.
☐ Make sure you have checked all the water sources in the area you'll be visiting.
☐ Try to plan your camps so they are near water.
☐ Know where you are going and where you are at all times in relation to the map you're carrying.
☐ Tell somebody where you are going and when you will be home.
☐ Check on the weather from more than one source.
☐ Don't overestimate your abilities.

Arizona is a land of diverse topography and climate extremes. What applies to desert survival doesn't always hold true for mountain travel. The key to surviving any situation, be it alpine tundra or austere desert, is your state of mind. And the best way to achieve the proper state of mind is to realize you have to make a sudden psychological transition from that of modern man, with all his comforts, to that of a caveman enduring a stone-age existence. Once you do that, your inherent will to live and a little common sense will take care of the rest. For additional reading material on the subject of *Survival*, see the reading list on page 135 of this book.

Day hikers enjoy the beauty of spring flowers in Organ Pipe Cactus National Monument.
James Tallon

7. Backcountry Ethics

"The richest values of wilderness lies not in the days of Daniel Boone nor even in the present, but rather in the future."

Aldo Leopold (1887-1948)

The days of the mountain man are over, and no one is disheartened by that fact more than I. The signs are everywhere, from the trampled shallows of Elves Chasm at the bottom of the Grand Canyon, to the lofty garbage dumps on Mt. McKinley. We continue to seek out that one spot where no one else has stood before, but just around the next bend in the canyon is a discarded pair of disco boots, a broken flashlight, and a ballooned-up baggie of rotten hot-dogs. Somebody has been there before.

The list of affronts against Mother Nature is endless. Too many backcountry users feel that nature is a sort of omnipotent garbage disposal, capable of digesting the endless swill of modern man. It is not. Gone are the days when you could pitch camp with little regard for the environment or those who followed in your footsteps.

Nobody wants to flee the harness of civilization only to have their wilderness experience restricted by government regulations, not you, not me, not the "free spirits" of tomorrows yet to come. However, that is exactly what is happening to wilderness areas adjacent to large cities, and it will happen to more remote wilderness areas if we don't change some of our bad habits and start living in harmony with nature. The U. S. Forest Service's *Backcountry Ethics* is the most succinct of several guides to wilderness etiquette.

☐ **Setting camp:** Avoid camping in meadows; you'll trample grass. Pick a campsite where you won't need to clear away vegetation or level a tent site. Use an existing campsite, if available. Camp at least 300 feet from streams or springs. State law prohibits camping within a quarter mile of an only available water source (for wildlife and livestock). Do not cut trees, limbs, or brush to make camp improvements. Carry aluminum tent poles.

☐ **Breaking camp:** Before leaving camp, naturalize the area. Replace rocks and wood used; scatter needles, leaves, and twigs on the campsite. Scout the area to be sure you've left nothing behind. Everything you packed into your camp should be packed out. Try to make it appear as if no one had been there.

(Left) Siesta time. A hiker rests beneath the emerald-like forest canopy in Havasu Canyon near the west end of the Grand Canyon. Tom Bean

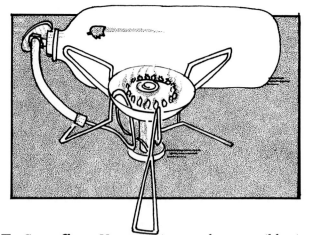

☐ **Campfires:** Use gas stoves, when possible, to conserve dwindling supplies of firewood. If you need to build a fire, use an existing campfire ring. If you need to clear a new fire site, keep it small and select a safe spot. Make your campfire away from rock ledges that would be blackened by smoke; away from meadows where it would destroy grass and leave a scar; and away from dense brush, trees, and duff where it would be a fire hazard. Clear a circle of all burnable materials. Dig a shallow pit for the fire. Keep the sod intact. Use only fallen timber. Even standing dead trees are part of the beauty of wilderness. Put your fire *cold out* before leaving, by mixing coals with dirt and water. Feel it with your hand. If it's cold out, cover the ashes in the pit with dirt, replace the sod, and naturalize the disturbed area.

☐ **Pack it in — Pack it out:** Bring trash bags to carry out all trash that cannot be completely burned. Aluminum foil and aluminum lined packages won't burn up in your fire. Compact it and put it in your trash bag. Cigarette butts, pull-tabs, and gum wrappers are litter, too. They can spoil a campsite.

☐ **Don't bury trash!** Animals dig it up. Try to pack out trash left by others. A good example may catch on.

☐ **Do not wash in streams or springs:** Wash yourself, your dishes, and your clothes in a container. Food scraps, toothpaste, even biodegradable soap will pollute streams and springs. Remember, it's your drinking water, too! Pour wash water on ground away from streams and springs.

☐ **Bury human waste:** When nature calls, select a suitable spot at least 100 feet from open water, campsites, and trails. Dig a hole 4 to 6 inches deep. Try to keep the sod intact. After use, fill in the hole completely burying waste and TP; then tramp in the sod. Improper disposal of human waste can spoil and pollute the backcountry. Fortunately, the top layer of soil is alive with bacteria that decompose human waste.

☐ **Don't short-cut trails:** Trails are designed and maintained to prevent erosion. Cutting across switchbacks and trampling meadows can create a confusing maze of unsightly trails. Federal law prohibits disturbing historic and prehistoric sites. Do *not* dig in sites or remove objects.

One additional bit of common sense: Leave gates, cabins, and other structures the way you find them.

This section, on hiking in your urban backyard, is included in this guide for several reasons. First, the following day hikes are a place to start if you have never hiked or backpacked. This taste of the wilds may help keep you from getting in over your head on some of the longer, more strenuous treks. If hiked regularly, or used in combination with other forms of aerobic exercise, these hikes will provide a convenient and reliable way to train for the more challenging hikes described later on in this book.

Also, these hikes offer urban Arizonans and visitors to the state more accessible places to hike if they can't break away for the entire weekend. Each of these hikes, taken by itself, is rewarding.

If you use these to train for longer hikes in this guide, please refer to the appended information at the end of each hike, specifically *elevation* and *mileage*. You should approximate, in your day hikes, the conditions you are likely to encounter in your planned overnighters. Build up slowly and regularly, and you'll find these day hikes can be stepping stones to greater horizons.

As Mount Everest conqueror Sir Edmund Hillary once said, "The only way to get in shape to climb mountains is to climb mountains."

The same holds true for hiking and backpacking in Arizona's wild lands.

Phoenix

① Squaw Peak

With the possible exception of the Bright Angel Trail in the Grand Canyon, no other hiking trail in Arizona is as popular as the 1.2-mile-long trail which switchbacks its way to the 2608-foot summit of Phoenix' beloved Squaw Peak. According to records, roughly 375,000 people hiked the trail in 1986. That was an average of 7211.5 people a week, or 1030 Phoenicians and tourists a day.

With those figures, you'd think we lived in Oklahoma and that Squaw Peak was the only mountain in the state. Hardly. It is simply one of the most accessible and rewarding hikes in the Phoenix metropolitan area. It is a wilderness beacon, drawing people out of the maw of civilization.

The trail climbs quickly through ocotillo, paloverde, creosote, barrel, and saguaro cactus. Fat, timid lizards called chuckawallas are a common sight. You shouldn't be totally surprised if you see a black, yellow, and orange beaded lizard called a Gila monster. Its winged namesake, the Gila woodpecker, is as common on Squaw Peak as the coveys of mourning dove and Gambel's quail.

If you don't quite have the snap to make the pull all the way to the summit, there's a good turnaround point about three-quarters of a mile up the trail. It's at the foot of the last series of switchbacks and is marked by a paloverde tree shading an old mine shaft.

(Left) Paloverde trees in bloom herald the coming of spring to Phoenix' Squaw Peak Park. Jerry Sieve

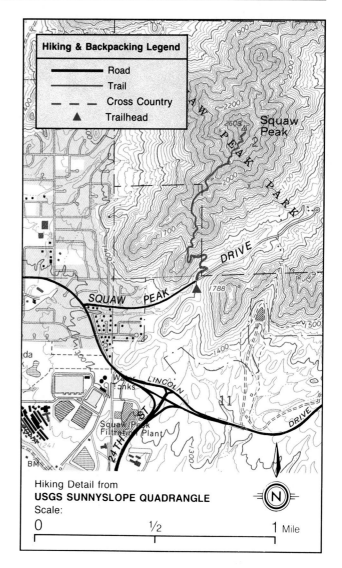

Hiking & Backpacking Legend

——— Road
——— Trail
— — — Cross Country
▲ Trailhead

Hiking Detail from
USGS SUNNYSLOPE QUADRANGLE
Scale:

0   ½   1 Mile

(Left) Brittle bush in bloom at the base of craggy Squaw Peak. John Annerino

(Below) The last Saturday evening before Christmas, thousands of people come to Squaw Peak Park to sing carols and hike the luminaria-lit Summit Trail. Frank Zullo

(Following panel, pages 22-23) Hikers take a break and enjoy the view from the most popular summit in Arizona, 2608-foot Squaw Peak. John Annerino

Squaw Peak was named by Dr. O. A. Turney in 1910, and from its craggy summit you'll have an uninterrupted 360-degree panorama of easily identifiable natural landmarks: The southern terminus of the Bradshaw Mountains can be seen to the north; Pinnacle Peak will be that lone finger of rock on the north end of the McDowell Mountains in the northeast; the main massif of the Superstition Mountains will be due east; South Mountain, shadowed by the sawteeth of the 4000-foot-high Sierra Estrellas, will be south-southwest; and the White Tank Mountains will be almost due west.

How To Get There

To reach the heart of Squaw Peak Park, and the 1.2-mile-long Summit Trail, drive on Lincoln Drive or Glendale Avenue (they join at 16th Street) to Squaw Peak Drive, which is just west of 24th Street. Take Squaw Peak Drive to the first ramada on the left (north) side of the road and park there, space permitting. The Summit Trail was designated a National Recreation Trail in 1974, so the trailhead is marked.

Primary Access: Squaw Peak Summit Trail via Squaw Peak Drive.

Elevation: 1400 feet at trailhead to 2608 feet on summit. So if you're using Squaw Peak to train for a hike in the Grand Canyon, as many people do, build up gradually until you can hike up and down the summit four times in a day, two days in a row with a pack on, and that'll be your best indication of the stamina required to hike up and down the Bright Angel Trail.

Mileage: 2.5 miles round trip.

Water: No perennial water en route: drinking fountain near trailhead.

Cache Point: Paloverde tree saddle.

Escape Route: Back down the Summit Trail.

Seasons: Fall through spring; summer it's best to hike it at dawn or dusk, as most of the regulars do.

Maps: USGS Sunnyslope quadrangle, or the Phoenix Mountain Trails Map (see address below).

Nearest Supply Point: Phoenix.

Managing Agency: City of Phoenix Parks and Recreation, 200 West Washington St., 16th Floor, Phoenix, AZ 85003, (602) 262-6861.

Backcountry Information: Permit not required: dogs not allowed. Fires and overnight camping prohibited. No mountain bikes on summit trail.

② South Mountain

Compared to the convenience and popularity of Squaw Peak, South Mountain can seem like a distant cousin. However, its 30 miles of main trails comprise a network that provides access to the largest municipal park in the world.

You can hike to the 2330 foot summit ridge from the general vicinity of 24th Street south of Baseline Road via the two-mile-long Mormon Trail, or from 7th Street south of Dobbins on the Holbert Trail. Or you can traverse the entire mountain via the 13.75-mile-long Sun Circle National Trail. You'll be traveling a mountain range long recognized by the Pima Indians as having spiritual significance. If you spend enough time out there studying the ancient petroglyphs, it will probably hold a similar significance for you.

One of the most popular hikes in South Mountain is the segment of the Sun Circle National Trail between Pima Canyon on the eastern end of the park, west to Buena Vista Lookout atop the summit ridge. This 3-mile-long segment of the National Trail meanders through the appropriately named Hidden Valley. There you'll be out of sight of metropolitan Phoenix, and surrounded by desert wilderness, enabling you to experience the land the way it was when the ancient Hohokam people roamed the area 2000 years ago.

This is an enchanting journey through primeval shapes of decomposed granite, like the natural slick-walled slot called Fat Man's Pass, the rock tunnel, and the natural bridge. If you're attentive, you may be able to pick out an elephant tree or two. South Mountain is as far north as this unusual desert tree grows.

How To Get There

You can reach the Sun Circle National Trail to Hidden Valley by driving south on Central Avenue to the park entrance (ask the park rangers for a free map) and continuing up the mountain to Buena Vista Lookout atop South Mountain. Take the trail east to Hidden Valley. Or, if you would like the challenge of hiking uphill, rather than downhill, take Guadalupe Road into Pima Canyon on the eastern end of the mountain and begin your hike at the parking lot there.

From either of these two trailheads you can do an out-and-back hike to Hidden Valley, or car shuttle with a vehicle at each trailhead. Either approach will take you into the heart of a desert wilderness in Phoenix' back yard.

Aerial view of Phoenix's South Mountain Park, looking southwest, with the Sierra Estrella Mountains in the background. At more than 16,000 acres, this is the largest city-owned park in the world. It contains 30 miles of well-marked hiking trails and a variety of lengths and degrees of difficulty. Landis Info Freeway

(Far left) The drive to the top of South Mountain begins at the southern end of Central Avenue and meanders up through some of the finest Sonoran Desert scenery to be found anywhere. Frank Zullo

(Left) A hiker examines the trail guide, obtained at the park entrance, before departing Buena Vista Lookout on the Hidden Valley trail. John Annerino

Primary Access: Buena Vista Lookout or Pima Canyon.
Elevation: Approximately 1500 feet at Pima Canyon to 2300 feet at Buena Vista Lookout.
Mileage: Approximately 3 miles one way.
Water: No perennial water en route.
Cache Point: Halfway between the beginning of your hike and the turnaround point.
Escape Route: Buena Vista Lookout or Pima Canyon.
Seasons: Fall through spring.
Maps: USGS Lone Butte, and Guadalupe quadrangles, or the Phoenix Mountain Trails map.
Nearest Supply Point: Phoenix.
Managing Agency: City of Phoenix Parks and Recreation, 200 West Washington St., 16th Floor, Phoenix, AZ 85003, (602) 262-6861.
Backcountry Information: Permit not required. Call for information on bike and horse trails.

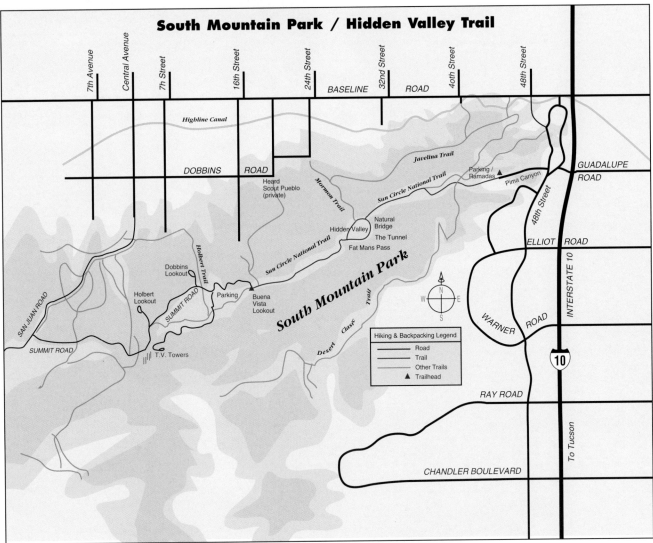

South Mountain Park / Hidden Valley Trail

W. Randall Irvine

Sarah Irvine

W. Randall Irvine

(Far left) A family of hikers enjoys a morning outing through South Mountain's Hidden Valley.
W. Randall Irvine

(This page) Hikers enjoy the flora and the fauna along the Hidden Valley Trail as well as its unique rock formations, such as Fat Man's Pass, the rock tunnel, and the natural bridge. Looking like a group of pre-historic hikers, this petroglyph panel was pecked into a rock near the trail's terminus at Pima Canyon parking area.

Wesley Holden

Wesley Holden

❸ Camelback Mountain

Echo Canyon

The most popular trail up Camelback Mountain leaves the east end of the Echo Canyon parking lot, which is located just south of the Tatum Boulevard/ McDonald Drive intersection. From the parking lot, head east uphill to the headwall which forms the foundation for a spire of conglomerate rock called the Praying Monk. The Camelback Mountain Trail contours the base of this headwall east/southeast, until it gains a prominent ridgeline which will take you all the way to the summit of Camelback.

Don't underestimate this trail. It is steeper and longer than the Squaw Peak Summit Trail. It's not as well maintained, but it's not nearly as heavily used either. You need sturdier shoes for hiking this trail than you might get by with on Squaw Peak, and they should also have good traction. Several stretches on the upper section of trail require some boulder-dancing as well as walking on a natural ball bearing-type surface. For these reasons, this trail requires more care coming down than hiking up.

Camelback Mountain Trail is approximately 4 miles round trip. Allow plenty of time not only to hike it, but to marvel at the amazing rock formations and spectacular views of the Phoenix area.

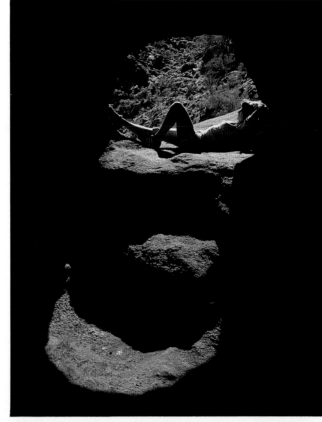

Fred Griffin

John Annerino

❺ McDowell Mountains

There are between 45 and 55 miles of well maintained trails in McDowell Mountain Regional Park. Among them is a portion of the historic military road that was once the cavalry trail between Fort McDowell on the Indian reservation and Fort Whipple at the territorial capital in Prescott. Nestled between the McDowell Mountains and the Verde River, this park displays the Sonoran Desert at its beautiful best, especially during the spring blooming time of mid-March to mid-April.

James Tallon

Located northeast of the Phoenix area, the park is best reached via Shea Boulevard east from Phoenix, or State Route 87 northeast from the Mesa-Tempe area, to Fountain Hills. The park entrance is approximately 4.5 miles north of this desert community on Fountain Hills Drive. Pick up a trail guide at the park.

James Tallon

James Tallon

❹ White Tank Mountains

Driving west of Phoenix about 20 miles on Olive Avenue will take you to White Tank Mountain Regional Park (Dunlap Avenue in Phoenix becomes Olive at 43rd Avenue.) The mountains were named for one of the granite catch basins, or tanks, located in the exposed bedrock outcrops. Numerous petroglyphs, prehistoric drawings on rocks, can be found in the area.

For details on picnic and camping facilities as well as the extensive and well-marked hiking trails, contact Maricopa County Parks Department, 3475 West Durango Street, Phoenix, AZ 85009, (602) 506-2930.

❻ Sierra Estrella

It is believed that the name Sierra Estrella, Spanish for Star Mountain, was derived from the outcroppings of white quartz that can be found throughout the length of the range. There are approximately 50 miles of well-maintained trails in Estrella Mountain Regional Park. Some trails extend into Rainbow Valley. You can pick up a trail guide at the park as well as information on park facilities — Camping is not allowed in the park.

To reach the Estrellas, drive west of Phoenix on Interstate 10, to Estrella Parkway, Exit 126, then south 5 miles to the park entrance, which is just south of Indian Springs Road.

What clearly sets Tucson's backyard apart from that of Phoenix and Prescott is the sheer scope of Tucson's day-hiking opportunities. For instance, if you were to continue a hike up from Sabino Canyon or Bear Canyon near the foot of the Santa Catalinas, you would soon be deep within the 56,430-acre Pusch Ridge Wilderness. Or if you continued a hike up the Tanque Verde Trail from Juniper Basin, you'd enter the 57,930-acre Rincon Mountain Wilderness. Even the 5.5-mile-long day hike up 4687-foot Wasson Peak in the 13,470-acre Tucson Mountain Wilderness rivals any hike you can do in the Prescott area.

What you should consider before embarking on any of the following hikes is the cutoff point between day hike and overnight backpack. In the Santa Catalinas, the consequences of stepping beyond that point would be unpleasant unless you are prepared for the rigors of genuine wilderness travel.

These 9157-foot-high mountains have been variously named the Santa Catalina Cuitchibaque and the Sierra de Santa Catarina; eventually the name was shortened and anglicized until it became the Santa Catalinas. Today, these rugged mountains form the northeastern skyline for the Tucson metropolitan area. The Pusch Ridge Wilderness comprises the front range of these mountains and is located only 10 miles from downtown Tucson, providing access to anyone who hankers to explore this wild section of the Coronado National Forest.

(Left) The major access to the Santa Catalina Mountains is through popular Sabino Canyon. The Phone Line Trail can be seen on the right side of the canyon.
(Below) A peaceful fall hike on the rugged slopes of the Santa Catalinas. Peter Kresan photos

⑦ Sabino Canyon

The most popular access point into the Santa Catalinas is the Sabino Canyon Recreation Area. It is to Tucsonans what Squaw Peak is to Phoenicians. The public no longer is allowed to drive into Sabino Canyon because of the congestion and the damage vehicular exhaust was doing to its riparian habitat.

That leaves the visitor three ways to visit this lush canyon: You can take a guided shuttle from the visitor information center up to road's end near the wilderness boundary and hike back down the paved Sabino Canyon Road; you can hike up the road to one of five streamside picnic areas and catch the shuttle back; or you can hike above Sabino Creek along the well-marked Phone Line Trail to the Sabino Creek junction 4.2 miles from the visitor information center.

Once at this junction, you have the option of hiking back the way you came, strolling along the blacktop paralleling Sabino Creek, or—if you're too winded from the hike up—catching the shuttle back. (Nominally-priced tickets are available adjacent to the visitor information center.)

(Left) The quiet waters of Sabino Canyon reflect the leaves of a cottonwood tree. Peter Kresan

(Right) Mother and daughter take a lunch break in Sabino Canyon. John Annerino

(Below) A mother javelina and youngster in the Catalinas. Robert Campbell

(Bottom) The Sabino Canyon shuttle splashes through runoff from a summer storm. John Annerino

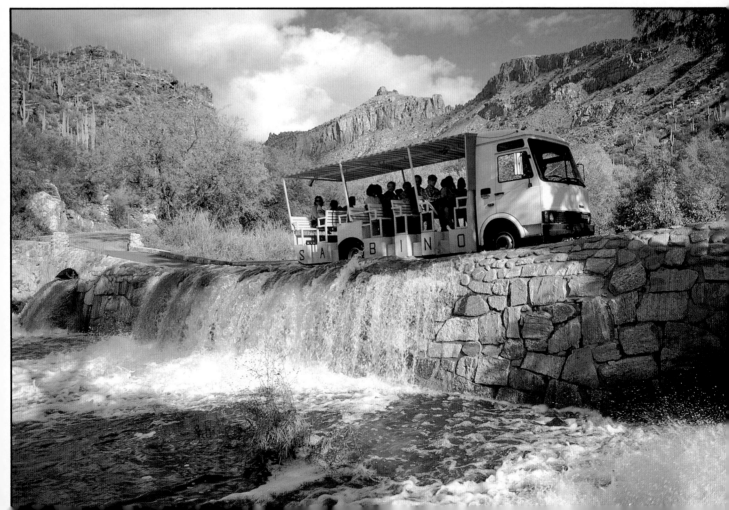

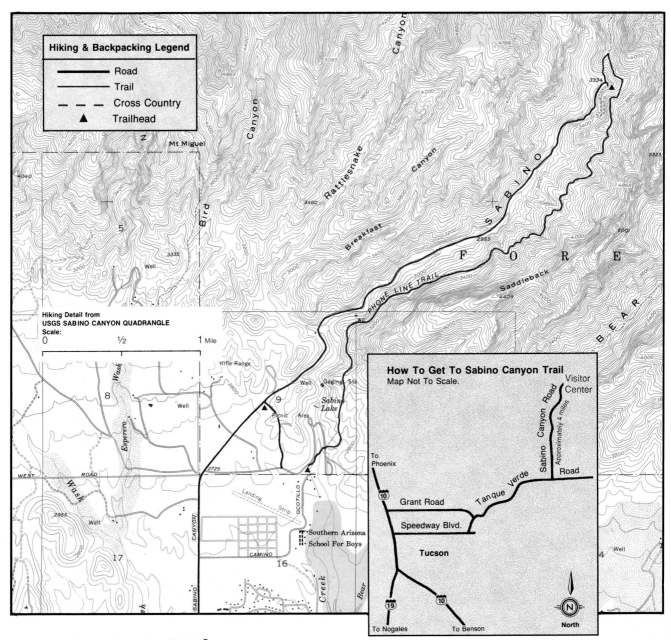

Hiking & Backpacking Legend

――――― Road
――――― Trail
― ― ― Cross Country
▲ Trailhead

Hiking Detail from
USGS SABINO CANYON QUADRANGLE
Scale:
0 ½ 1 Mile

How To Get To Sabino Canyon Trail
Map Not To Scale.

How To Get There

To get to the Sabino Canyon visitor center from the west side of Tucson, take the Grant Road exit from Interstate 10 to Tanque Verde Road on the northeast side of town. Turn left on Tanque Verde Road and follow it to Sabino Canyon Road. Make another left onto Sabino Canyon Road. Approximately 4 miles later you will find the visitor center parking area, which is well marked.

(Right) Known to Tucsonans as "The Thimble," this rock pinnacle is the lone sentinel dividing the headwaters of lower Sabino and Bear Canyons. Jack W. Dykinga

Primary Access: Visitor center on north end of Sabino Canyon Road.
Elevation: 2800 feet at visitor center to 3460 feet at north end of Sabino Canyon Road.
Mileage: 4.2 miles one way.
Water: No perennial water along Phone Line Trail; numerous water stops on Sabino Canyon Road.
Cache Point: Not applicable unless you're hiking Phone Line Trail, then choose secluded area two miles out.
Escape Route: Via Phone Line Trail to visitor information center or end, or the safest-looking descent line to Sabino Canyon Road.
Seasons: Fall through spring; summer can be hot on Phone Line. Beware of dangerous runoff in Sabino Creek during storms.
Maps: USGS Sabino Canyon quadrangle.
Nearest Supply Point: Tucson.
Managing Agency: Coronado National Forest, 300 West Congress, Tucson, AZ 85701, (520) 670-4552 or Santa Catalina Ranger Station, (520) 749-8700.
Backcountry Information: Permit not required; dogs and camp fires prohibited. No bikes on Wednesdays and Saturdays. Bikes allowed other days before 9:00 a.m. and after 5:00 p.m.

⑧ Hugh Norris Trail
Saguaro National Monument West

The 20,738-acre Tucson Mountain Unit, established in 1961, contains the western section of Saguaro National Park, which also includes the 63,360-acre Rincon Mountain Unit established in March 1933. The units preserve incredible stands of saguaro cactus growing in this rich biotic community. The best way to visit this small desert wilderness and view these stately giants is to day hike up the Hugh Norris Trail in the Tucson Mountains.

The 5.5-mile-long Hugh Norris Trail is, for all practical purposes, a ridge trail. Its appeal lies not only in the airy views it offers while hiking most sections of it, but you actually get to the top of 4687-foot high Wasson Peak where the 360-degree panorama is even better. To get there, you have to pay some minor dues in the form of switchbacks that begin about one-half mile after you leave the trailhead. The trail is well marked and maintained its entire length.

Three miles out you'll come to the junction of the Sendero Esperanza Trail. This is a good cache point, or turnaround point if you're not feeling your oats. Wasson Peak is 2.5 miles beyond this junction, but you must first climb over the 4500-foot-high saddle on the south side of Amole Peak before tackling the spiral of switchbacks that will take you up to the summit ridge of Wasson Peak.

From the summit of Wasson, you can clearly see 7750-foot Baboquivari Peak to the southwest; 9453-foot Mount Wrightson to the southeast; the Rincon Mountains due east; the front range of the Catalinas northeast; and 4508-foot Newman Peak northwest. This is without a doubt the best view on any day hike in the Tucson area.

How To Get There

Drive west from Tucson on Speedway Boulevard until it turns into Kinney Road. Turn right on Kinney Road and drive to the Red Hills information center. The 6-mile-long Bajada Loop Drive is located 1.5 miles beyond; turn right onto the Bajada Loop Drive, and the Hugh Norris trailhead is located one mile farther.

Primary Access: Hugh Norris and Sendero Esperanza trailheads.
Elevation: 2600 feet at trailhead to 4687 feet on Wasson Peak.
Mileage: 11 miles round trip.
Water: No perennial water en route.
Cache Point: Sendero Esperanza Trail junction.
Escape Route: Via Hugh Norris or Kings Canyon trail.
Seasons: Fall through spring: summer can be a very hot trek.
Maps: USGS Avra quadrangle.
Nearest Supply Point: Tucson.
Managing Agency: Saguaro National Park, 3693 South Old Spanish Trail, Tucson, AZ 85730-5699, (520) 296-8576 or Saguaro National Park West, (520) 883-6366.
Backcountry Information: No camping is permitted in the Tucson Mountain Unit; therefore no permits are issued for overnight hiking. Camping is permitted in the Rincon Mountain Unit. Permits are issued at the visitor center. Permit not required for day hiking. Dogs and campfires are prohibited. Bikes on established roads only. Park is open daylight hours only.

(Right) Saguaro National Park was established to preserve stands of saguaros such as these near the Hugh Norris Trailhead. Peter Kresan

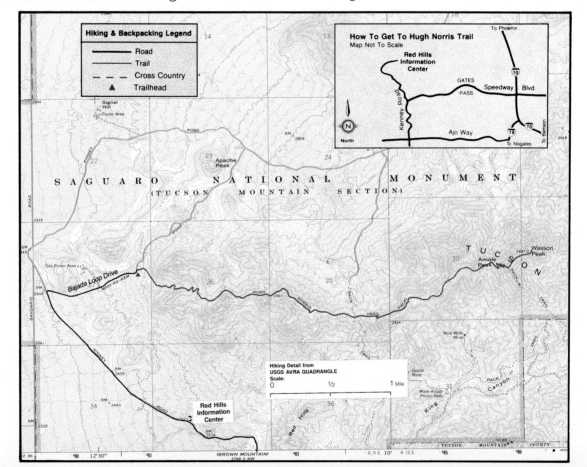

View looking north from
the Hugh Norris Trail, in the
Tucson Mountains. Peter Kresan

(Right) Now and then, the paths of hikers and coyotes converge. Robert Campbell

(Far right) The rich desert vegetation along the Hugh Norris Trail is among the finest to be found, and the 360-degree view from Wasson Peak is one of the best in the Tucson area. John Annerino

(Below) The saguaro blossom, with its waxy white petals, is the state flower. Peter Kresan

⑨ Bear Canyon/Seven Falls

From the Sabino Canyon visitor center take the shuttle train to the lower Bear Canyon Picnic Area and Bear Canyon Trailhead. Seven Falls is one of the prettiest waterfalls in southern Arizona. The hike up Bear Canyon is 2.2 miles one way. Be sure to wear comfortable shoes, however, because of the rocky, uneven trail. Also, they should be shoes you don't mind getting wet, because you'll cross the creek numerous times.

Finally, a choice loop hike goes up Sabino Canyon and down Bear Canyon. Start at the visitor center and take the shuttle up Sabino Canyon to the end of the road. Hike another 2.5 miles up-canyon, a well marked trail, to Sabino Basin. The trail that crosses the ridge to the east into Bear Canyon is 2.1 miles long. From there on it's 4.3 miles to Seven Falls and another 2.2 miles back to the picnic area and the shuttle to your car.

(Left) Seven Falls, an impressive sight in Bear Canyon. However, this is not a continuously running stream so check with the Sabino Canyon information center before taking the hike. Larry Ulrich

⑪ Catalina State Park

Located just off U.S. Route 89, about 10 miles north of Tucson, Catalina State Park contains a nice variety of well marked hiking trails. But what makes Catalina State Park hikes different from other Tucson area hikes are the views of the sheer rock cliffs of Pusch Ridge. They are spectacular! As with Tucson's other backyard hikes, the best time of year is fall through spring, although dawn and late afternoon are delightful in summer.

⑩ Tanque Verde Ridge

Saguaro National Monument East

The 63,360-acre Rincon Mountain Unit comprises the eastern section of Saguaro National Park; it also serves as park headquarters. From downtown Tucson take Broadway east about 9 miles to Old Spanish Trail. Turn right (south) about 4.5 miles to the park entrance. Before you charge up Tanque Verde Ridge, stop in the visitor center for a brief orientation. From there take Cactus Forest Drive a mile to the Javelina Picnic Area. The trailhead is off to the right (south).

If you're just interested in an hour's stroll, the mile-long hike up to an unnamed peak at 3574-feet is as good a view of Tucson as you will get without climbing all the way up to 7000-foot Tanque Verde Ridge. From peak 3574, this well-marked trail begins climbing in earnest, 500 vertical feet per mile in the five miles to the Juniper Basin campsite area. You can turn around at any point, but if you hike all the way to Juniper Basin, you will have climbed completely through the desert scrub biotic community, while having some magnificent views of the saguaro forest and the Tucson Basin below, and 8482-foot Rincon Peak above.

Because of the rapid elevation change, this is a strenuous day hike. Prepare yourself accordingly.

"From Mount Union's summit, one can view thousands upon thousands of square miles, not only the length and breadth of the land, but from alpine heights to distant low deserts."

Pauline Hensen
Founding A Wilderness Capital

That not only sums up the incredible panorama from the highest peak in the Prescott area, 7971-foot Mount Union, but pretty well characterizes the views from most of the other craggy summits that ring the former territorial capital. Rugged mountains like the Bradshaws, Sierra Prietas, and Granite Mountain offer some of the coolest and most rewarding summer hiking in central Arizona. Each of these individual mountain ranges still typifies the beauty of the Old West; yet each can be explored via a comprehensive system of hiking and equestrian trails that snake, twist, and climb through the 1,407,596-acre Prescott National Forest.

⑫ **Thumb Butte Trail**

There's an old saying sometimes used in these parts when a fellow can't make up his mind: "It's six of one, half a dozen of another." It is a toss-up when you try to decide which is *the* most popular hiking trail in the Prescott National Forest, the Thumb Butte Trail or Granite Mountain Trail. At 2.5 miles roundtrip, the Thumb Butte Trail is certainly the shortest and easier of the two. It makes one of the best introductory hikes to the area before you tackle one of the longer, steeper, and less-accessible summits.

This well maintained trail climbs about 600 feet in the first mile to the main saddle on the southwest ridge of Thumb Butte. A half-mile up this trail, you will see the remains of a rough-hewn, one-room log cabin. It is characteristic of those once used by gold seekers who prospected near Miller Creek and dug "glory holes" elsewhere in the Bradshaw Mountains during the 1800s. Aluminum placards posted along this enchanting trail identify some of the local flora such as gambel oak, manzanita, and agave.

(Left) Thumb Butte was a landmark for Arizona's first territorial capital. This view is from downtown Prescott during the annual 4th of July parade. Thumb Butte is in the background.
(Right) Hikers study the sign at the Thumb Butte trailhead before starting their trek.
Christine Keith photos

From Thumb Butte saddle, you can picnic or nap under a nearby alligator juniper before heading back the way you came. Or you can tackle the summit of Thumb Butte. To reach the actual summit, you need to follow a secondary trail northeast from the saddle several hundred yards to the foot of the easiest-looking rock gully. Several unexposed boulder moves will take you up to the fluted summit of Thumb Butte.

From either the summit of Thumb Butte or its saddle, you'll be able to see monolithic Granite Mountain almost due north; the standing wave of the 7000-foot-high Sierra Prieta rim will be immediately to your west; and 7696-foot Spruce Mountain and neighboring Mount Union will be competing for your attention in the maze of green peaks to the southeast.

You can return to the trailhead and picnic area by the same route, or you can complete a loop hike by descending a shorter and steeper, well marked trail that switchbacks off the northwest side of Thumb Butte.

How To Get There

To reach the Thumb Butte trailhead, drive west through Prescott on Gurley Street as far as you can (it's the main drag through town) and when it turns into the Thumb Butte Road, drive 3 miles farther to the Thumb Butte picnic area and trailhead. The 6514-foot-high volcanic landmark will be off to your left; a large sign highlighting the Thumb Butte trail system marks the trailhead.

Primary Access: Thumb Butte picnic area.
Elevation: Approximately 5700 feet at the trailhead to 6514 feet on summit.
Mileage: 2.5 miles round trip.
Water: None en route.
Cache Points: Thumb Butte Saddle.
Escape Routes: Back the way you came.
Seasons: Spring through fall is the most popular time, though winter can offer excellent cross-country skiing.
Maps: USGS Iron Springs quadrangle and Prescott National Forest recreation map.
Nearest Supply Point: Prescott.
Managing Agency: Prescott National Forest, 344 S. Cortez, Prescott, AZ 86303, (520) 445-1762.
Backcountry Information: No permit required.

(Left above and below) For some Prescottonians, the pristine surroundings of Thumb Butte are the major attraction. For others it's the picnic area. Christine Keith photos

(Above right) A great backyard hike: Some people, even with baby packs on their backs, challenge Thumb Butte's 6514-foot peak on a regular conditioning schedule. John Annerino

How To Get To Thumb Butte
Perspective Map Looking West

Thumb Butte

Thumb Butte
Picnic Area

Hiking & Backpacking Legend

————	Road
———	Trail
– – –	Cross Country
▲	Trailhead

Thumb Butte Road

To Wickenburg

89

Prescott

Gurley Street

89

To Williams

69

To I-17

⑬ Granite Mountain Wilderness

Only a couple areas in Arizona share the peculiar characteristics of the 9800-acre Granite Mountain Wilderness: Cochise Stronghold in the Dragoons of southeastern Arizona and Hualapai Mountain County Park in the northwest. They all look more like islands of exposed stone than mountains.

In the case of 7626-foot-high Granite Mountain, nearly 50 percent of the wilderness is exposed granite. Rock climbers come from all over the Southwest to climb its immaculate-looking, 500-foot-high, south-facing buttress. It also makes for some exceptional hiking, if you stick to its main trails.

Trail 261 is known locally as the Granite Mountain Trail, and it is the main access into Granite Mountain Wilderness. Go west from the trailhead gate a little more than a mile to the junction at Trail 37 and 261. The trail to the right is Trail 261. Walk through the wooden chute and hike up 1.5 miles of moderate switchbacks to Granite Mountain Saddle. If you keep your eyes open enroute, you may see rock climbers plying their craft on the mountain's main buttes. You can turn back at the saddle, or you can continue hiking another mile through the ponderosas to Granite Mountain Overlook.

Looking south from the overlook, you'll see 7089-foot Little Granite Mountain immediately in front of you, a small finger of granite called Lizard Head a bit to the southeast, and Thumb Butte rearing its gnarly head at the foot of the Sierra Prietas.

The summit area of Granite Mountain is sheltered by huge granite boulders and tenacious-looking ponderosas. It is an ideal place to camp if you're not troubled by the fact that you'll be sleeping in prime mountain lion habitat. This is one of the densest concentrations of that magnificent animal in the state. They like rocks, too.

How To Get There

Hiking Trail 261 up to the Granite Mountain Saddle, or to its summit, makes for an exhilarating day's outing for walkers and hikers of all ages. To reach the trailhead, take the Iron Springs Road 3 miles west from Prescott to the Granite Basin Lake turnoff. This is Forest Service Road 374, where you'll turn right and drive (or pedal) 5 miles to Trail 261.

Primary Access: Granite Mountain trailhead.
Elevation: 5600 feet at trailhead to 7626 feet on summit.
Mileage: 7 miles round trip.
Water: No perennial water en route.
Cache Point: Blair Pass and Granite Mountain Saddle. Use a tree; the local squirrel population has developed a voracious appetite for Cordura and Gore-Tex-type products.
Escape Route: Back the way you came.
Seasons: Spring through fall is the best time.
Maps: USGS Iron Springs and Jerome Canyon quadrangles or FS recreation map.
Nearest Supply Point: Prescott.
Managing Agency: Prescott National Forest.
Backcountry Information: No permit required. Use existing fire rings and dead and down wood. Beware of fire danger. For camping information, call the Prescott National Forest, (520) 771-4700.

(Above) 7626-foot Granite Mountain, nearly 50 percent exposed granite, is a haven for rock climbers. This view is from nearby Granite Basin Lake. David Brown

(Above right) Hikers on the trail to the summit of Granite Mountain. John Annerino

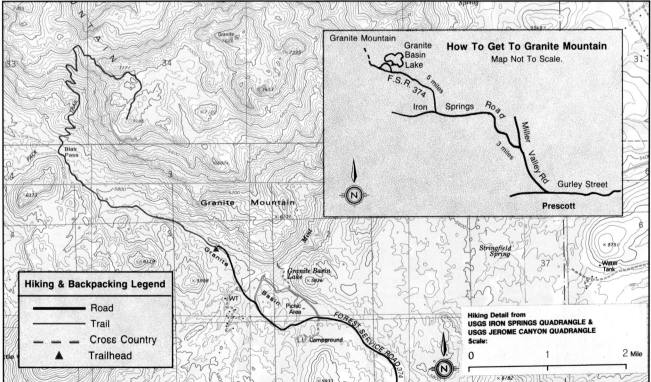

⑭ Spruce Mountain

The trees on Spruce Mountain are actually Douglas fir, and the area is surrounded by ponderosa pine with nary a spruce tree in sight. Nevertheless, either of the two main loop trails up Spruce Mountain provides an excellent forest hike.

Drive 6 miles south from Prescott on the Senator Highway to the first Groom Creek Loop Trail sign. At 3.5 miles to the lookout, it's the shortest and steepest of the two trails. To reach the south loop, drive another .7 mile on the Senator Highway to the obvious trailhead on your left. It's 5.5 miles to the lookout from here.

There's a picnic area near the top, and a road, so don't be surprised to find cars up there too.

⑮ West Spruce Mountain

Not to be confused with Spruce Mountain, West Spruce Mountain is approximately 5 miles west of Thumb Butte via Forest Service Road 373 to the trailhead.

The trail, which follows the crest of the Sierra Prieta Range, is about 2.5 miles one way to West Spruce Mountain's summit at about 7100 feet. The spectacular views enroute overlook Copper Basin, so named in 1864 for the copper claims within it, and Skull Valley, whose name was derived from the piles of bleached Indian skulls found by the first white man who entered the area.

⑯ Mingus Mountain Woodchute Trail

From Prescott take U.S. Route 89A east across the pass on Mingus Mountain to Potato Patch campground. Then take Forest Service Road 107 to Powerline Tank. Woodchute trailhead is a few hundred yards beyond the pond.

It's 2 miles from Powerline Tank to Woodchute Tank, and another mile to the summit and some great

(Left) A youngster challenges one of the many stone obstacles on the west face of Granite Mountain. John Annerino

views of the Verde Valley, Sedona's famous red rock country, Sycamore Canyon Wilderness, San Francisco Peaks, Kendrick Peak, and Bill Williams Mountain. There is an 800-foot elevation change from the Woodchute Trailhead, at about 7000 feet, to the top of Woodchute Mountain.

Once upon a time a giant wooden trough brought logs splashing down the mountain. They were used in the copper mines of Jerome, which is about 5 miles beyond Potato Patch. Today Jerome is Arizona's liveliest "ghost" town.

"The desert holds a mystique, a subtle fascination, which is difficult to pinpoint and more difficult to describe. Not all people are so affected by it, but those who have experienced the desert in this way are the richer."

Peggy Larson
The Deserts of the Southwest

To a frail city boy fresh off the streets of 1950s Chicago, the cinnamon-red humps of Phoenix' Papago Buttes were beyond civilization, a stark no-man's land.

If diamond-eyed rattlesnakes didn't drag me into their steamy subterranean dens, herds of saber-tusked javelinas would munch on my spindly legs at their leisure. For a 12-year-old, this ghastly picture of the Papago Buttes nether world became a dare; they were visible from my family's cinder-block "fortress". To tread that desert vastness and return alive soon became an obsession.

Equipped with little more than a giant can of Franco American spaghetti, my mother's wool comforter, and two G.I. canteens, I struck along McDowell Road toward this great Back of the Beyond. How long would it be, I wondered, before I'd be forced to defend myself from these lower Sonoran gorgons with my dad's pruning shears? I would find out just as soon as I crossed 56th Street.

Almost five hours later, I reached a cave high on the south side of Papago Buttes. Not only was I still unscathed, but I discovered other less sinister creatures inhabited this desert wilderness. I had seen a flight of Mearn's quail, heard the cooing of mourning dove, and watched both jackrabbits and roadrunners race through the creosote and paloverde. To top it all off, I saw my first wily coyote. A startling contrast to life I had known in Chicago.

But I was lucky, I knew, because in the distance I could clearly see the dreaded Superstition Mountains. It was an area, I was told, where rattlers really were as thick as a man's forearm, where marauding desert pigs would just as soon eat you as run around you, and where pistol-toting prospectors were just itchin' to boil up another kettle of pilgrim stew.

I'm not sure how many times I made that overnight expedition to Papago Buttes before I got up enough nerve to visit the legendary Superstitions, but each time I did I was able to stand back from myself in an unenlightened sort of way and glimpse a part of myself that remained hidden in civilization.

More than half of Arizona is desert. Contrary to legend, it is not characterized by turkey vultures roosting on the bleached bones of some poor pilgrim who did not quite make it to the next water hole. Natural scientists identify four great and complex deserts in North America, and each finds it way into Arizona at some point: the Mojave, the Great Basin, the Chihuahuan, and more than any other, the Sonoran, which comprises most of southern Arizona.

But where do you begin? The prudent newcomer does not just go marching off to the Hidden Quarter without some idea of where he is going and what he might see when he gets there. The following pages might be a good place to start your desert adventures.

(Opposite page) Though hot, spiny, and sometimes forebidding, Arizona's deserts can show color and beauty to be found in few other places.
David Muench

(Below) The massive front range of the Superstition Mountains. Jerry Sieve

⑰ Superstition Wilderness Area

"There is no way of getting away from treasure...once it fastens itself upon your mind."

Joseph Conrad, Nostromo

They say there is something haunting about these mountains of the Superstitions: that they *kill* people. They do. At least 36 people have died in the Superstitions since Charles Mallett Dobie was found murdered near the J.F. Ranch. That was May 31, 1892, and according to James Swanson and Tom Kollenborn's *History of the Superstition Wilderness*, it was the last documented attack in the Superstition area by Apaches.

Movies like the classic *Lust for Gold* starring Glen Ford and book titles like *Killer Mountains* and *Thunder On Forbidden Mountain* have contributed to the lore which, over the years, has bred upon itself.

But if these mountains inspired dread and foreboding, you couldn't tell by the anxious smiles of my backpacking class. Counting Randy Mulkey and Tony Mangine, my two assistants, we were 15 strong (which is the maximum group allowed). We had come to traverse one peak in the range that Pima Indians once knew as *Kakatak Tamai*, "Crooked-Top Mountain," otherwise known as Superstition Mountain, one of the peaks in the Superstition range.

This was the last weekend outing of a month-long backpacking and wilderness survival course I had been teaching at Scottsdale Community College. In the three weekends previous, this diverse crew of high school and college students, housewives, attorneys, nurses, and retirees had hiked up Chiricahua Peak, trekked down the Boucher Trail into the Grand Canyon, and made a winter-style ascent of 12,670-foot Humphreys Peak.

Superstition Mountain was the last hurdle I could throw at them before they went on to become explorers in their own right.

Teacher had a minor problem, though. I was carrying 30 pounds too much, and that wasn't my backpack. I worried about my balance. I knew if I didn't lean into the mountain as we tackled the last steep section of the West Boulder Travelway, I could slip and roll all the way back down to Carney Springs. And how would that stand up to the legends of the Superstitions? "Overweight Instructor Falls In Superstitions: Flattens 14 Students Like Bowling Pins."

So I leaned into the mountain as we climbed, locking my knee with each step. The "reststep," we called it; it was the technique I would use to haul all this weight up to the 5057-foot south summit of Superstition Mountain, our objective for the first day.

(Left) Halley's Comet as it appeared in the pre-dawn sky above the Superstition Mountains in 1986. Frank Zullo

The cheese crisps were melting off me by the time we reached an unnamed pass at 3600 feet. But we had this area to ourselves. That was one reason we had voted on this particular trek. We were trying to avoid the would-be gunfighters who funnel through the Peralta Canyon Trailhead every weekend. They come armed to the teeth to wage their imaginary battles on the spirits of the Lost Dutchman. The scarred and disfigured saguaros in Peralta, Needle, and La Barge canyons seemed to take the brunt of the mindless firepower. And it was just too nice a spring day to be mistaken for a saguaro.

From this pass, we headed west-southwest cross-country to Peak 4391. It was a minor summit on the prominent ridgeline which led directly to the South Summit. Between the manzanita and the steepness of the climb, however, we were starting to get too spread out. So I volunteered Randy, and a couple of the others who were chomping at the bit to be the first on the summit, to bring up the stragglers and push the crew together.

It was 3:30 p.m. when we topped out on the South Summit of Superstition Mountain, and echoes of both relief and fulfillment filled the air.

We had climbed more than 2,600 vertical feet in about 3½ miles, and fortunately the dog work of climbing this mountain was over. What lay at our feet was the entire Phoenix metropolitan area on one side of the mountain and all of the 150,000-acre Superstition Wilderness on the other. But suddenly, almost imperceptibly, this group turned their backs on civilization and stared into the heart of these legendary desert mountains. Sticking out of its cauldron of canyons, ridges, bluffs, and mesas was 4,553-foot Weavers Needle. It was one of the last things Dutchman Jacob Walz talked about on his deathbed in 1891: "There's a great stone face looking up at my mine. If you pass three red hills you've gone too far. The rays of the setting sun shine on my gold. Climb above my mine and you can see Weavers Needle."

See it we could, framed through two pillars of golden dacite, stone, not gold, colored by the now setting sun and known to some legend makers as "Fingers of Fire."

The temptation to push on was strong; we still had a good hour-and-a-half of daylight left. But from here on out, all the way to the 5024-foot North Summit of *Kakatak Tamai*, it was *terra incognita*. When medieval cartographers pointed to the blank spots on their maps and said, "Here be the dragons," they might as well have been talking to us about what lay ahead of us tomorrow. All we knew about that ridgeline was the route we'd circled across it on our maps—trying not to press too heavily as we skirted the overhanging contour lines.

No, we'd camp here tonight and build an Indian fire. "White man builds big fire, stands back; Indian builds little fire, huddles close." We'd swap lies and stare into the sea of lights we knew as Phoenix, and wager what time tomorrow we'd be chomping through mesquite-broiled steaks; that's what we promised ourselves if we succeeded.

Still staring into the burning red embers of our fire while everybody else drifted off to sleep, I knew we'd succeed tomorrow. Each of us. Because we would traverse "The Shadow of the Crooked Mountain" the same way we had climbed it, as a team.

That was treasure enough for me.

(Above) Prickly pear cactus blossoms along West Boulder Trail in the Superstition Mountains. Peter Kresan

(Above right) The "Fingers of Fire," dacite formations, comprise the southern summit of the Superstitions. John Annerino

How To Get There

From Apache Junction, drive southeast on U.S. Route 60 approximately 8 miles to the Peralta Road turnoff. This is also Forest Road 77, and you take it 7 miles to the Carney Springs junction. Turn left and take this road another mile to the Carney Springs Trailhead. This is your jump-off spot for the West Boulder Canyon Travelway; it's also where you can park one shuttle vehicle. You can park another shuttle vehicle near the mouth of Siphon Draw by taking the Lost Dutchman State Park turnoff 5 miles northeast of Apache Junction on State Route 88.

Take the West Boulder Canyon Travelway one mile to the unnamed pass at 3600 feet. Make your way cross-country west-southwest to the prominent ridgeline leading to the South Summit. You can eyeball a route all the way to this summit, but the exact course is up to you.

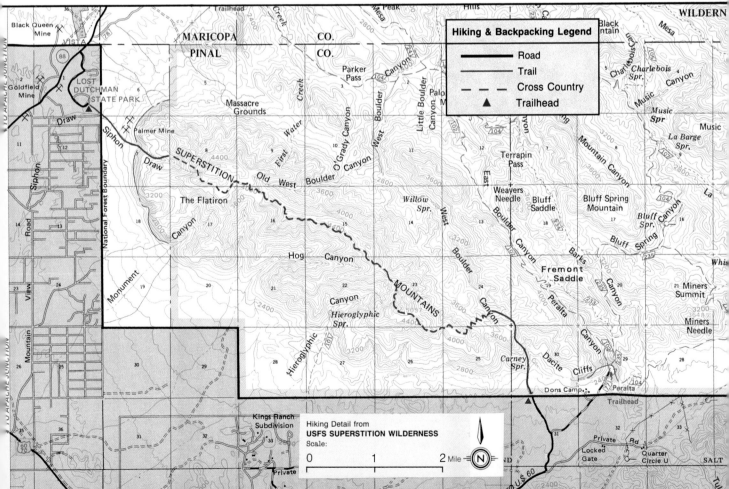

Hiking & Backpacking Legend

▬▬▬▬	Road
———	Trail
– – – –	Cross Country
▲	Trailhead

Hiking Detail from
USFS SUPERSTITION WILDERNESS
Scale:

0   1   2 Mile (N)

South Summit makes an excellent turnaround point for a challenging day hike or rewarding overnighter. From the South Summit, skirt the base of the dacite pillars on their west side until you can again regain the summit ridge. Stay atop this ridgeline all the way to Peak 4402; this is the first dragon to slay on the U.S. Geological Survey map of the Goldfield quadrangle.

This notch can be safely negotiated if you first remove your pack, then scramble down a series of interconnecting ledges on the north-northeast side. If you get into an exposed situation, you're definitely off the route. Once you have lowered your pack, scramble out of this notch on its east-northeast side by making a series of unexposed boulder moves. Regain the summit ridge and proceed to the saddle between Peak 4861 and the 5024-foot North Summit of Superstition Mountain. This is your exit into the head of the Siphon Draw, the second dragon on your chart. After you view your descent line, you'll see the initial section is as steep and loose as any talus slope in Arizona, but this challenging, unexposed section completes one of the most rewarding hikes anywhere in these mountains.

Primary Access: West Boulder Canyon Travelway via Carney Springs Trailhead, though you may find it easier negotiating the head of Siphon Draw at the beginning of the hike.
Elevation: 2400 feet at Carney Springs Trailhead to 5057 feet on the South Summit.
Mileage: Approximately 10-11 miles one way.
Water: No perennial water en route, though you may make use of Willow Spring in West Boulder Canyon during an emergency.
Cache Points: None for the traverse; though the saddle at 3600 feet makes an ideal cache point for a hike to the South Summit.
Escape Routes:
Depending on where you are, back the way you came: Old West Boulder Canyon to Willow Springs and West Boulder Canyon Travelway to Carney Springs or the Siphon Draw exit.
Seasons: Fall or early spring; summer can be unforgiving, and winter can be treacherous if you get caught in a snowstorm.
Maps: USGS Goldfield and Weavers Needle quadrangles and Tonto National Forest "Superstition Wilderness" map.
Nearest Supply Points: Apache Junction, Mesa, Phoenix.
Managing Agency: Tonto National Forest, 2324 East McDowell Road, Phoenix, AZ 85006, (602) 225-5200.
Backcountry Information: No permit required. Fires allowed but wood is scarce. Bikes are not allowed in wilderness. A guide to designated bike trails (Recreation Opportunity Guide) is available on request from Tonto National Forest.

(Below) A hiker surveys the Superstitions' rugged interior wilderness and its famous landmark, Weavers Needle. (Right) To hikers camped on the south summit of the Superstitions, the lights of the Phoenix metro area gleam like diamonds on velvet. John Annerino photos

(Right below) Blossoms on a hedgehog cactus brighten a desert hike. (Far right) The roadrunner is a bird with a personality. Frank Zullo photos

⑱ Organ Pipe Cactus National Monument

"On the brightest and warmest days my desert is most itself because sunshine and warmth are the very essence of its character. The air is lambent with light; the caressing warmth envelops everything in its ardent embrace. Even when outlanders complain that the sun is too dazzling and too hot, we desert lovers are prone to reply, 'At worst that is only too much of a good thing.'"

Joseph Wood Krutch
The Voice of the Desert

It is sublime Sonoran desert. In fact, it's hardly a desert at all. The relatively lush vegetation seems to be spaced as orderly as though it had been placed by a landscaper. After a wet winter, the spring (February and March) bloom of brittle bush and annual wildflowers can set the scene ablaze with color. Again in late summer, thunderstorms bring more moisture and the active chlorophyll green in the plants seems out of place against the stark red-yellow-orange volcanic cliffs of the Ajo Mountains.

If you live in Mexico, just a few miles south, Organ Pipe Cactus National Monument would be just an extension of your own backyard. But for many of us, coming from the United States, it has a unique blanket of plants. This part of southwestern Arizona is virtually frost-free, and at the same time gets enough summer rains for tropical plants to reach their northern limits. To the west the land is too dry and to the east, too cold. So here grow smoke tree, senita cactus, limber bush, and most notably, the best population of organ pipe cactus in the United States. Largely, it is warmth that makes this an extraordinary place.

Ajo Mountain Drive, a 21-mile loop road, provides access to viewpoints, trails, and cross-country hiking with spectacular vistas of this Sonoran Desert landscape. Just as the loop road begins to parallel the imposing front of the Ajo Mountains, look for a prominent cliff with a window, framing the azure sky. Farther on, a dense forest of teddy bear cholla quells any immediate anxiety to explore, at least until you find the trail to Estes Canyon and Bull Pasture.

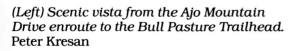

(Right) A Gambel's quail sentinel takes a high perch.
James Tallon

(Left) Scenic vista from the Ajo Mountain Drive enroute to the Bull Pasture Trailhead.
Peter Kresan

There is no finer display of organ pipe cactus in the monument than on the southwestern flank of the Ajo Mountains, along the trail to Bull Pasture. It is approximately a 4-mile loop up switchbacks to Bull Pasture and back through Estes Canyon. Bull Pasture is at the end of a short but steep side trail. Each step toward Bull Pasture opens up more magnificent vistas of the basins and ranges in southwestern Arizona and New Mexico. The mountain ranges seem like layered shingles, stacked westward, one after another. Between them are wide and somewhat desolate valleys or basins, which from this vantage point seem rather insignificant. It is the mountains that captivate my attention, for the rugged Ajo Mountains dominate the foreground.

Rising to 4808 feet at Mt. Ajo, the Ajos are the highest and most massive range in southwestern Arizona. It is probably more effective than any nearby range at deflecting the moist gulf air high enough to condense into rain. The orographic effect of this large hunk of rock probably sets the stage for the Organ Pipe plant community by inducing more rain than typically falls to the west.

Like most ranges and basins in southern Arizona, the elevaton differences of about 3100 feet between Mt. Ajo and the valley floor is primarily a result of vertical movements of these large crustal blocks during earthquakes. In fact, the fracture or fault along which this movement occurs can be found in some places along the loop road at the base of the mountains. Yet another geologic story is told by the layers of brown lava and alternating tan and yellow volcanic tuffs. These are rocks born from fiery origins, when, around 25 million years ago, cataclysmically explosive volcanic eruptions shook the Southwest.

Although the view from Bull Pasture is spectacular, there is nothing like being on top. The summit of Mt. Ajo is still above Bull Pasture, but it beckons to anyone inclined to cross-country hiking. It is a very strenuous trek with some traverses along ridge crests. Constantly remind yourself not to climb up anything you couldn't safely get down. The topographical map for Organ Pipe Cactus National Monument shows a spring just above Bull Pasture, but don't count on water. Except for Dripping Springs in the Puerto Blanco Mountains and Quitobaquito in the southwest corner of the monument, other oases are marginal and cannot be counted on for perennial water.

Quitobaquito is a special place for both its natural history and for its role in human history. It is the most dependable source of water between Sonoyta, Sonora, and the Colorado River. It is a milepost on a route know as *El Camino del Diablo*, or Devil's Highway. The Camino was a southern trade route for Indians traveling from Arizona and Sonora to the Colorado River and southern California. Many sleeping circles, bedrock metates, and petroglyphs are found along this trail of the ancient people. In 1540 Melchior Díaz, one of Coronado's lieutenants, ventured across. Father Eusebio Francisco Kino followed the route in

1699, and eventually pioneers followed the Camino in wagons to bypass the absolutely dry, active sand desert to the south.

West of Quitobaquito, water, if there is any, is found in depressions in bedrock, called "tinajas," which trap rainfall. The tinajas are scant and undependable water holes. Because of this, some early travelers died as they tried to hurry on to the Colorado River across this parched and sandy corner of Arizona.

From your perch at the edge of Bull Pasture, the great expanse of stark mountains and desert valleys lay parched before you, making it difficult to understand why Organ Pipe is as rich in life as it is. Yet, surviving out there are two desert denizens, bighorn sheep and pronghorn antelope. If you walk quietly, maybe you'll glimpse one.

— *Peter Kresan*

(Above) Northward view from Bull Pasture; note trail lower left corner. Peter Kresan

(Above right) Bull Pasture trailhead. Jerry Sieve

(Right) There is no designated trail from Bull Pasture to the summit. Carefully study your options before starting out. John Annerino

PETS NOT ALLOWED ON TRAIL
ANIMALES DOMÉSTICOS SE
PROHIBEN EN LAS VEREDAS

BULL PASTURE TRAIL
THIS IS A 2 MILE SELF
GUIDING TRAIL LEADING
INTO THE AJO MOUNTAINS
HIKING TIME   3 HOURS ROUND TRIP
WEAR STURDY SHOES - TAKE WATER
ELEVATION HERE   2440
ELEVATION BULL PASTURE   3135

How To Get There

To reach Organ Pipe Cactus National Monument from Phoenix, drive south on U.S. Route 80 and State Route 85 140 miles; from Tucson, take State Route 86 and State Route 85 142 miles to monument headquarters.

The trek up to Mt. Ajo is an excellent day hike or overnighter. However, make sure you can observe the route to the summit crest before leaving Bull Pasture. The route alongside the conical turrets, though longer, is probably safer. For those wishing to spend the night on this incredible perch, there are several ledges suitable for two on the east-southeast side of the peak. Remember, it's farther from the Bull Pasture hiker register than it looks.

Primary Access: Estes Canyon picnic area on Ajo Mountain Drive, via Bull Pasture.

Elevation: 2400 feet at Estes Canyon picnic area to 4808 feet atop Mt. Ajo.

Mileage: Estes Canyon — Bull Pasture, 4.1 miles round trip. Approximately 4 miles one-way to Mt. Ajo.

Water: No perennial water en route. Rangers recommend that hikers not use seasonal water anywhere in Organ Pipe unless it's an emergency because animals rely on it.

Cache Points: Bull Pasture and summit crest.

Escape Route: Via Bull Pasture to Estes Canyon.

Seasons: Late fall through early spring. Summer can be deadly.

Maps: USGS Mt. Ajo, Diaz Peak, Kino Peak, and Lukeville quadrangles or topographical map sold at visitor center.

Nearest Supply Points: Gila Bend, Ajo, Lukeville, and Sells.

Managing Agency: Organ Pipe Cactus National Monument, Route 1 Box 100, Ajo, AZ 85321, (520) 387-6849.

Backcountry Information: No campfires. Overnight hiking by permit only. Bikes on scenic loop roads only.

(Left above) Hiker surveys Organ Pipe Cactus National Monument from the summit of Mt. Ajo. John Annerino

(Left below) The Ajo Mountains. Peter Kresan

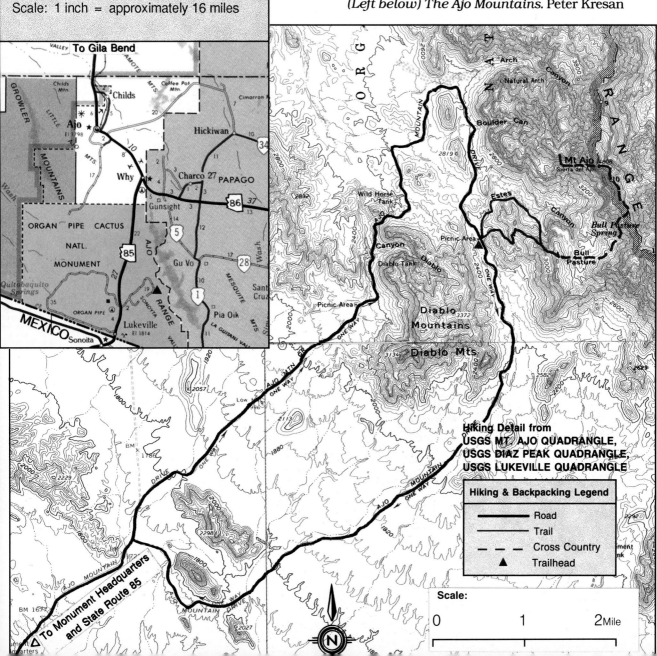

How To Get To Organ Pipe Cactus National Monument
Scale: 1 inch = approximately 16 miles

⑲ Kofa

"You will note with profound surprise that these Arizona deserts are not barren and desolate wastes, but literally teeming with life...Go with an open mind; for the voices of the arid wastes are entitled to a hearing. If you cannot endure a certain amount of thirst, heat, fatigue and hunger without getting cross with Nature, it is best to stay at home."

—William Hornaday

The observations of Hornaday, a naturalist born and bred in New York City, are worth remembering in the beautiful desolation of the Kofa Mountains. This kind of desert is not for everyone. In fact, the Kofa Wildlife Refuge, more than any other area of Arizona, may be close to the image of a desert that someone from New York or Connecticut carries in his mind.

Aside from the well-trod Palm Canyon trail, there are no developed trails in this 663,700-acre refuge. There are faint game trails, and traces of Indian trade routes. It was always thus. William Keiser described prospecting in the range in the 1890s: "An old Indian trail went over the mountain and going up the trail he (Charlie Eichelberger) discovered a small cave, and overhanging rock where the evidence showed that the Indians cooked there. He sat down under the shade as it was fairly warm. Where the smoke covered the wall he noticed some bright yellow spots—gold..." Charlie and his grubstaking partner sold the find in 1897 for $250,000. It became the King of Arizona Mine. The initials KOFA stenciled on the crates of mine supplies replaced the former scatalogical name for the mountain range that once appeared on maps.

The rust-colored volcanic rocks, which stack up to form the Kofa Mountains, remind one of a gigantic layer cake without icing. They rise dramatically from a broad valley, called La Posa Plain. The desert floor slopes gently to the abrupt mountain front and appears paved with a mosaic surface of interlocked volcanic pebbles and cobbles. This so-called desert pavement is formed as wind blows the fine dust away, leaving those fragments too big to be moved by the wind. These in turn protect the ground from further wind erosion. Some of the cobbles in the pavement are such a shiny blue-black that you might think the desert is littered with meteorites. But the shiny "desert varnish," formed by the precipitation of iron and manganese oxides, coats only the top sides of the pebbles.

(Left) Jutting out of the desert floor, the ragged skyline of the Kofas has been sculptured by the elements into a sheer mountain front of high cliffs, spires, and jagged peaks. Willard Clay

Winter and spring are my favorite times to explore the Kofas. March can be windy, but the dust kicked up into the atmosphere creates spectacular sunsets. There are no dependable water holes, so bring plenty of water.

The Kofa Mountains contain the most extensive natural groves of Washingtonia Palm trees in Arizona. These palms are in Palm Canyon, and such adjacent canyons as Fishtail, Four Palms, and Old Palm. The sheer orange cliffs of Palm Canyon provide a dramatic setting for the grove.

(Above) The Desert bighorn, one of the rarest sheep in the world, is master of this terrain. James Tallon

(Right) Day's end comes to the Kofa Mountains. Jerry Sieve

(Below) View looking west from the doorway to Palm Canyon. James Tallon

Cross-country hikes in these adjacent canyons might reward you with a glimpse of a bighorn sheep. One of my best sightings of a bighorn was one spring day in Fishtail Canyon. We decided to trek along the mountain front to the south in search of more palms. It was relatively easy going across the open desert, skirting the rugged mountain face. Beavertail prickly pear cactus were blooming, and occasionally a hummingbird would dive bomb my red day pack, perhaps thinking it was a huge ocotillo bloom.

Instead of entering Fishtail, as we had planned, we decided to quietly climb the nose of a ridge at the entrance, in hopes our presence would go unnoticed. It worked. From the ridge crest we spotted a beautiful ram with massive curled horns wandering along the canyon bottom. It was some time before he caught our scent and disappeared up the boulder-choked canyon.

Studies have shown that the bighorn can go three to five days without water. Then they find moisture in tinajas, or bedrock tanks, which erosion has carved in the bottoms of the steep upper canyons. If you do discover tinajas, it is best not to disturb them, unless your need for water is dire. Bighorns usually travel in family groups, so if you spot one, look for others.

We got into Fishtail Canyon and worked our way through the dense brush lining the channel of the wash. It was like walking in a tunnel. Vines engulfed some of the larger palm trees, creating a promenade which contrasted sharply with the much browner desert just 100 feet away. At dusk, the hoot of a screech owl and the howl of coyotes out on the plain reminded us of other timorous inhabitants of the desert.

—*Peter Kresan*

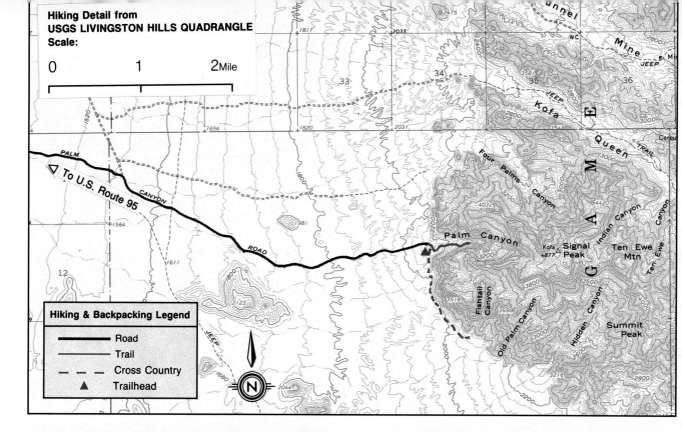

How To Get There

From U.S. Route 95, turn left (east) on the Palm Canyon Road and follow it approximately 7.5 miles to the mouth of Palm Canyon. This is the most popular hike in the Kofas because it's the only place in the state where Arizona's native palm trees grow in the natural habitat. The estimated 42 native palms that

(Above left) Hikers on the trail into Palm Canyon. Tom Bean

(Above right) Most of the native palms are found in a steep side canyon on the right side of the picture. Wesley Holden

(Right) For a unique vantage point, an energetic hiker can scramble up among the palms. Willard Clay

remain grow in the steep, sheltered tributary drainages above the floor of Palm Canyon.

This is an easy to moderate hike for the first .5 mile. The most popular time to hike Palm Canyon is during the spring when the cacti and annuals are in their full glory.

Primary Access: Palm Canyon Road approximately 7.5 miles.
Elevation: 2200 feet at Palm Canyon parking lot.
Mileage: Approximately .5 mile into Palm Canyon. Cross-country hiking mileage is at your discretion.
Water: No perennial water, though you may find tinajas (natural tanks) full after a rain. However, these are key water resources for the desert bighorn and should only be used in emergencies.
Escape Routes: Back the way you came.
Seasons: Late fall through early spring. Summer can be deadly.
Maps: USGS Livingston Hills quadrangle. U.S. Fish and Wildlife has a map available in leaflet boxes at most entrances.
Nearest Supply Points: Quartzsite and Yuma.
Managing Agency: U.S. Fish and Wildlife Service, Kofa National Wildlife Refuge, P.O. Box 6290, Yuma, AZ 85364, (520) 783-7861.
Backcountry Information: No Permit required. Fires allowed, but wood is scarce. Bikes on designated roads only.

⑳ Organ Pipe Cactus National Monument

Several trails in the monument offer close looks at the beauty of the desert. From shortest to longest:

Quitobaquito Nature Trail (.5 mile roundtrip) is one of the most fascinating, refreshing, and enjoyable short hikes you will take anywhere. Starting at milepost 20 on Puerto Blanco Drive, this well marked trail provides an excellent introduction to Organ Pipe's rich flora and fauna. Many different species of birds have been sighted at this oasis. Bring your binoculars.

Campground Perimeter Trail (1 mile loop). This trail makes an ideal leisurely walk to start or end the day.

Desert View Nature Trail (1.2 mile loop). Starting at the group campground parking lot, this circular route provides some delightful vistas of the monument and the Sonoyta Valley all the way into Mexico.

Victoria Mine Trail (4.5 miles roundtrip). Starting at the south end of the campground, this hike takes you over rolling desert terrain to the monument's richest and oldest gold and silver mine.

Alamo Canyon. For those looking for a longer hike, here's a good one. Immediately north of Alamo Wash Bridge, about 8 miles south of Why on State Route 85, is a 3-mile dirt road which takes you eastward to four primitive campsites at the mouth of Alamo Canyon. Although there are no defined trails, this open desert country provides a great opportunity for cross country treks. A casual hike to explore magnificent Alamo Canyon can easily take all day. On the alluvial plain at the base of the Ajo Mountains, brittle bush and spring wildflowers put on a spectacular display in early March during wetter years. A permit is required from the visitor center for overnight stays.

(Below) Located in the western portion of Organ Pipe Cactus National Monument, and next to the border with Mexico, Quitobaquito was the last oasis for early pioneers and 49ers heading west across the infamous Camino del Diablo—Highway of the Devil. Art Clark

㉑ Petrified Forest National Park

and the Painted Desert

The open and expansive badlands of this area furnish great opportunities for cross country hiking, as well as some exceptional nature walks. The best introductory hikes are within the park. Shortest to longest, they are:

Agate House Trail (.5 mile roundtrip). This hike is unique for the pre-historic Indian dwellings made of petrified wood. Of the original seven rooms, two have been reconstructed.

Crystal Forest Trail (.5 mile loop). The landscape on this hike is covered with all sizes of petrified wood from small pieces to whole logs. Take your camera.

Wesley Holden

Blue Mesa Trail (.8 mile loop). Hike off the mesa top and down into the blue, grey, and brown arroyos. You'll think you're on the moon. This is perhaps the park's most dramatic display of erosion.

Long Log Trail (.8 mile loop). Here one finds the petrified remains of a giant logjam, with logs up to 170 feet long. This is the largest concentration of petrified wood in the world.

Painted Desert. There are some outstanding day and overnight hikes in this area too. From the northwest section of the park a trail leads into the Painted Desert. From Kachina Point, one can strike north across Lithodendron Wash about 2 miles to the Black Forest, or 6 miles to Chinde Mesa. The terrain is very open and the low mesas, hummocks, spires, and pedestals seem to blend with the vast sky and sometimes mimic puffy clouds. Bring a polarizer for your camera if you have one.

Petrified Forest National Park and the Painted Desert are located 25 miles east of Holbrook on Interstate 40. A permit is required for all hiking and overnight stays off established trails. There is no water or wood so bring plenty of canteens and a gas stove if you are going overnight. One could easily get lost in this maze of low hills and mesas, so be sure your backpack includes a compass and topographic map. Fall and spring are especially nice times of the year to explore this part of Arizona. For more information contact: Petrified Forest National Park, P.O. Box 217, Petrified Forest National Park, AZ 86028, (520) 524-6228.

㉒ Picacho Peak State Park

Jerry Sieve

Thrusting out of a broad desert plain, the jagged, black peak can be seen 60 miles away. It beckons to be climbed. At the west end of the Picacho Mountains and 40 miles north of Tucson off Interstate 10, Picacho Peak is a striking landmark. It is often mistaken for a volcanic neck. It is mostly volcanic rock, but the type that becomes plastered onto the flanks of a volcano, not the magma that cools within the neck. The layers have been tilted on end and erosion has sculptured the material into a prominent peak.

Hunter Trail climbs 1500 feet in 2.2 miles to the summit. if you are not psyched for a rigorous climb, stroll along the .5 mile Calloway Trail at the base of the peak. Picacho Peak is well known for dazzling displays of desert wildflowers in the spring. There is a day use fee. For additional information contact: Picacho Peak Visitor Center, P.O. Box 275, Picacho, AZ 85241, (520) 466-3183. No bike trails.

㉓ Buckskin Mountain State Park

James Tallon

In the low, hot desert along the Colorado River near Parker Dam, 11 miles north of the city of Parker on State Route 95, Buckskin Mountain State Park has three developed trails — Wedge Hill, Lightning Bolt, and Buckskin. They are about .5, 1, and 2.5 miles long, respectively. These trails ascend steep bluffs to the mesa top and overlooks of the river.

For additional information contact: Buckskin Mountain State Park, 54751 Highway 95, Parker AZ 85344, (520) 667-3231.

Superstition Mountains

There are 35 named trails that lead into the back-country of the Superstition Wilderness, and they run the gamut from the primary trails to unmaintained trails. A total of 12 trailheads provide access to these trails, with the Peralta and First Water trailheads being the most heavily used. So plan your hike into this area based on your temperament, level of experience, and available time. Just remember, you've got about 150 miles of trail to explore.

(Above) Winter sunset view near Lost Dutchman State Park. J. Peter Mortimer

24 Lost Dutchman State Park

The area around the park contains some of the Sonoran Desert's more dramatic landscape. A 2.4-mile Treasure Loop Trail gradually climbs along the base of the Superstition Mountains. Two short trails, Jacobs Crosscut and Prospectors View, connect the Treasure Loop to Siphon Draw Trail. Jacobs Crosscut is now a 7.5 mile hiking, horse, and bike trail. Trailheads are at the end of East Broadway and off of First-water Road (.6 miles from State Route 88). From the campground, Siphon Draw Trail follows a canyon about 3 miles to the top of the cliffs.

Lost Dutchman State Park entrance is 5 miles northeast of Apache Junction on State Route 88. There is a small day-use fee for hiking and picnicking. For additional information contact: Lost Dutchman State Park, 6109 North Apache Trail, Apache Junction, AZ 85219, (602) 982-4485.

㉕ Fremont Saddle

From U.S. Route 60, turn left onto the Peralta Canyon Road and drive 8 miles to the Peralta Canyon trailhead. This is the most popular day hike in the Superstitions, with as many as 500 people filing through the Peralta Canyon trailhead on a busy spring day, with good reason. The view from Fremont Saddle is one of the classics in the Southwest. On a clear spring morning, it'll seem like you can reach out and touch Weavers Needle. Stand there and ponder the words of Pedro de Castenada, diarist for early Spanish explorers, who wrote in 1545: "Granted that they did not find the riches of which they had been told; they did find the next best thing—a place in which to search for them."

This is a moderate hike, which climbs 1400 vertical feet in the 2.25 miles it takes to reach Fremont Saddle. It makes a excellent day's outing fall through spring. It is most heavily hiked during colorful springtime.

Steve Bruno

㉖ Angel Springs

From Apache Junction take U.S. Route 60 16 miles to Florence Junction; 2 miles farther east, turn left on the Queen Valley Road; 1.5 miles out, you'll make a right on the Hewitt Station Road, or Forest Road 357. Follow this road approximately 3 miles to Forest Road 172, turn left and take it 11 miles to the seldom used Woodbury trailhead. If you found this trailhead, chances are you won't have much problem finding the utopian setting of Angel Springs.

This is an excellent overnight hike into the less frequently hiked, upper elevations of the Superstition Wilderness eastern end. From the Woodbury trailhead, take the J.F. Trail 106 approximately 3 miles up to a gnarly-looking alligator juniper sitting in the middle of 4000-foot high Tortilla Pass; this is an excellent cache point and/or lunch stop. Descend the Rogers Canyon Trail 110 (overgrown with just about every bush that's found in the Sonoran desert mountain transition zones) to the junction of the Frog Tanks Trail 112. Make a right here and take the Rogers Canyon Trail across the meadow and through the sycamore trees up canyon about three-quarters of a mile to one of the prettiest springs and best preserved Indian ruins in the Southwest. Camp no less than a quarter mile away from Angel Springs, and *don't* climb on these precious ruins. According to James Swanson and Tom Kollenborn's fine *History of the Superstition Wilderness*, this Pueblo-style cliff dwelling was occupied by 25 to 30 Salado Indians *circa* A.D.1000. No doubt, the area was as idyllic then as it is now, and it should remain so.

John Annerino

*"Only the mountain has lived long enough
to listen objectively to the howl of a wolf."*
—*Aldo Leopold*
A Sand County Almanac

The first time I saw the San Francisco Peaks was through the foggy windows of a high school bus. From Phoenix we traveled 140 miles north on a cold January day to ski the noble flanks of Arizona's highest mountains. When we stormed out of the bus, I looked up and saw through the swirling winter mist what I thought was the 12,670-foot summit of Humphreys Peak. It had my name on it.

Until that time, the steepest thing I had climbed were the kitchen cupboards when I was five; that's where Mom always hid the Oreos.

This dearth of mountaineering experience obviously wasn't going to stop me or my ski date, Ricarda Matt. I pretended I was polar explorer Rear Admiral Edwin Peary and broke trail. Ricarda patiently trudged behind me, thinking I knew a quicker way to the top of the mountain than using the chairlift like our classmates. We weren't a half-hour above the lodge, however, when my head started to feel like a rugby ball. Somebody had obviously turned off the oxygen. I looked up and, through the dots spinning in front of my eyes, saw another ridge behind what I thought was the summit; behind that was yet another snow-swept ridge. I turned around and expected Ricarda to be swimming up through the hip-deep snow drifts a half-mile behind me, but she was practically standing on top of the skis I'd been pulling behind me, *and* she was smiling.

"Ricarda," I said, trying to hide the fact I was breathing like a sled dog, "this is high enough for your first time out." She laughed, obviously unaffected by the extreme altitude, and said, "Let's ski, then."

I stepped into my skis as if I were Jean Claude Killy and instructed Ricarda to do exactly as I did. She did not know the only other time I'd been skiing was on the grassy hill at Encanto Park in Phoenix, on snow from a giant ice machine.

"Now, watch this," I further instructed Ricarda. I tucked into an FBI crouch, planted the silver tips of my poles into the icy crust, and pushed off...

(Left) Descending the slopes of San Francisco Peaks near the Snow Bowl. John Annerino

(Above right) Camping in an aspen glade during fair summer months is a more traditional mountain experience. Tom Bean

Ten feet down my skis shot out from under me, and I exploded into the air as if I were a Raggedy Ann doll being torn apart by the neighbor's dog.

The only thing I remember during that painful flight is "When am I going to hit a tree?" I was lucky, though, because when I finally did come to a screeching, skin burning halt, my poles were hanging in the trees like Christmas ornaments, and my skis were still rocketing downslope into the hinterlands far below. And Ricarda was now skiing with a bronze ski god named Hans.

I vowed never to ski down a mountain again. What I enjoyed more was the struggle up toward the mysterious heights beckoning me through the swirling mist. To me, it looked no less daunting than the *National Geographic* pictures of Tenzing Norgay and Sir Edmund Hillary climbing Everest. But, I promised myself, still brushing the icy snow off my Levis, I would start with Arizona's other mountains and use them as stepping stones for conditioning and experience until I could one day scale these lofty peaks.

There were certainly enough peaks to choose from. While the 12,633-foot Humphreys Peak and its sister peak, 12,356-foot Agassiz, are Arizona's highest, they aren't our only sub-Alpine peaks; 11,404-foot Baldy Peak and 11,357-foot Mt. Ord reign over the Mt. Baldy Wilderness and the rest of the White Mountains. Two more peaks comprise the rest of the San Francisco Peaks: 11,460-foot Doyle Peak and 11,969-foot Fremont Peak. The list of Arizona peaks 8000 to 11,000 feet high is impressive.

Phoenix, however, has an elevation of about 1100 feet above sea level, and you just don't march up these 12,000-foot mountains without suffering the ill effects of hypoxia and altitude sickness. Better to start on some lesser peaks in the state.

㉗ San Francisco Peaks
Humphreys Peak Trail

"If there was courage needed it was only the same courage required to meet all the everyday problems of life, to go for an interview, to bring children into the world, to propose to a girl, to take any new step. If we had shown courage in going up to bury four fellow climbers, the only difference was that our everyday problems were located on the side of a mountain and we were on the spot and suited to the task."

—*Joe Tasker*, The Savage Arena

It is daybreak when the three of us begin struggling along a perilously icy ridge 12,000 feet above sea level. We are weary from our rapid ascent and our throats are parched from thirst. Worse, an arctic front has swept in from the west and a fierce westerly wind has sent the chill factor well below zero.

We are not survivors of a plane crash fighting our way down off a remote Alaskan mountain. We are, at the moment, clawing our way up toward 12,356-foot Agassiz Peak. It is the second highest mountain in Arizona, and we have voluntarily gone out of our way to attempt a winter ascent of a peak we can only occasionally see.

These delightful winter conditions are characteristic of alpine climbing, a sport that is as popular in Europe as jogging on the canal bank is in Phoenix. And the San Francisco Peaks are the only mountains in Arizona where climbers can "practice" before

journeying to the distant ranges of the world for something more ambitious.

So we have come prepared for the extremes of both altitude and weather. We are equipped with ice axes, crampons, lightweight stoves, down sleeping bags, and a mountain tent. We are wearing cumbersome layers of wool, down, and nylon. Yet if we do not force each other to keep moving—up or down—we could freeze to death. Some sport.

This endeavor began the week before, at the urging of a friend. "Let's climb the Peaks," he said, well fortified with ale.

"It's too cold," I told him. "Wait until spring." I then explained to him that in the course of teaching outdoor education the previous ten years, I'd been on the Peaks 40-odd times; that my time might now better be spent sitting in front of the fireplace or running around in the desert. He suggested that perhaps I was getting soft.

A week later, I am snowshoeing up the west flank of 12,633-foot Humphreys Peak with Randy Mulkey and Ken Akers. Both experienced climbers, they will take longer to adjust to the altitude because they live nearer sea level in Phoenix. Since I have the advantage of living and training around 6000 feet, I agree to break trail through the hip-deep powder snow.

By the time we reach the tree line above 11,000 feet several hours later, my companions are beginning to feel the effects of mountain sickness: nausea, headache, general malaise. Mountaineers call it "going too high, too fast." So we heat up a cup of mocha while we wait for our lungs to catch up with our legs.

(Opposite page) The trailhead to Humphreys Peak.
John Annerino

Autumn on the peaks is a time of golden elegance.
Martos Hoffman

(Above) Snowshoeing up Humphreys Peak can test the most experienced hikers.
Ken Akers

(Right) Mule deer in velvet.
Tom Bean

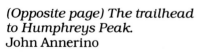

An hour later, we begin climbing a 45-degree slope, "front-pointing" with the tips of our crampons in the icy snow. By sundown, our tent is pitched and we have wolfed down a dozen homemade tostadas, a jar of frozen jalapeno peppers, and a pound of Oreos.

I stick my head outside the tent to check the weather. The sky is clear and a near-full moon shrouds the vast Coconino Plateau with a diaphanous white glow. Crawling outside the tent for a better view, I can clearly see that dark gash in the earth we call the Grand Canyon. Far to the northeast is the ebony-blue hump of 10,416-foot Navajo Mountain on the Utah border. And to the west-southwest, Kendrick Peak, Sitgreaves Mountain, and Bill Williams Mountain float on ethereal mist. If we get no higher this time, the awesome view is enough.

Conditions deteriorate around midnight, and throughout the early morning hours it feels as though our tent will be blown off the mountain. We grow restless. Near dawn, Randy crawls outside and sees that the mile-long ridgeline leading to Humphreys Peak is being hammered by 30- to 40-mph winds and heavy cloud cover. Over frozen ham sandwiches, we discuss our options: bash our way toward Humphreys and hope conditions improve; bail off the mountain; or make a dash for nearby Agassiz Peak.

The choice is obvious. We strike camp and agree to go for Agassiz as long as conditions don't further deteriorate into a whiteout. With every few yards gained, however, we are blown a step or two back, sometimes thrown to our knees. We soon understand why traditional Navajos sometimes refer to the Peaks as "the mountains through which the wind blows." To compound matters, it is the first time I have ever seen overhanging cornices on this ridgeline. If we do not concentrate on where we put each step, the unstable snow could avalanche, hurtling us into the inner basin far below.

When we finally reach the second highest summit of this sacred mountain an hour later, the ice-laden cloud cover lifts long enough for us to see that we have just enough time to get off the mountain before the full force of the storm hits us.

But standing on the summit is almost anti-climactic: It was the journey, not the destination; and in journeying together to this stormy summit we had, if not glimpsed the spirits of others, rekindled our own. That was good enough for us.

Climbing the "Peaks," as nearby Flagstaff residents fondly call them, is most frequently done during the fair summer months. While they are not technically difficult mountains to climb, the winds on the Peaks are fickle: They can reach gale force, creating weather as unforgiving as any mountain range in the Southwest. So whether you day hike up to the summit, or plan on spending the night on the slopes, you must be

(Right) Pay careful attention to the weather reports if you hope to enjoy a quiet winter camp on Arizona's highest mountain. The city of Flagstaff can be seen in the distance. Tom Bean

(Above) Autumn nights get chilly, but day hikes on the peaks are very popular. Tom Bean

(Left) The mountain vastness is fun for hikers of all ages in all seasons. Gill C. Kenny

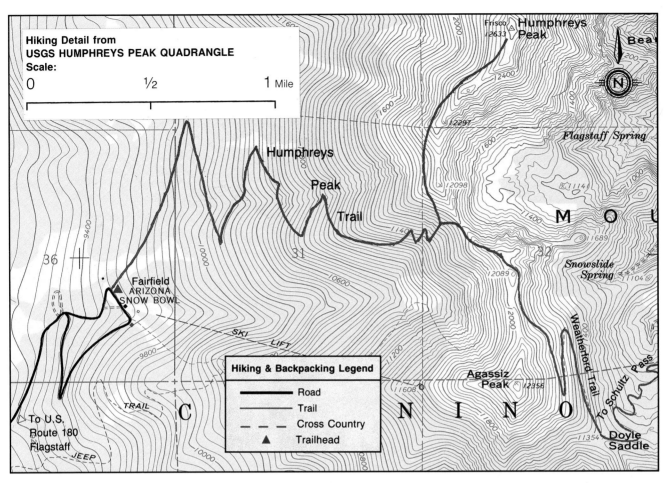

**Hiking Detail from
USGS HUMPHREYS PEAK QUADRANGLE
Scale:**

0   ½   1 Mile

Hiking & Backpacking Legend

——————— Road
——————— Trail
— — — — Cross Country
▲ Trailhead

conditioned for the altitude and be prepared for the sudden onset of extreme mountain weather. A winter ascent of the Agassiz or Humphreys summit is a marvelous adventure, but it is not for your everyday hiker, or even for the majority of the so-called experienced hikers. In winter, these mountains are no place for anyone but the most experienced with the best equipment.

There are numerous approaches to take: any of the most obvious routes leading out of the inner basin; the old Waterline Trail paralleling White Horse Canyon up to Philomena Spring; the Weatherford Road, now a wilderness trail, which leaves 8024-foot Shultz Pass and switchbacks up to the Agassiz-Humphreys ridgeline; or the Humphreys Peak Trail. Of these, the new, 4.5-mile-long Humphreys Peak Trail is the most popular way to hike the Peaks. It's well-marked and easy to follow all the way to Agassiz-Humphreys ridgeline. Hiking above timberline is restricted to designated trails only. Indiscriminate cross-country hiking is prohibited. This restriction is necessary to protect the fragile tundra habitat and, specifically, the San Francisco groundsel, a small endangered species found nowhere else in the world. Summer hikes to Agassiz Peak are prohibited, but Humphreys Peak provides breathtaking views over the 18,200-acre Kachina Peaks Wilderness and the rest of northern Arizona—assuming a storm isn't in the offing.

How To Get There

To reach Humphreys Peak Trailhead, drive 5 miles north from Flagstaff on U.S. Route 180 to the turnoff for the Snow Bowl: drive 8 miles up this steep mountain road to the upper lodge. That's where you pick up the trailhead.

Primary Access: Humphreys Peak Trail and Weatherford Trail.
Elevation: 9500 feet at Humphreys Peak trailhead to 12,633 feet on Humphreys Peak.
Mileage: 4.5 miles one way to Humphreys Peak.
Water: No perennial water en route, however, seasonal snow can be melted and boiled.
Cache Points: 11,800 foot saddle on Humphreys-Agassiz ridge line, or anyplace else you get tired.
Escape Routes: Scree slope below Humphreys-Agassiz saddle down to lodge.
Seasons: June through September is the most popular time. Beware the summer monsoons; you don't want to be anywhere on the Humphreys-Agassiz ridge line when lightning starts. Wintertime be prepared for severe alpine conditions.
Maps: USGS Humphreys Peak quadrangle, though the new Humphreys Peak Trail is not yet marked on it.
Nearest Supply Points: Flagstaff, Williams.
Managing Agency: Flagstaff Ranger District, 5010 N. Highway 89, Flagstaff, AZ 86004, (520) 527-7450
Backcountry Information: Permits are not required; however, there is a hiker's register near the trailhead. Fires are not permitted above the tree line. If you need to build a fire, use existing fire rings, dead and down wood, and beware forest fire danger. Bikes on designated trails only.

28 Mogollon Rim

"Mountain, forest, valley, and streams are blended in one harmonious whole...few worldwide travelers in a lifetime could be treated to a more perfect landscape, a true virgin solitude, undefiled by the presence of man."

—*Captain George M. Wheeler, 1873*

Captain Wheeler's impression of the Mogollon Rim country, as he saw it while surveying northern Arizona in 1871, is perhaps a bit idealized. The country is a "harmonious whole" from the air, but not if you're trying to hike it, or otherwise traverse the ragged country above and below the Rim.

Captain John G. Bourke, who traveled along the crest of the Rim, also in 1871, called it, "a strange freak of nature, a mountain canted up on one side." The Mogollon escarpment is a scar across the face of Arizona, from its cheek at the New Mexico border to its eyebrow in the area of Lake Mead. It is one of the state's distinctive landmarks, and deeply rooted in the consciousness of travelers.

This, the southern boundary of the Colorado Plateau, is not quite a mountain, but it offers just about everything a mountain range can offer. The precipice zigs and zigs, rising one or two thousand feet above the land below.

Travel is not bad right along the crest. That is why

in 1872, General George Crook built a wagon road there. To the north, the plateau immediately breaks up into steep canyons that fall away to Chevelon Creek, Clear Creek, and ultimately the Little Colorado River.

The land to the south, on the watershed of the Verde and Salt rivers, is even more ragged. Bourke, aide to General Crook, wrote of the Tonto Basin more than a century ago: "The 'Basin' is a basin only in the sense that it is all lower than the ranges enclosing it — The Mollogon, the Matitzal (Mazatzal) and the Sierra Ancha — but its whole triangular area is so cut up by ravines, arroyos, small stream beds and hills of a very good height that it may safely be pronounced one of the roughest spots on the globe."

It has been said that to visit the Mogollon Rim is to stand on the edge of the world. This sunset view from along State Route 260 looks west across some of the greatest hiking country in Arizona.
Jerry Jacka

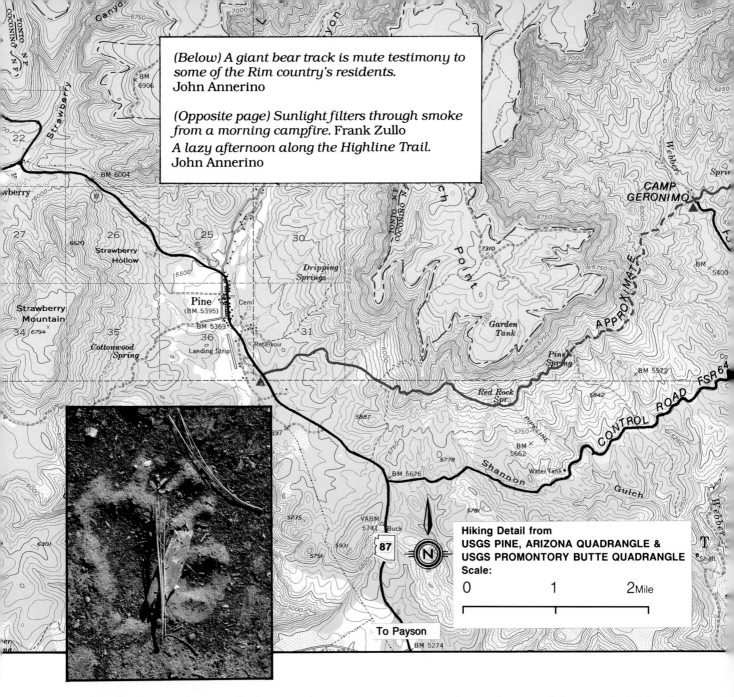

(Below) A giant bear track is mute testimony to some of the Rim country's residents.
John Annerino

(Opposite page) Sunlight filters through smoke from a morning campfire. Frank Zullo
A lazy afternoon along the Highline Trail.
John Annerino

Hiking Detail from
USGS PINE, ARIZONA QUADRANGLE &
USGS PROMONTORY BUTTE QUADRANGLE
Scale:

0   1   2 Mile

To Payson

Martha Summerhayes, wife of an Army lieutenant, wrote years later of a trip across the Rim in 1874: "The scenery was wild and grand; in fact, beyond all that I had ever dreamed of...but oh! would any sane human being voluntarily go through what I have endured on this journey, in order to look upon this wonderful scene?"

Summerhayes did it the easy way, along the crest. The Rim averages a little above 7500 feet in elevation along its most clearly defined stretch, north of the Pine-Payson-Christopher Creek area. Pioneer families coming into the country in the nineteenth century—the Randalls, the Fullers, the Pyles—all told of stopping at the top of the Rim to chain logs to the rear of their wagons to act as brakes so the rigs would not run away or overtake the horses pulling them.

You might expect to find piles of skinned-up logs all along the Highline Trail, but they are not there.

Maybe the settlers used them to build log houses. About 1,000 feet below the crest of the Rim, the Highline cuts across the heads of the ridges and canyons in the basin, bobbing up and down, and zigging in and out with the points of the Rim. The trail begins at State Route 87, south of Pine and meanders eastward for 51 miles.

My companions and I had started to hike the 36 miles to the western terminus of the trail a day and a half earlier. Beginning our trek where FR 289 crosses the trail near the Tonto Fish Hatchery, we hiked through the blackened spars and luxuriant undergrowth past the spot where author Zane Grey's Cabin once stood. The land here is recovering from the Dude Fire of July, 1990, which burned 28,480 acres below and above the Rim, including Grey's cabin. But like the phoenix emerging from the ashes, this fire-ravaged land now sprouts verdant

Continued to Page 90

grasses and native shrubs that provide an exceptional wildlife habitat. Also, plans are underway to build a replica of Grey's cabin at Payson's Museum of the Forest.

The second night we camped among the tall pines of the western portion of the Highline near the head of Bray Creek. There we spent a restless night, our sleep interrupted by what sounded like someone throwing a garbage can through the woods. We never did find out what animal caused the ruckus.

The Highline, an old trail used by homesteaders and cowboys, crosses the tops of a number of tributaries to the Salt River system: Hells Gate Canyon, Walk Moore (we called it "Walk More"), Dry Dude Creek, Cow Canyon, Poison Spring. It also intercepts several trails from atop the Rim, including the

Col. Devin Trail, named for Col. Thomas Devin who pursued a band of Apaches off the Rim at this point in 1868. The trail became a wagon road, built in 1883 to haul supplies for the Arizona Mineral Belt Railroad, which was trying to tunnel through the Rim to connect Globe and Flagstaff by rail. Money ran out before the tunnel was completed, but the wagon road continued as an important route for a long time.

Even though volunteer groups maintain the Highline, it requires a great deal of up and down hiking — more than is apparent at first glance.

That incipient elevation gain and loss had hammered us, taking its toll both physically and mentally. But we had to gather our strength and hit the trail if we expected to reach our car that day.

You needn't hike the entire 51-mile Highline

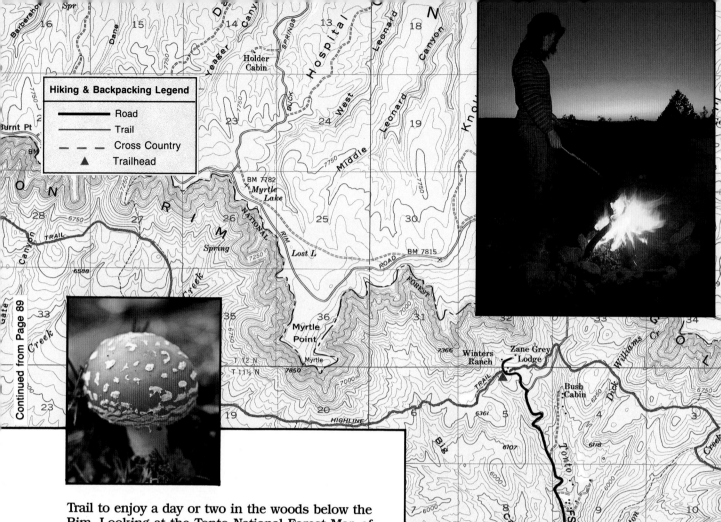

Continued from Page 89

Trail to enjoy a day or two in the woods below the Rim. Looking at the Tonto National Forest Map of the Highline Trail, compiled by Peggy Newman and the Payson Ranger District, you'll see any number of ways to hike various stretches of this trail. There are no less than 11 routes that link up with the Highline Trail from below (off State Route 87, Forest Road 64, and State Route 260), and nine trails that descend off the Mogollon Rim from Forest Road 300, the Rim Road, to intersect with the Highline from above. However you hike the Highline, you'll find the trail a well-marked, cool respite in summer from the desert lowlands, with adequate perennial water sources along most of its length.

How To Get There

To reach the Pine trailhead for the Highline Trail, drive a half-mile south of Pine on State Route 87; the turnoff and trailhead are on your left. Three other major trailheads provide access to the Highline; on that same Highline Trail map you'll see they are Camp Geronimo, Washington Park, and Forest Service Road 289. If you plan on hiking the entire 51 miles, however, you'll need to leave a shuttle vehicle at the east end of the Highline, about 4 miles east of Christopher Creek on State Route 260.

Primary Access: Pine, Camp Geronimo, Washington Park, FR289, FR284 off State Route 260 out of Christopher Creek.

Elevation: The trail ranges in elevation from 5400 feet to 6800 feet with a good portion of it between 6100 and 6500 feet.

Water: Perennial Streams: Weber Creek, Bray Creek, Chase Creek, Paloverde Creek, Dude Creek, Perely Creek, Tonto Creek, Horton Creek, and Christopher Creek.

Cache Points: Not applicable on this point-to-point hike. However, if you want to fudge a bit, use your vehicle to drop caches near the primary access points.

Escape Routes: Back the way you came. Or the most direct trail or forest road to the primary access points on State Route 87 or State Route 260.

Seasons: Due to its southern aspect, or exposure, the Highline Trail has been historically used all year long, midwinter included. Just prepare and dress for prevailing weather and you should have a fine time whenever you go.

Maps: USGS Woods Canyon, Porcupine Ridge, Weimer Point, O W Point, Dane Canyon, Knoll Lake, Diamond Point, Promontory Butte, Pine, Kehl Ridge, Buckhead Mesa and Payson north. USFS Tonto National Forest Recreation Map, and Payson Ranger District/ Highline Trail map by Peggy Newman.

Managing Agency: Tonto National Forest, Payson Ranger District, 1009 East Hwy. 260, Payson, AZ 85541, (520) 474-7900. Permits are not required. Fires are permitted. However, use existing fire rings and wood that is dead and down. Avoid fires during forest fire season, when conditions can be explosive. Bikes are allowed on the Highline Trail. Inquire at the ranger station about other mountain bike trails.

(Far left) The Rim country is a land of marvels, some only inches high. Inge Martin

(Left) Evening around the campfire is one of the most delightful times of day. Tom Bean

(Right) Should you choose to hike up one of the many trails connecting the Highline Trail to the Rim above, you will find the views spectacular. Jerry Sieve

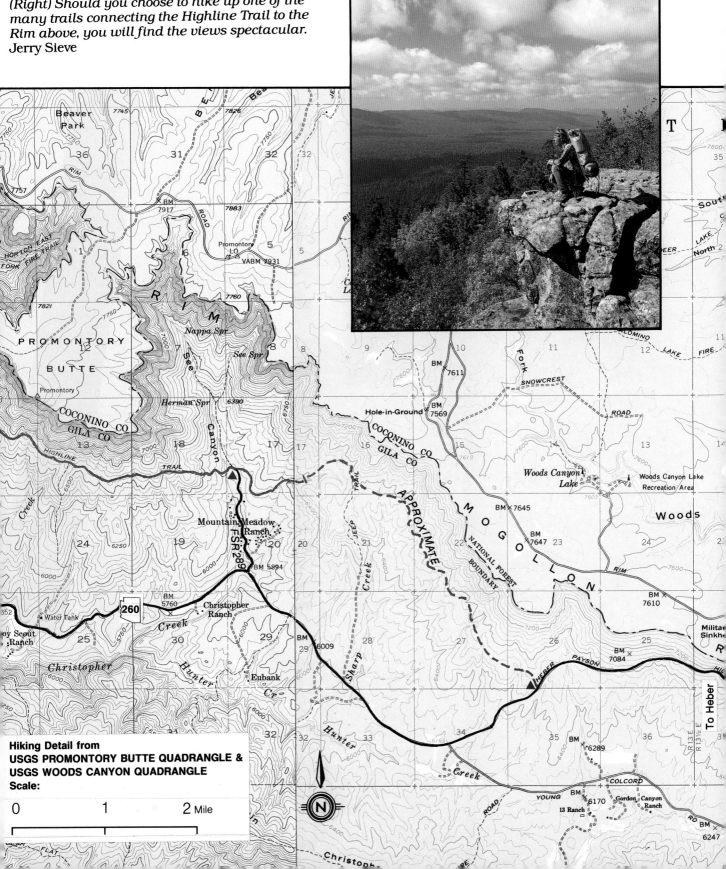

Hiking Detail from
USGS PROMONTORY BUTTE QUADRANGLE &
USGS WOODS CANYON QUADRANGLE
Scale:

0   1   2 Mile

N

㉙ Chiricahua Wilderness

"Do you fear the force of the wind? The slash of the rain? Go face them and fight them, be savage again. Go hungry and cold, like the wolf; go wade like the crane. The palms on your hands will thicken, the skin on your face will tan. You'll grow ragged and weary and swarthy, but you'll have walked like a man."

—*Hamlin Garland*

The Chiricahua Mountains, a "sky island" rising out of the flatlands in extreme southeastern Arizona, have a special place in the hearts of Arizonans, for their natural wonders and for their history as ancestral home of the Chiricahua Apaches, the people of Cochise. The peaks rise more than 9000 feet into the Hudsonian life zone and harbor a diversity of plants and animals.

There is a maze of hiking trails in this range, and the backbone of the system is the Chiricahua Crest Trail. On the north end of the mountains, you can reach the crest trail from Rustler Park via Pinery Canyon Road. For families and the not so gung ho, Pinery Canyon Road provides a way of reaching the crest trail without the steep climb otherwise necessary. If you want less driving and more hiking, start at Morse Canyon Trailhead at the end of West Turkey Creek Road.

Morse Canyon Trail climbs through ponderosa pine forest to a saddle near Johnson Peak, then follows a ridge east to Monte Vista Peak. Your dividend for this relatively steep four-mile climb of 2600 vertical feet is one of the best panoramas in southeastern Arizona. Looking north, you can see Cochise Head rise above Chiricahua National Monument, and to the northwest the salt-crusted mud of Willcox Playa reflects the sun brightly. In Pleistocene Time, about 20,000 years ago, Sulphur Springs Valley held Lake Cochise. As the climate became hotter and drier, Lake Cochise shrank to Willcox Playa. If you are hot and dry from your climb, Bear Springs is a refreshing water supply about half a mile down the southwest flank of Monte Vista Peak.

(Above) Wild iris are found in many of the alpine meadows of the Chiricahua Mountains. Peter Kresan

(Left) A hiker strides out on the Chiricahua Mountain trail. John Annerino

(Opposite page) Turkey Creek near the Monte Vista Trailhead. David Muench

Monte Vista Peak via Morse Canyon Trail is a good full-day hike. But we had three days so we went stalking the wild iris. Between Chiricahua and Flys peaks, along the Crest Trail, lie two alpine meadows: Anita and Cima. Each is carpeted with Rocky Mountain Iris—Western Blue Flag—and surrounded by Cathedral-like stands of spruce and fir. Anita Springs, and Booger Springs are dependable. With most of the elevation gain under our belt, the crest trail was a casual walk through moss-covered fir and groves of aspen.

Just before we reached Anita Park, we heard quite a ruckus in the forest ahead. We were on the lookout for black bear, which I have often spotted in the Chiricahuas, but it turned out to be three white-tailed deer browsing on young aspen.

It was early June, and the Blue Flag was just beginning to bloom. Lady bugs swarmed over some of the plants. The blue and purple of the delicate plants stand out from the dark wall of the forest like striking gems.

In Cima Park, I was saddened to see iris trampled by someone insensitive enough to camp in the middle of the meadow. There are excellent campsites just under the trees around the periphery of the meadows, and you have the added comfort of a soft blanket of pine needles.

From Round Park below Flys Peak, the Crest Trail runs about another 5 miles north to Barfoot Lookout on Buena Vista Peak. At the northern terminus of the Crest Trail, Barfoot Lookout provides a whole new, but equally spectacular vista. With Monte Vista Lookout barely visible to the south, we were now 13.5 miles from the West Turkey Creek trailhead, so back we traveled, but at least it was mostly downhill.

There are 111 miles of developed trails in the Chiricahua Wilderness, and the Morse Canyon trailhead is only one of four main trailheads leading into backcountry. South to north the other three are Rucker Lake, south fork of Cave Creek, and Rustler Park. Once at the Morse Canyon trailhead, you can follow the well-marked, steep trail 2 miles to Johnson Saddle; that makes a vigorous introductory hike into the area. If you want to tackle a more ambitious day hike or an equally pleasant overnighter, it's another 2 miles to the lookout on Monte Vista Peak. The Chiricahua Crest Trail links Monte Vista Peak with Chiricahua Peak and its northern satelite, 9666 foot Flys Peak. This 6.5 miles of trail is as fine as any in Arizona. So if you've driven this far plan on spending another night in the Chiricahuas.

The best way to take in these three peaks might be for you to spend your first night atop Chiricahua Peak; day hike over to Flys Peak and back, pick up your pack and spend your second night atop Monte Vista. That way you have a leisurely downhill stroll

(Right) View from Monte Vista Peak in the Chiricahua Wilderness. David Muench

(Left) Sunlight filters through an aspen leaf. Peter Kresan

(Below) A hiker reflects on the beauty to be found in the Chiricahua Mountains. Fred Griffin

back to your car in the morning before tackling the drive back home.

How To Get There

To reach the Morse Canyon trailhead from Tucson, drive east on Interstate 10, 81 miles to Willcox. Drive south from Willcox on State Routes 186/181, 43 miles to the turnoff for the West Turkey Creek Road, also known as USFS Road 41: its 11 miles to the Morse Canyon trailhead.

Pinery Canyon Road provides access to the Chiricahua high country trails and Coronado National Forest campgrounds. From its junction with State Route 181, just before the entrance to Chiricahua National Monument, Pinery Canyon Road climbs 16 miles to Onion Saddle. It is another 3 miles to Rustler Park at 8400 feet. The graded gravel road is steep and winding, and no combination of vehicle and trailer over 41 feet long is permitted on the road. Snow can close the road in winter.

The Rattlesnake Fire in the summer of 1994 burned a patchwork pattern near the crest of the Chiricahua Mountains. However, much of the area

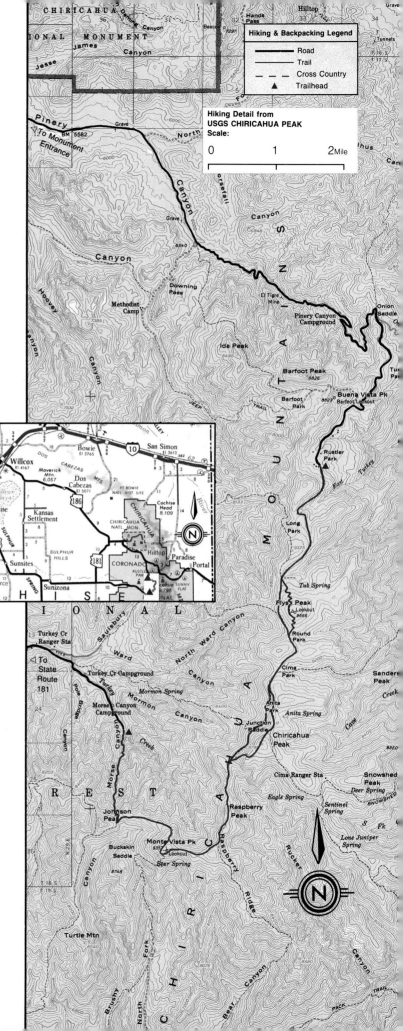

was left untouched and still offers terrific hikes through spectacular scenery. The aftermath of a forest fire presents some hazards you'll want to watch out for including loose boulders, falling trees and branches, and flash floods and mudslides when it rains. The Forest Service recommends these safety precautions: Stay on designated trails to minimize impact to burned forest floor. Camp in designated campgrounds and away from burned trees. Watch for flash floods in water courses during storms.

Primary Access: Morse Canyon Trailhead or Rustler Park.
Elevation: 7000 feet to 9357 feet on Monte Vista Peak.
Mileage: 4 miles one-way from Morse Canyon to Monte Vista.
Water: Lower Morse Canyon (seasonal). Treat all water.
Cache Points: Johnson Saddle.
Escape Routes: From Monte Vista Peak, back the way you came.
Seasons: All year long. Summer is naturally the most popular time to seek relief from the heat in this cool refuge. Fall is incredibly colorful. Winter you may need cross-country skis.
Maps: USGS Chiricahua Peak quadrangle. USFS Douglas District Coronado National Forest Recreation Map.
Managing Agency: Douglas Ranger District, R.R. 1, Box 228R, Douglas, AZ 85607, (520) 364-3468 and (520) 364-3231.
Backcountry Information: Permits are not required. Fires are permitted. Use existing fire rings and wood that's dead and down. Avoid fires during forest fire season.

㉚ Kendrick Peak

At 10,418 feet, Kendrick Peak is more than 2000 feet lower than the crest of the San Francisco Peaks; however, unlike the San Francisco Peaks, Kendrick Peak offers an unrestricted 360-degree panorama from its summit. Kendrick thrusts itself out of the 7000 foot high Coconino Plateau more than 3000 feet, providing the greatest vertical relief in the southern half of the Kaibab National Forest.

Martos Hoffman

While the 4 mile climb to the summit is an invigorating hike, it's the destination, not so much the journey, that is your reward. As early as 1902, cartographer Francois Matthes used Kendrick as his key triangulation point for the first topographic map of the Grand Canyon. From the summit of this natural lookout you can clearly see the Grand Canyon to the north, the Little Colorado River gorge to the northeast, and San Francisco Peaks to the east. However, if you turn in any other direction you'll need a good set of maps to identify all the other mountain ranges.

To reach Kendrick Peak, drive northwest from Flagstaff on U.S. Route 180 for 17 miles to USFS Road 193. Turn west on 193 and drive 4.5 miles to USFS 171. Take 171 for 3 miles to 171A. Turn right and 171A will deadend at the Kendrick Peak trailhead a mile farther.

㉛ Bill Williams Mountain

For all practical purposes, you can drive all the way to the summit of 9256-foot-high Bill Williams mountain on a narrow, twisting road which corkscrews its way up its southern flank to the lookout and radio towers crowded onto its small, forested summit. However, the hiking trail leading to the summit gives you a fine taste of what it was like when mountain man Bill Williams trapped the area in the

John Annerino

mid-1800s. Appropriately enough, it's called the Bill Williams Trail.

You can reach the trailhead by driving 2 miles west of the community of Williams on old U.S. Route 66 to the Camp Clover Ranger Station. It's a stout, 2000-foot climb in 3 miles up the north side of Bill Williams Mountain. The well marked trail parallels the upper fork of West Cataract Creek through the "quakies" and Douglas fir to a fine lunch spot just before you reach the summit road. Bill Williams Trail makes an excellent day hike spring through fall.

㉜ Chiricahua National Monument

There is great year-round hiking on well-maintained trails and the visitor center can give directions to spectacular hikes lasting from a few hours to all day. Here are just a couple. "Day use" only.

Wesley Holden

Echo Canyon Trail. The Echo Canyon Trail wanders down through an Alice in Wonderland labyrinth of hoodoos, balanced rocks, and narrow passages. This maze of pinnacles and spires stands like chessmen, sculpted out of volcanic rock layers formed by an eruption millions of years ago. The trail starts at the Echo Canyon parking area. A nice loop trip of 3.5 miles takes you down Echo Canyon Trail and returns by Hailstone Trail through Rhyolite Canyon. But however you climb out of the canyon it's steep and can be hot in summer.

Heart of Rocks Trail. Some of the most distinctive rock formations and inspiring views in Chiricahua National Monument are seen along Heart of Rocks Trail. Unlike many other trails that take you into canyons, the 7-mile round trip Heart of Rocks Trail is carved into the top of a mesa. The Heart of Rocks Trail starts at the Massai Point parking area. This is an exhilarating full-day hike. Bring plenty of water.

For additional information contact: Superintendent, Chiricahua National Monument, Dos Cabezas Rt., Box 6500, Willcox, AZ 85643, (520) 824-3560.

Jack W. Dykinga

㉝ Mt. Lemmon
Santa Catalina Mountains

Not far from downtown Tucson, the Mt. Lemmon Trail skirts the top of the Santa Catalina Mountains at 9157 feet. It meanders through ponderosa pine forest and crosses beautiful grassy meadows. In summer and early fall, sunflower and Indian paint brush decorate the mountain side. Even in the middle of summer, when Tucson's temperature soars over 100 degrees, this is a refreshingly cool place to hike.

From Tanque Verde Road in Tucson, take the Mt. Lemmon Highway 30 miles to the top. The last mile of road, just past the ski lift, is especially steep and narrow. The trailhead is very close to a fenced compound of telescopes and communication towers. A topographic map of Mt. Lemmon, or the Southern Arizona Hiking Club's trail and recreation map and Pusch Ridge Wilderness map of the Santa Catalina Mountains, shows various trail options.

㉞ Hualapai Mountain Park
Hualapai Mountains

The Hualapai Mountains, south of Kingman, provide magnificent vistas of the surrounding basin and range landscape of northwestern Arizona. From the campground at about 7000 feet, three relatively easy trails meander up Hualapai, Hayden, and Aspen Peaks. A short trail climbs Hualapai Peak at 8417 feet, and a 2.7-mile trail reaches Hayden Peak. From the top, one can see four states, Utah, Nevada, California, and of course, Arizona. Other trails are marked on the USGS Hualapai Peak and Dean Peak quadrangles.

To get there from U.S. Route 93, on the east end of Kingman take the Hualapai Mountain Road about 12 miles up Sawmill Canyon to Hualapai Mountain Park. For information contact Hualapai Mountain Park, Pine Lake Route, Kingman, AZ 86401, (520) 757-3859.

㉟ Lockett Meadow
San Francisco Peaks

At 8000 feet, Lockett Meadow provides cathedral-like groves of aspen, mingled with pine, spruce, and fir. Surrounded by high San Francisco Peaks, this is a fabulous place to catch the rich fall color of aspens. There is good access to casual hiking along old dirt roads. The peaks tend to make their own weather and snow often arrives early.

Peter Kresan

To reach Lockett Meadow, turn west off U.S. Route 89 onto a Coconino National Forest Service Road about .75 mile north of the Sunset Crater National Monument turnoff. Just past a cinder mine, the gravelly road turns right and climbs steeply around Sugar Loaf Mountain and, in 4 to 5 miles, reaches Lockett Meadow.

James Tallon

㊱ Mt. Wrightson
Santa Rita Mountains

At the head of Madera Canyon beginning the climb up Mt. Wrightson, you already are in ponderosa pine forest at 5500 feet elevation. You have a choice of Old Baldy or the newer Mt. Wrightson trails. As usual, you do not get something for nothing. Old Baldy is shorter, but steeper. You might want to try

Jack W. Dykinga

this combination: Start on the Mt. Wrightson trail, which leaves from the lower end of Roundup Picnic Area parking lot and follows a gorge 3.7 miles to Josephine Saddle. The Old Baldy trail also crosses this saddle, and is a good way to travel the next 1.6 miles to Baldy Saddle. You pass dependable Sprung and Bellows springs along the way. The final mile to 9453-foot Mt. Wrightson is an exposed trail, providing awesome views of southern Arizona.

You can climb Wrightson year-round, but high mountains create their own weather. Bring more clothing and food than you might think you need.

To get there take the Continental exit from Interstate 19, about halfway between Tucson and Nogales. Follow the signs 13 miles to the head of Madera Canyon, where there are Coronado National Forest campgrounds and picnic sites. The Southern Arizona Hiking Club sells a trail map of the Santa Rita Mountains. Coronado National Forest, (520) 670-4552.

㊲ Mt. Baldy

White Mountains

At 11,403 feet, Mt. Baldy is one of the highest mountains in Arizona. The extinct volcano is sacred to White Mountain Apaches and figures in the lore of other tribes. A forest of Engelmann spruce, blue spruce and Douglas fir harbors elk, beaver, golden-mantled ground squirrels, Audubon's warbler, gray jays, and red-breasted nuthaches.

From the trailhead at Sheeps Crossing, the trail meanders through alpine meadows and along the West Fork of the Little Colorado River. In about 6 miles, it climbs from 9300 feet to near timberline at 11,200 feet. The last mile to the top of Mt. Baldy is on the Fort Apache Indian Reservation. Hiking in this sacred area is forbidden.

Summer through fall is the best time to explore the Mt. Baldy Wilderness. It is always cool. Thunderstorms develop quickly.

To reach the trailhead, turn off State Route 260 east of McNary onto State Route 273, the Big Lake road. Sheeps Crossing is about 10 miles farther. Topographic maps of the Mt. Baldy Wilderness and the surrounding Apache-Sitgreaves National Forest are available from the district ranger's office in Springerville, (520) 333-4372. No bikes in the wilderness.

Peter Kresan

"There is a Japanese sport, called sawan- *abori, in which you follow streams to their origins.... Sawanabori is not only a sport, it is a kind of a ritual, like many ancient games: a pilgrimage along the natural pathways of free-running water. In the desert the ritual has a more intense kind of beauty; following water is the holiest kind of quest in a dry land."*

Rob Schulthesis, The Hidden West

Galen Snell was a soft-spoken country boy from Kansas. He was my psychology professor at Scottsdale Community College, and he had been inviting me and another student named Gary to hike down the Boucher Trail in the Grand Canyon. The Boucher Trail, I'd thought, what's that? We've got the Superstition Mountains right here. I'd been backpacking in those mountains since my early teens. They represented everything that was wild about Arizona.

Galen pressed on, subtly, and by semester's end Gary and I relented. We would hike his canyon before resuming our adventures in the Superstitions.

... I'm not sure how many miles of hiking it took us; it wasn't many. But we were walking along the enchilada-red Hermit formation when it hit me. Here we were hiking one of the airiest stretches of trail I'd ever been on, and it felt like I could fly. The Colorado River was at our feet—I don't know how many thousands of feet below; the North Rim, well, it felt like I could just reach out with my right hand and grab a handful of ponderosas. East or west as far as you could see, up-canyon and down, awesome tributary canyons drained into the Colorado River. Seventy-some canyons in all, Galen told his two slack-jawed students.

Galen didn't have to say anything more about his little ol' canyon. It did all the talking during the peaceful night the three of us camped near Boucher Creek. Needless to say, that hike taught me Arizona was more than my Superstition Mountains. It also was canyon country, and not just the Grand Canyon.

Arizona is criss-crossed with canyons. The Salt River Canyon is one; we drove through it in June, 1960, when we first moved to Arizona. I remember my mom covered her eyes while my father bravely drove on into the abyss. His three wide-eyed children had their noses pressed flat against the window. There is gentle Sycamore Canyon on the Arizona-Sonoran border, which is often mistaken for its more rugged counterpart near Sedona. There is Aravaipa Canyon at the foot of the Galiuro Wilderness, Burro Creek near Bagdad, Tsegi Canyon, and on and on.

That list doesn't include mountain-based canyons like Bear and Sabino Canyons in the Santa Catalinas, the magnificent Cliff Canyon draining the southwest side of 10,388-foot Navajo Mountain, or Deadman Creek in the Mazatzal Wilderness; nor does it include the major canyons draining the Mogollon Rim like Wet Beaver Creek, West Clear Creek, Fossil Creek, Tonto Creek, Canyon Creek, Cibecue Creek.

The Superstitions, I confessed to Galen, might have to wait awhile; well, maybe I'd just take a look at one canyon I'd heard about in there. Fish Creek, someone said, was the place to be in the spring: deep pools of water to swim in.

What follows are some of the favorites I "discovered" with other friends not long after Galen introduced me to Arizona's canyon country.

(Left) Hikers look over the Grand Canyon from Plateau Point on the Bright Angel Trail. Martos Hoffman

(Right) Although the Grand Canyon is the ultimate, Arizona is blessed with a wide variety of canyon hikes. Fred Griffin

㊳ Aravaipa Canyon

The Land of 'Little Running Water'

"Certainly, there is nothing commonplace about the vigorous, laughing, crystal-clear stream which has carved this remote, little known canyon through the heart of a desert mountain range."
— *Weldon F. Heald, 1950*

It was quiet in Aravaipa Canyon, except for nature's soft voice. The sound of running water was soothing. We heard the rustling leaves of magnificent cottonwood trees, which dominate the many other kinds of trees lining Aravaipa Creek.

Aravaipa Canyon is full of contradictions. The high-walled canyon apparently was a refuge for Indians before the Spaniards came, and after. Father Eusebio Francisco Kino took note of the place in 1697, although he called it by another name. And white settlers irrigated small farms from Aravaipa Creek before the Civil War.

Near the end of the 18th Century, Apaches and Pimas merged to form a group which white men labeled Aravaipa Apache. History books almost always equate Aravaipa with the Camp Grant Massacre in 1871, when vigilantes from Tucson, frustrated with the government's "kindness" toward Apaches, wiped out most of the band. But that occurred outside the canyon's west end, near the junction of Aravaipa Creek and the San Pedro River. Certainly the canyon was a passageway for red man and white soldiers in Arizona's more restless days.

Yet today, Aravaipa is a symbol of primitive nature in the minds of many people. It is so rugged that a Bureau of Land Management brochure warns hikers it is "not a picnic ground." But a hiker who is in shape can walk through it handily, from one side of the Galiuro Mountains to the other. It is a tough environment, containing a fragile ecology.

Getting to know where water flows in Arizona— when it flows—is one of those customs that makes you feel at home. Aravaipa empties into one of the odd north-flowing rivers, the San Pedro, shortly before the San Pedro joins the Gila.

Another tradition says that an Arizona creek is more likely to have water in it than an Arizona river. Aravaipa Creek is one of the few perennial streams in the Southwest. The Tohono O'Odham call it *A Aly Waipia* for "little wells," and the Apache call it "little running water."

The sound of running water has a soothing, almost placental quality to it. The farther we hike into the confines of this riparian sanctuary, the more distant the sounds of civilization become. Soon they are washed away completely by the rustling of leaves

(Right) The soft green foliage of magnificent cottonwoods contrasts with the rocky walls of Aravaipa Canyon. Peter Kresan

in the magnificent cottonwoods which protrude from this silver strand of water like giant stalks of broccoli.

The two of us have been hiking since morning, but not too early morning. There is no need for a daybreak attack when your day's objective is the other end of this 11-mile-long canyon. In *The Gila: River of the Southwest*, Edwin Corle wrote, "Aravaipa Creek and its upper canyons look exactly today as they did in the days of Esteban de Dorantes in 1539 and Coronado in 1540. Here is a corner of the Gila watershed that is little known, even to Arizonans."

True enough. Until this trip, I'd always been on the receiving end of the comment, "You haven't been to Aravaipa, yet!" Well, once before, but that was so long ago I might as well have read about it. That's why I invited Caroline Wilson to hike with me. She is an interpretive specialist at Organ Pipe Cactus National Monument. If anybody could identify and interpret the myriad species of flora and fauna in this lush canyon, she could. I don't mean the heavy hitters that normally get top billing on the desert marquee: saguaros, bighorns, sycamore, javelina, mourning

dove…ad infinitum. I mean the exotic-sounding animals, like the Ash-throated Fly Catcher, the Tiger rattlesnake, and the Loach minnow. They take a trained eye and a sense of wonder to become familiar with.

As we wade beyond the knee-deep confluence of Booger Canyon, my mind wanders, as do my eyes. What I assume is a golden eagle is soaring over the lip of the canyon wall a thousand feet above, carving long graceful arcs in the warm June sky.

So lush is Aravaipa's riparian habitat that seven species of fish, eight amphibians, 46 reptiles, 46 mammals, and over 200 birds inhabit this small 6699-acre wilderness. Those are just numbers, though. We're not taking into account what each of those critters eats, how long it lives, or how the presence of 3000 or 4000 hikers a year affects it.

We have sloshed and hiked almost 6 miles, and we have not seen one hiker yet. Not that I came out here to see other people, but the U.S. Bureau of Land Management office in Safford advised us that all the permits (50 per day) had been spoken for.

(Above) It's nice to cool off in Aravaipa Creek, and the scenery is so beautiful you don't mind having your feet wet most of the time. John Annerino

(Far left) This aerial view shows a portion of the rugged terrain surrounding Aravaipa Canyon. Peter Kresan

(Left) Wildlife abounds in the canyon, from squirrels to bighorn sheep, and from hummingbirds to hawks. John Annerino

(Right) The wide variety of vegetation includes the lovely, but poisonous, sacred datura. Peter Kresan

In the fading late afternoon light, we see three barrel-thick cottonwood logs perched on a rock ledge 20 feet above the stream bed. They have been carried down and deposited there by a previous summer flash flood.

That's not hard to imagine. Aravaipa Canyon drains a watershed on the east side of the Galiuros, cuts clean through the mountain range and delivers the water to the San Pedro. It has 14 major tributaries, four of them perennial, and drains an area of 541 square miles. That area includes the seldom-visited Galiuro Wilderness immediately to the south, and part of 10,713-foot-high Mount Graham, the highest mountain in southern Arizona.

But we don't see, or hear, a soul. We have the place to ourselves, and that's fine by me. Sitting next to our small fire drying out wet tennis shoes, it's not hard to imagine how this canyon once was seen by the barefoot-and sandal-clad Hohokam and Salado Indians; archeologists believe they used Aravaipa Canyon as a primary migration route. So did the wolf. According to David E. Brown's *The Wolf In the Southwest,* "No epitaph for the wolf in the southwest United States could be written, however, without mentioning the Aravaipa wolf ... " Staring into the primal light of our fire, you can almost hear it howl.

Campfires are like that, though; they're good for "the dreamtime," what the aborigines of Australia call *Uluru.* They spark the imagination the way nothing else does; then, so does this canyon and the way some

of the people—the *only* people—we see playing in it the next day.

A mile short of our car, about where you normally see empty pop cans on most other hikes, we see a family rafting (!) down Aravaipa Creek. Mind you, we're not talking Crystal Rapids here; the creek at this point is maybe two dozen feet wide and a foot or so deep. But mom, pop, and the kids are floating down Aravaipa Creek in inner tubes as if that's the *only* way to see Aravaipa Canyon. Edwin Corle wrote if you go to Aravaipa, prepare to hike. Staring down at our prune-toed feet, and listening to the distant echoes of their laughter, I think we might have literally missed the boat on this one.

No matter how you try, you're not going to keep your feet dry. So avoid time-consuming detours you *think* will keep them dry. If you are day hiking without a heavy pack, you can get by with tennis shoes and two pairs of socks. Some canyon hikers swear by a neoprene walking shoe called a Reefwalker. Take extra socks and a second pair of sneakers or thongs for camp.

If you're carrying a heavy pack, or if your ankles are prone to injury, wear hiking boots. Although they'll get wet, they provide needed support for walking the rocky stream bed. Again take plenty of socks—wool socks make a difference in cool weather.

Because Aravaipa is such a short canyon, you have several hiking options: day hike from either entrance; do an overnight back pack from either

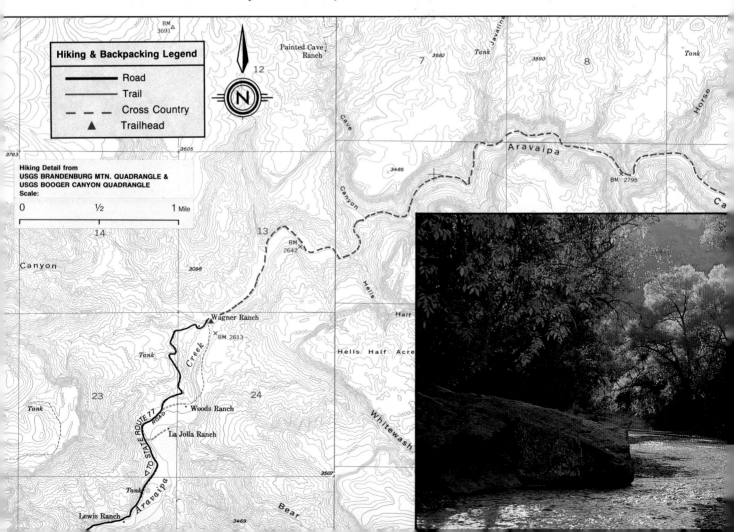

entrance; or pack in and set up a base camp from where you can spend days exploring Aravaipa's tributary canyons: Parsons, Virgus, and Half-Acre canyons on the south side and Hell Hole, Paisano, Booger, Horse Camp, Javelina, and Painted Cave Canyons on the north side. However you plan to hike the main stem of Aravaipa Creek, the route is obvious; stay in the creek bed, on dry ground when you can, and on faint pieces of trail when you find them. And *always* make a high camp; look for the "bathtub ring," or old high water line, and try to camp above it to be safe from flash floods during the wet seasons.

How To Get There

To reach the west entrance, take State Route 177 south from Superior through Kearny, Hayden, and Winkelman. At Winkelman, turn south on State Route 77 for 11 miles to the Aravaipa Canyon Road. The turnoff is well marked, and the 13 miles of paved and gravel road which follow are suitable for passenger cars. To reach the east entrance, drive approximately 15 miles northwest of Safford on U.S. Route 70, then turn southwest on Klondyke Road. Follow Klondyke Road for approximately 45 miles to the entrance. Klondyke Road is a graded dirt road, maintained by Graham County and suitable for passenger cars.

Primary Access: West entrance and east entrance: the east entrance is a longer drive but is far prettier than the other.
Elevation: East entrance: 3060 feet. West entrance: 2640 feet.
Water: All water from Aravaipa Creek and tributaries should be purified.
Cache Points: If you're doing an overnighter, figure on making a cache on high ground halfway between the beginning of your hike and camp.
Escape Routes: Back the way you came; or if you're closer to one entrance than the other and you *know* there's a vehicle there.
Seasons: Springtime through fall: winter can be bone-cold unless your idea of a good time is hiking in a wetsuit or hip waders. Summer can be hot though refreshing. And the July/August monsoons can cause deadly flash floods.
Maps: USGS Booger Canyon and Brandenburg Mountain 7 ½ minute quadrangles.
Nearest Supply Points: Tucson, Willcox, Safford, Superior, Hayden.
Managing Agency: Bureau of Land Management, Safford District Office, 711 4th Ave., Safford, AZ 85546, (520) 428-4040.
Backcountry Information: Permits required (fee). Recommend requesting permits up to 13 weeks in advance. Fires permitted. use driftwood and existing fire rings.

(Bottom) Changing colors makes Aravaipa Canyon a favorite place for autumn hikers.
Peter Kresan

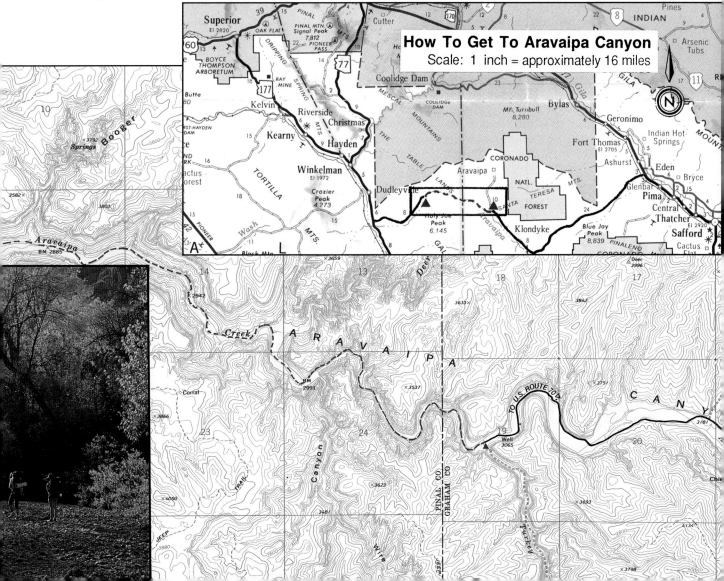

③⑨ Paria Canyon

"Secret doors: there are so many of them out on the Colorado Plateau. Secret doors to other lost worlds, spinning their own time, turning on their own occult axes."
Rob Schultheis, The Hidden West

Buckskin Gulch was one such secret door. Through it, we had hoped to enter the heart of Paria (Pah-ree-uh) Canyon, a narrow sandstone defile which twists through a land every bit as sublime as the Grand Canyon. Buckskin at its best is a fissure carved through the soft sandstones of the Colorado Plateau by the relentless forces of erosion.

Rich Nebeker, Kimmie Johnson, and I were half an hour into our journey when Buckskin pinched together, forming a passageway no more than two feet wide. We squeezed through this first secret door, holding our packs over our heads. Paria Canyon was used as an access route by Pueblo Indians and later by Mormon settlers traveling between northern Arizona and southern Utah. Its tributary of Buckskin seemed to serve primarily as a storm drain for spring runoff and summer flash floods. It was clogged with log jams and boulder slides that served as strainers for any and everything traveling through Buckskin, us included.

Now, that wouldn't be such a big deal if you could see where you were going. But with overhanging walls hundreds of feet high, there were few places that sun could actually penetrate the gold and copper depths of this labyrinth. When it did, it was as if we were walking through the incandescent glow of a light bulb. Otherwise, we either had the ambient light of the sun to guide us from one shaft of light to the next, or we were walking in almost complete darkness.

We didn't think that was a major concern either, because we knew where two major dropoffs occurred. But where the water pooled up and formed stagnant ponds of quicksand, we started thinking about what the Spanish explorers Dominguez and Escalante said of the canyon country in 1776: *Salsipuedes*. Literally, "if you can." Get out if you can. Except for one, possibly two, places along its 15-mile course, there is no way out of Buckskin Gulch. That leaves you with the option of retreating the way you came, assuming a flash flood isn't thundering toward you, or continuing to probe your way downstream as if you were spelunking. Our immediate course lay approximately 7½ miles downstream from the Wire Pass trailhead where we knew we could climb out of the canyon, make camp, and assess the weather. But first we had to get there.

Our progress was barred by a Volkswagen-sized boulder. We voted to climb over it, because if the boulder did fall, we could ride it down—we thought. That was only slightly more appealing than being caught underneath it while crawling on our hands and knees, in the growing darkness, through the tangle of logs and trees.

I removed my pack, stemmed the walls on both sides with hands and feet, and shimmied down until I could see how the footing looked.

"What's it look like?" Kimmie shouted. "Clear to me." I jumped, landing like two wooden fence posts in the knee-deep muck. Quicksand, some call it. Having encountered this several times in the Paria Canyon "narrows," I knew the farthest I would sink would be up to my thighs, not necessarily an encouraging thought.

This area is appropriately called the Cesspool. We slogged through this sucking, pudding-like substance in the twilight until we reached firmer ground. Our legs and feet were encased in a good half-inch of mud that felt like it was drying almost as fast as Super Glue.

When Kimmie looked up, she saw clouds, and we decided we should check the weather topside. It was the wrong season, but it would be awkward to be flushed out of the canyon by a sudden storm. Finding a way to get up to a pinon-studded mesa on the north side of Buckskin, we discovered a view that took our breath away.

Writer Gregory Crampton, in *Standing Up Country*, said the Grand Canyon is easier to comprehend and explore than the maze of canyons upstream in southern Utah. We could see that Buckskin and Paria were but two canyons lost in a maze of reefs, buttes, and mesas.

The rock at White House Ruin, in Buckskin, and in the Paria narrows will remind you a bit of Zion Canyon. It is carved through the same massive Navajo Sandstone formation, with its colors ranging from white to bright, rust-colored orange. Navajo sandstone is a vast blanket of fossilized dunes, once traversed by dinosaurs.

(Above) Pudding-like mud covers the feet and ankles of hikers in Buckskin Gulch. Tom Bean

(Right) A hiker stands spotlighted by one of the shafts of sunlight that penetrate Buckskin's convoluted depths. Tom Bean

Below Wrather Canyon, the Paria River broke through about 1,700 feet of Navajo sandstone into generally softer rock. These softer layers cannot support the massive cliffs of sandstone, and so landslides have widened the canyon, which opens up for a view of the majestic Vermilion Cliffs.

There are several ways to hike the Paria Canyon area. The most popular way is to start from the White House Ruin entrance and spend three or four days hiking the 34 miles downstream to Lees Ferry. There is no trail, although the way is obvious and the footing, although wet, is relatively pleasant. The streambed is strewn with flat sandstones and siltstones, as opposed to the more troublesome round stones and boulders encountered while hiking most other canyons in Arizona.

Drinking water from Paria is safe if you purify and if you let it stand overnight in order for the heavy sediments to settle.

Although the Paria runs all year around, Bush Head is the last reliable spring before Lees Ferry, 13 miles below. So bring large, collapsible containers to fill at the spring in Bush Head.

The second way to hike Paria is to hike down Buckskin either via the Wire Pass trailhead, or the Buckskin trailhead. Make sure you plan this hike during a dry season. If you don't plan on hiking Buckskin to Paria in a single day, you'll want to camp on the rimrock above Buckskin. One certain place to get out of Buckskin is via the Middle Trail located 6 miles below the confluence of Wire Pass and Buckskin Gulch. It's a bit of a scramble, but it is marked by cairns on the north side.

Buckskin Gulch can be like a refrigerator, so bring a jacket. And if you're taking photographs, bring a tripod. Light levels inside Buckskin and the Paria narrows are amazingly low; exposures can require tens of seconds.

In addition to the Cesspool 6.6 miles below the Wire Pass and Buckskin confluence, one other obstacle may impede your progress. A rock jam is located 11 miles below the confluence. It is safe-guarded by your choice of weathered nylon ropes and contemporary Moqui steps chipped into the rock, or you may bring a rope to safeguard your 20- to 30-foot descent to the canyon floor. The jam can be safely negotiated without much difficulty, but you may find it more comforting to be belayed by your partner with your own climbing rope.

Once you reach the confluence with Paria Canyon, you have two attractive options: a 28-mile hike through the length of Paria Canyon to Lees Ferry; or complete a loop hike by hiking 6.8 miles up (north) to the White House Ruin trailhead.

Below the confluence with Bush Head Canyon, you can choose to follow an undeveloped trail through a boulder slide on the south side or continue walking in the Paria River bottom. Farther along, a well-beaten path often shortcuts the wide meanders.

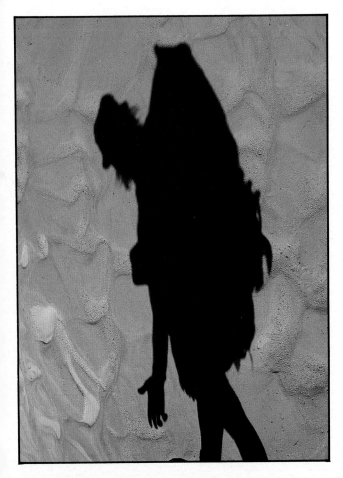

(Above) Self-portrait of a Paria Canyon hiker's shadow on the wall. Peter Kresan

(Left) At the lower end, the scenery and vegetation change as Paria Canyon widens out. Peter Kresan

(Right) A canyon resident. Peter Kresan

How To Get There

To enter Buckskin Gulch, take U.S. Route 89 between Kanab, Utah, and Page, Arizona, to the House Rock Valley Road and turn south. The Buckskin Gulch trailhead is approximately 4.3 miles south of Route 89; the Wire Pass trailhead is 4 miles farther.

To enter the White House Ruins trailhead for Paria Canyon, drive 28 miles west of Page on U. S. Route 89 to the White House Ruins turnoff; turn left (south), and the trailhead is 1.8 miles beyond the turnoff.

Due to flash flood danger, both Buckskin and Paria are almost always hiked top to bottom. However, if you are hiking all the way through Buckskin and Paria, you need to first park your shuttle vehicle at Lees Ferry. To reach the Lees Ferry trailhead, turn north off U. S. Route 89A at Marble Canyon and drive 6.5 miles to the parking area on the left side of the road.

Several concessions provide shuttle services for Paria Canyon hikers; contact the Bureau of Land Management in Kanab, Utah at (801) 644-2672 for further information.

Primary Access: Wire Pass, Buckskin Gulch, and White House Ruin trailheads: You should not attempt to hike the length of Paria Canyon upstream from Lees Ferry due to flash flood danger.

Elevation: White House Ruin: 4400 feet. Buckskin Gulch: 5500 feet. Wire Pass: 5500 feet. Lees Ferry 3151 feet.

Mileage: Wire Pass to Lees Ferry: 40.4 miles. Buckskin to Lees Ferry: 43.4 miles. White House to Lees Ferry: 37 miles.

Cache Points: Not applicable on these point-to-point hikes.

Escape Route: Back the way you came; via the Middle Trail out of Buckskin or the closest trailhead.

Seasons: Fall, winter, late spring, and early summer, though you should obviously avoid summer monsoons and heavy spring runoff.

Maps: USGS Nephi Point, Eight Mile Pass, Five Mile Valley, Lower Coyote Spring, Nipple Butte, Tibbet Bench, Petrified Hollow, Pine Hollow Canyon, West Clark Bench, Bridger Point, Glen Canyon City, Lone Rock, Buckpasture Canyon, Coyote Buttes, Poverty Flat, Wrather Arch, Water Pockets, Ferry Swale, Cooper Ridge, House Rock Spring, One Toe Ridge, The Big Knoll, Navajo Bridge, Lees Ferry, and BLM Paria Canyon hiker's map.

Nearest Supply Points: St. George and Kanab, Utah; Page, Marble Canyon, and Flagstaff, Arizona.

Managing Agency: Bureau of Land Management, Kanab Resource Area, 318 N. 100 East, Box 459, Kanab, UT 84714. (801) 644-2672

Backcountry Information: Permits are required; campfires permitted. Use existing fire rings and dead and down wood.

(Below) A hiker emerges from Buckskin Gulch into Paria Canyon.
(Right) With the help of a rope, a hiker climbs down Buckskin Gulch on steps chipped into the rock by other hikers.
John Annerino photos

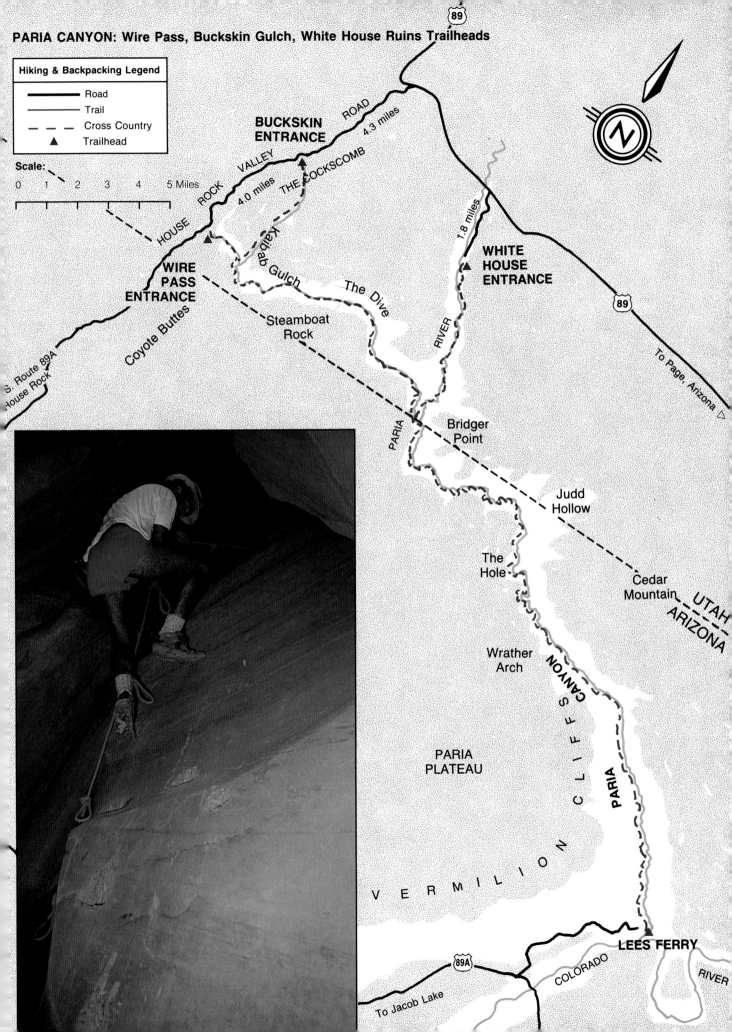

PARIA CANYON: Wire Pass, Buckskin Gulch, White House Ruins Trailheads

Hiking & Backpacking Legend

——	Road
―	Trail
– – –	Cross Country
▲	Trailhead

Scale:

0 1 2 3 4 5 Miles

89

BUCKSKIN ENTRANCE

VALLEY ROAD

ROCK

HOUSE

THE COCKSCOMB

4.3 miles

4.0 miles

Kaibab Gulch

WIRE PASS ENTRANCE

Coyote Buttes

U.S. Route 89A

House Rock

Steamboat Rock

The Dive

PARIA RIVER

1.8 miles

WHITE HOUSE ENTRANCE

89

To Page, Arizona

Bridger Point

Judd Hollow

The Hole

Cedar Mountain

UTAH

ARIZONA

Wrather Arch

PARIA PLATEAU

VERMILION CLIFFS CANYON

PARIA

LEES FERRY

89A

To Jacob Lake

COLORADO RIVER

⑩ West Fork of Oak Creek

"The red walls seemed to dream and wait under the blaze of sun; the heat lay like a blanket over the still foliage; the birds were quiet; only the murmuring stream broke the silence of the canyon. Never had Carley felt more the isolation and solitude of Oak Creek Canyon."

—*Zane Grey*, The Call of the Canyon

Hiking the West Fork of Oak Creek is one of those very special outdoor experiences peculiar to Arizona. Knowledgeable hikers put it right up there with Paria, Bright Angel, or the San Francisco Peaks, but it is different from any of them.

West Fork has been a Research Natural Area for many years and is now a part of the Red Rock Secret Mountain Wilderness. And much that is sought after in Arizona comes together along the Mogollon Rim, a zone of transition between the Basin and Range region to the south and the Colorado Plateau to the north.

In these canyons, prickly pear cactus, agave, pinon, and juniper, common to the lower zone, meet ponderosa pine and Douglas fir. Where they converge with the rich streambed vegetation, the mixture is luxuriant.

West Fork offers several options: a few hours or a full day from its lower end, or an arduous overnight bushwhack beginning on the plateau above, southwest of Flagstaff, and ending where West Fork joins the main Oak Creek Canyon. The latter option requires even the experienced hiker to commit to a point-of-no-return situation, so we'll concentrate on the lower end, which provides spectacle enough for most hikers.

Faulting allowed the canyons to break through the resistant cap of lava on top of the plateau. Once through that rock, water carved the spectacular canyons through the softer, red layers of sedimentary rock below. Faulting and fracturing also made it possible for springs to feed the canyon streams today.

Where West Fork joins Oak Creek, the trail begins in an apple orchard near the ruins of Mayhew Lodge, which burned several years ago. Towering cliffs of sandstone form a cathedral-like entrance, through which you pass into what seems to be another world.

(Above left) An old stone buttress marks the site of a washed out foot bridge and the beginning of the trail into West Fork. Peter Kresan

(Left) The trail passes through an apple orchard near the ruins of the old Mayhew Lodge. W. Randall Irvine

(Right) Weekdays are an especially good time to enjoy the beauty of West Fork, simply because there is less traffic. Peter Kresan

A well-traveled path criss-crosses the creek. Just beyond this meadow, a long, shallow pool extends upstream from the first crossing. Water seeping from the sandstone overhang splashes into the pool as though tiny fish were jumping. If you see a larger splash, it might be a water ouzel, a slate-grey bird shaped like a large wren. The ouzel builds its nest of a ball of moss hung on the rock walls along streams. Listen for the canyon wren, whose distinctively clear whistle descends in tempo; watch for the bridled titmouse, yellow warbler, and Bullock's oriole.

Although the canyon of the West Fork twists and turns, essentially it runs east and west, dropping from the high country west of Oak Creek. It is generally cool and damp, and so contains abundant fern and moss gardens. Tight clumps of horsetails, which look like green soda straws capped with crowns, grow on the muddy banks. One of the earliest land plants, the horsetail grew in the ancient forests and swamps when the red rock of this canyon was being deposited more than 100 million years ago. Dogwood and boxwood form prominent and denser stands along the banks, adorned occasionally by yellow monkey flower. In the fall, the canyon and its shadowy glens are accented by the fire red to brilliant yellow big-tooth maples, which become a blaze of color in direct sun. The mixture of pines with deciduous trees, and a forest floor of ferns and white violets, reminds some hikers of New England.

Half-mile posts are embedded along the trail for the first several miles. Just beyond the two-mile mark, watch for a flat, bare rock platform undercut by the stream. This is a great place for a snack, a snooze, or for contemplating the dramatic canyon before you. Across the creek and somewhat hidden behind the dense streamside vegetation is a "wave cave," another overhang with a striking resemblance to a huge ocean wave. This, like many other alcoves and overhangs, was sculpted by water when the stream was at a higher level.

Not far beyond this point, the path becomes less defined. Those with a zeal for exploring can continue, but the route gets tangled in trees and brush. In some places you can walk in the creek to avoid the tangle of dense streamside vegetation. Occasionally the canyon is blocked by boulders, log jams, and deep, wall-to-wall pools. You have to climb or swim to get past these obstructions.

Regardless how far up West Fork you hike, it is an inspiring and revitalizing place to explore.

West Fork is a great day hike all year. Weekdays are

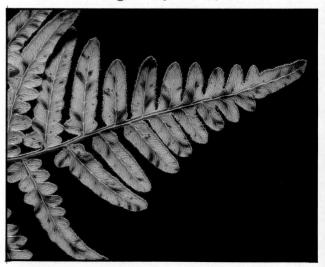

(Above far left) Be prepared to get your feet wet in West Fork. The trail criss-crosses the creek often. Peter Kresan

(Above left) Looking like a giant ocean wave turned to stone, this wave cave is about 2 miles up West Fork. W. Randall Irvine

(Above) A colorful view of the high, cathedral-like walls surrounding West Fork. Peter Kresan

(Left) An artistic study of a fern leaf in morning sunlight. Fred Griffin

(Right) Beauty on the canyon floor. Wesley Holden

(Left) If you want to hike farther than 3 miles up West Fork you will have to hike in the creek and/or do some bushwhacking. Peter Kresan

(Below) In autumn, hikers make special efforts to walk the lower end of West Fork. John Annerino

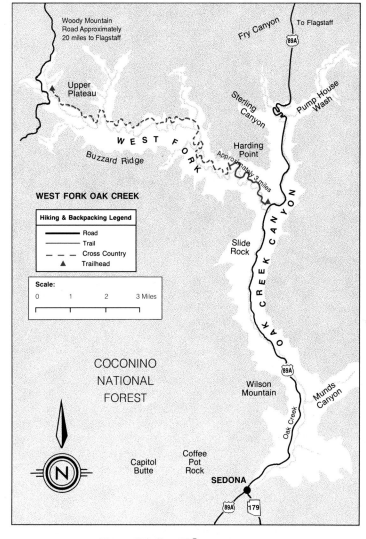

the most pleasant; the lower reaches of the canyon get crowded on weekends. Camping and campfires are forbidden in the first 6 miles above the confluence with Oak Creek.

Because wading through the creek is unavoidable, it is most comfortable from late spring through the fall. Heavy wool socks help keep feet warmer during colder weather, even when wet. Rocks in the creek are usually slippery, especially when covered with slimy green or black algae. Although I was able to recover from a slip once by catching myself on all fours, the camera around my neck swung right into the water.

Flash flooding is the principal danger in hiking these canyons. Streams swell very quickly when it storms. Localized summer thunderstorms a few miles up the drainage can go unnoticed by hikers in the lower ends of the deep canyons. It is important to check local weather forecasts before starting the hike. Take some extra food and clothing in case you do need to wait out a storm and its flood waters, which usually pass in a few hours. We tend to underestimate the power of rushing water. Water knee-deep and flowing only a few miles per hour is capable of sweeping a person away.

At the end, if you are carrying a walking stick to help with the stream crossings, it's a local custom to leave it at the trailhead for the next person who comes along to explore one of Arizona's most special places.

— Peter Kresan

How To Get There

The West Fork trailhead is 10.75 miles north of the Sedona junction of U.S. Route 89A and State Route 179. Take 89A through Oak Creek Canyon. Parking space is limited along 89A at the trailhead, but .2 of a mile farther up the canyon, a large parking lot is located off the west side of the road.

A paved path leads past a private home and down to the crossing of Oak Creek. Wade across the stream near the old stone buttresses which mark the site of a washed-out foot bridge. Then follow the path past the ruins of Mayhew Lodge and through the orchard to the mouth of West Fork.

Primary Access: U.S. Route 89A. Day use area parking lot: fee: $2 per day.
Elevation: 5200 feet at the mouth of West Fork to 6500 feet on the plateau above.
Mileage: Approximately 3 miles one-way.
Water: More than enough, but purify.
Cache Points: Only applies if you're doing an out-and-back overnighter, in which case you want to make a cache on high ground halfway between the beginning of your hike and camp.
Seasons: Late spring through early fall for the upper end.
Maps: USGS Dutton Hill, Wilson Mountain, Munds Park quadrangles and the Coconino National Forest map.
Nearest Supply Points: Flagstaff and Sedona.
Managing Agency: Sedona Ranger District, 250 Brewer Road, Sedona, AZ 86336, (520) 282-4119. Mailing address: P.O. Box 300, Sedona, AZ 86339
Backcountry Information: Permits are not required. However, no camping or campfires are permitted in lower 6 miles of West Fork. If you do build a fire, use existing fire rings and dead and down wood.

"If a person does not fear to look into the Canyon and see distance such as he has never seen elsewhere, depths such as he has never dreamt of, and if he becomes lost in shades of gentian and cherry and trout-like silver, watches the unceasing change of hue and form in depth, distance, and color, he will have feelings that do not well go into words and are perhaps more real on that account."

—Haniel Long

On a warm day early in the summer of 1540, three Spanish soldiers tried to reach the bottom of the Grand Canyon. General Francisco Vasquez de Coronado, camped near present-day Zuni, New Mexico, had heard of a gorge far to the west. He thought perhaps it might be part of a fabled waterway across North America. He sent a small detachment to explore it.

The words of these first Grand Canyon hikers are not recorded, but their impressions are. The diary of Pedro de Castaneda, another soldier, reveals that they succumbed to a common illusion that distances are shorter than they seem. The Spaniards would not believe that the Canyon was as deep, or the Colorado River as wide, as their Hopi guides claimed.

They returned exhausted late in the afternoon, having climbed perhaps one-third of the way into the Canyon.

Hiking the Canyon is not nearly that challenging today (although it can be if you want it that way). Some of the well-maintained trails are like boulevards compared to hiking elsewhere in Arizona. Yet hiking in the Canyon is the ultimate outdoor experience for many. If earlier sections of this book, particularly the backyard hikes, prepare you for Grand Canyon hiking, that would be entirely fitting.

One of the contributors to this guidebook suggested, "Each one of us, on each trip to the Canyon, writes a new chapter on the Grand Canyon for ourselves." That is as it should be. We'll provide you with a framework here, and you can write your own chapter. And if words fail you, and your color slides do not capture what you see—if the experience is adequately recorded only by your mind and soul— then you are in good company.

The same contributor, in a memo delineating all the things a Canyon experience could be, mentioned "sole searching." Assuming the pun was a typing error, we still find it appropriate. Hiking even the best of the Grand Canyon trails is arduous. Morning temperatures are brisk at the South Rim, 6876 feet elevation, and the North Rim at 8200 feet. But summer temperatures of 110 are common in midday at the bottom of the Canyon.

(Right) Bird's-eye view of the Bright Angel Trail into the Grand Canyon from the South Rim. Collier/Condit

It is likely that a hiker's first experience will be with the Bright Angel Trail. It is easy to be lured down, down, down Bright Angel with no intention of going all the way to that tiny silver strand of water at the bottom—actually a roaring river. Many hikers, particularly summer tourists, find themselves at the bottom, facing the climb back out. Hikers need to be aware that they face the equivalent of hiking a mile-high mountain, in reverse, and prepare accordingly. You need food, water, proper clothing, and footwear.

If you go properly prepared, the greatest danger is being stunned by the Canyon's grandeur.

For the very same reasons Grand Canyon is so awesome, we cannot adequately summarize in this chapter all the potential human experiences it offers. Let us guide you over a couple of trails. Numerous books and trail guides are available to enhance your future adventures in the grandfather of all canyons.

A fine rim-to-rim hike starts on the North Rim (preferably) and ends at the South Rim. If you hike north-to-south, it is best to emerge via Bright Angel Trail. If you begin at the South Rim, you will find South Kaibab a shorter but steeper way to enter the Canyon than Bright Angel.

㊶ Bright Angel Trail

Havasupai Indians, and prehistoric people before them, followed the route of the Bright Angel Trail to reach their gardens near the place now called Indian Gardens on a plateau midway to the canyon bottom. In more modern times, miners developed the trail to reach mines in the Canyon. It was named the Cameron Trail for Ralph R. Cameron, one of the mine owners. Cameron realized there was more money in tourists than in minerals, so the Cameron Trail became a toll road. He charged visitors $1 each to use it.

The Santa Fe Railroad, which wanted a piece of the tourist action, challenged Cameron's claims, which were invalidated about 1920. The trail became the property of Coconino County, which in turn traded it to the federal government in 1928. In 1937 the U.S. Board of Geographic Names named it Bright Angel Trail.

Major John Wesley Powell, who explored the Colorado River in wood boats in 1869 and 1872, first applied the name to Bright Angel Creek, which enters the Colorado from the north. The name spread. In fact, the trailhead is a short walk west of Bright Angel Lodge at the South Rim.

The 9.5-mile trail is plainly marked and impossible to mistake. It leads down through thick layers of Kaibab limestone and Coconino sandstone. The Civilian Conservation Corps of the 1930s built the rest houses which still serve 1.5 and 3 miles down the trail. At a switchback called Two-Mile Corner, pictographs date back to A.D.1300, showing how long the trail's natural course has been followed. Any of these three points would be a likely destination for a short hike.

Switchbacks called Jacob's Ladder lead down

through the 500-foot-thick layers of a formation called Redwall limestone. Indian Gardens is a welcome refuge to hikers going up or down the trail. It is 4.7 miles from the trailhead, and its towering cottonwood trees are visible from several areas. There is a ranger station here, corrals, a developed campground, water and toilets. It makes a good turnaround for a one-day hike from South Rim. This also is the beginning of the relatively flat, 1.5 mile trail out to the end of Plateau Point, which offers gorgeous views of the Inner Gorge.

After Bright Angel leaves Indian Gardens, it descends through Tapeats Narrows and then into the Devil's Corkscrew, winding hairpins of trail through the Vishnu Schist, some of the earth's older rocks. The trail bottoms out along the bed of Pipe Creek. At Pipe Creek resthouse near the Colorado River, you pick up River Trail and follow it east 1.7 miles to the suspension bridge leading to Bright Angel Campground on the north side of the river. Continue straight on River Trail, and you reach the foot of South Kaibab Trial; the old suspension bridge is a mile farther east. _Text continued on page 128_

(Above) Bright Angel Trailhead. Tom Bean

(Opposite page) A rainbow arches over the Grand Canyon. The trees visible in the lower part of the Canyon shelter Indian Gardens campground. Diane Hoffman.

(Right) The cool shade of Indian Gardens provides a restful interlude for Canyon hikers. Tom Bean

(Opposite page) Walls of the world's oldest exposed rock line the banks of the Colorado River at the bottom of the Grand Canyon. A bridge for hikers and mules spans the Colorado about 1.5 miles from Phantom Ranch. Tom Bean photos

(Right) A collared lizard, one of the Canyon's residents. Diane Hoffman

(Below) Hikers enjoy a cool plunge in Bright Angel Creek along Bright Angel Trail near Phantom Ranch. Martos Hoffman

㊷ North Kaibab Trail

To reach the head of the modern North Kaibab Trail, drive 2 miles north of Grand Canyon Lodge. The parking lot is on the right (east) side of State Route 67. Like the Bright Angel, the North Kaibab is easy to follow all the way to the river. The only difficulties you may encounter, aside from its length and steepness, are the rock slides that occasionally cover upper sections of the trail during spring thaw or after a summer squall.

By far the steepest section of the North Kaibab Trail is the 4.7-mile stretch from the trailhead down Roaring Springs Canyon to its confluence with Bright Angel Canyon, dropping some 3400 vertical feet. En route to the confluence, you'll pass Roaring Springs day use area on the right. Nearby buildings are occupied and maintained by Park Service personnel who operate the Roaring Springs pumphouse, sending water to both rims.

From this confluence it's another 2 miles down Bright Angel Creek to Cottonwood Campground, where there is a seasonally manned ranger station. A mile farther on, you'll come to Ribbon Falls Trail junction. The non-maintained trail leading to Ribbon Falls is marked by cairns, as is its fording of Bright

Angel Creek. (You may also use the bridge .5-mile north of the fording.)

It is another 6 miles down Bright Angel Creek to the Phantom Ranch-Bright Angel Campground Area.

If you're planning a rim-to-rim hike from the North Rim to the South Rim—and you will find it easier hiking north to south—consider coming out the Bright Angel Trail; it's a few miles longer than the South Kaibab, but it's not as steep, so your legs will have more of a chance to recover. Besides, there's water on the Bright Angel, and there isn't any on the South Kaibab.

—*James E. Cook*

(Above) This view from the North Rim shows why early autumn is a great time to hike the Canyon. Tom Bean

(Right) Hikers on the North Kaibab, as on the Bright Angel, occasionally have to share the trail with mules. Inge Martin

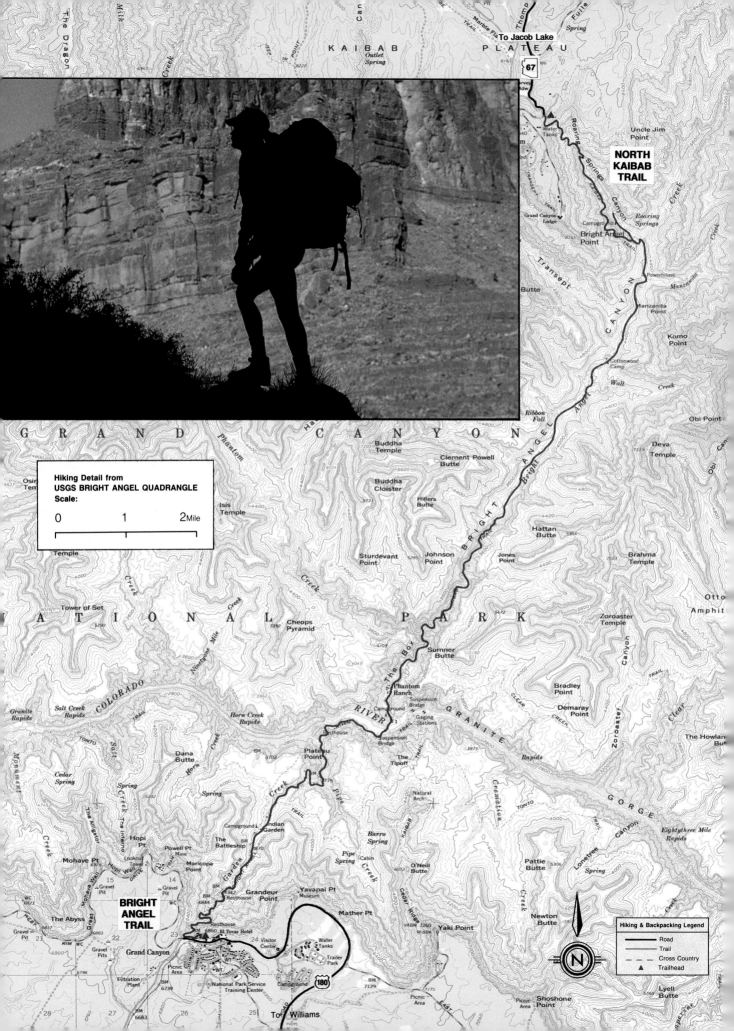

Hiking Detail from
USGS BRIGHT ANGEL QUADRANGLE
Scale:

0   1   2 Mile

NORTH KAIBAB TRAIL

BRIGHT ANGEL TRAIL

To Jacob Lake

Hiking & Backpacking Legend
——— Road
——— Trail
- - - Cross Country
▲ Trailhead

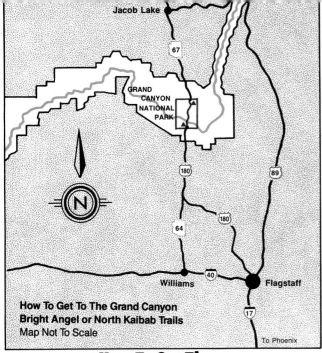

How To Get To The Grand Canyon
Bright Angel or North Kaibab Trails
Map Not To Scale

How To Get There

To reach the South Rim from Flagstaff drive north on U.S. Route 180 for 81 miles; from Williams drive north 28 miles on State Route 64 to U.S. 180 and follow it north another 31 miles. To reach the North Rim, drive south from Jacob Lake 44 miles on State Route 67.

BRIGHT ANGEL TRAIL

Primary Access: South Rim, and River Trail from Phantom Ranch..
Elevation: 6876 to 2400 feet.
Mileage: 9.5 miles to Bright Angel Campground.
Water: Indian Gardens, Colorado River, and Bright Angel Campground; seasonal water at 1.5- and 3-mile rest houses.
Cache Points: Contact the Grand Canyon Backcountry Reservation office.
Escape Points: South Rim, Indian Gardens or Phantom Ranch by trail, whichever is closest.
Seasons: Fall through spring are best; summer can be hot.
Maps: USGS Grand Canyon, Phantom Ranch, and Bright Angel Point.
Nearest Supply Points: Grand Canyon Village, Flagstaff, Williams, and Cameron.
Managing Agency: Grand Canyon National Park.
Backcountry Information: Permits are required for all overnight hiking. No fires are permitted. Backcountry reservations office: P.O. Box 129, Grand Canyon, AZ 86023. Backcountry information line, (520) 638-7888, 11 a.m. to 5 p.m. Monday through Friday.

NORTH KAIBAB TRAIL

Primary Access: North Kaibab Trailhead. Old Kaibab Trail, Bright Angel Trail, South Kaibab Trail.
Elevation: 8241 feet at trailhead to 2400 feet at Colorado River.
Mileage: 14 miles one way.
Water: Roaring Springs, Bright Angel Creek, Transept Springs, Ribbon Springs (heavy lime), Phantom Creek, Bright Angel: seasonal water at Cottonwood Campground, Roaring Springs residence, Supai Tunnel.
Cache Points: Contact the Grand Canyon Backcountry Reservation office.
Seasons: June through September from North Rim, all year from South Rim — but expect snow, ice, rock falls, and harsh conditions above Roaring Springs during winter.
Maps: USGS Bright Angel point.
Nearest Supply Points: Fredonia, Page, Vermilion Cliffs, Jacob Lake, North Rim, Grand Canyon Village.
Managing Agency: Grand Canyon National Park.
Backcountry Information:
Permits are required for all overnight hiking. No fires permitted.

(Far left) For cross-canyon hikers it is easiest to arrange a van shuttle from the South Rim to the North Rim, then hike back. Gary Ladd

(Below) Ribbon falls is a delight for the eyes just off the North Kaibab Trail at the bottom of the Grand Canyon. Jack W. Dykinga

㊸ Navajo National Monument

These prehistoric cliff dwellings mark the end of the Anasazi culture in northeastern Arizona. It is fascinating to stand in the stony silence of Betatakin or Keet Seel and speculate on what life must have been like in these pueblos seven hundred years ago.

Rangers lead tours to Betatakin, Memorial Day to Labor Day, on a first-come, first-served basis. From the visitor center at 7286 feet there is an elevation drop of 700 feet into the canyon below. The round trip is 3 miles long and takes four hours.

Keet Seel is the largest cliff dwelling in Arizona. The arduous trail, at 16 miles round trip, makes a pleasant overnight backpack. It is open from Memorial Day to Labor Day. Permits are required for both hiking and overnight camping at Keet Seel. Reservations should be made two months in advance, and permits must be obtained from monument headquarters at least one day before your hike. To get to Navajo National Monument, travel 68 miles north of Flagstaff on U.S. Route 89. Turn east and go 62 miles on U.S. Route 160, then 10 miles north on Arizona Route 564. For information or reservations contact: Navajo National Monument, HC71 Box 3, Tonalea, AZ 86044, (520) 672-2366, or 2367.

㊹ Island Trail

Walnut Canyon National Monument

Two-hundred-forty steps and a paved trail three-quarters of a mile long lead to more than a dozen individual prehistoric cliff dwellings in Walnut Canyon. At 7000 feet, this beautiful canyon has a mixture of vegetation from prickly pear cactus to stands of Douglas fir. This is an interesting one-hour walk, open year-round.

Walnut Canyon is 4 miles east of Flagstaff on Interstate 40, and 3 miles south on an access road to the monument entrance. For information contact: Walnut Canyon National Monument, Walnut Canyon Road, Flagstaff, AZ 86004, (520) 526-3367.

㊺ Lower Paria/Lees Ferry Vermilion Cliffs

If you're not inclined to take a three- to four-day trek through Paria Canyon, Lees Ferry is a great place to explore for an hour or a full day. The towering Vermilion Cliffs, constructed of rocks from the age of the dinosaurs, dominate the scene.

A short hike along the Paria River leads you past the old cemetery and the remains of Lonely Dell, the farm established by John Doyle Lee when he founded the ferry across the Colorado River in 1871. This was the route used by the Church of Jesus Christ of Latter-day Saints (Mormon) for its people to colonize Arizona from Utah. A one-mile hike up the river from the boat launching ramp takes you along the old wagon road, past Lee's fort building and the wreck of the steamboat Charles H. Spencer. Where the road ends at the main ferry site (the ferry was replaced by Navajo Bridge in 1929), look across the Colorado for remains of the old road hugging the cliffs.

There is a small campground at Lees Ferry. For information contact: Glen Canyon National Recreation Area, P.O. Box 1507, Page, AZ 86040, (520) 645-8405.

Wesley Holden

㊻ Havasu Canyon

Located in a remote area at the western end of the Grand Canyon, Havasu Canyon has often been called Shangri-la because of its high waterfalls, turquoise-colored pools, and beautiful scenery. It is a strenuous 10 miles from the parking area at Hill Top to the campground. And although you can

hike in and out in two days, allow three or four days to enjoy the waterfalls and hike farther down the canyon. It is nine beautiful, but difficult miles beyond the campground to the Colorado River. May through October is best.

This is the home of the Havasupai Indians. Permits for hiking and camping must be acquired in advance. Contact: Tourist Manager, General Delivery, Supai, AZ 86435. (520) 448-2121.

To get there drive 55 miles northeast of Kingman on Old U.S. Route 66. Turn north on Indian Route 18, and in 60 miles you'll arrive at Hualapai Hilltop parking area and trailhead.

㊽ Canyon de Chelly
White House Ruin Trail

This certainly has to be one of the most spectacular settings ever for a "house" (not to be confused with White House ruin at the head of Paria Canyon). The streaks of blue-black varnish across the massive sandstone cliffs of Canyon de Chelly draw your attention to the pueblo ruin. If you are at

White House overlook on the opposite rim of the canyon (reached by road from Chinle), the view of White House beckons you to closer exploration. A trail leads 500 feet down into the canyon and across the streambed to the base of the ruins. It is an enjoyable hike, and the only part of Canyon de Chelly accessible without an authorized Navajo guide. The trail frequently is used by Navajos who sometimes move sheep over it. In the fall, cottonwoods which line the canyon bottom are ablaze with color.

For information contact: Canyon de Chelly National Monument, P.O. Box 588, Chinle, AZ 86503, (520) 674-5500.

㊼ Sycamore Canyon   Southern Arizona

There are several Sycamore Canyons in Arizona. Not to be confused with a better-known Sycamore which empties into the Verde Valley, the southern Sycamore Canyon is west of Nogales. Running generally north to south, the canyon extends 5 miles to the Mexican border. Walking through shallow pools, the intermittent stream meanders past pin-

nacles and cliffs of volcanic rock rising above a lush canyon bottom. With care, and a little luck, you might see a rare coppery-tailed trogon.

Take Interstate 19 about 6 or 7 miles north of Nogales, turn west on State Route 289 for 10 miles to Pena Blanca Lake, then continue another 10 miles on a narrow graded gravel road to Sycamore Canyon.

Wesley Holden

1. Clubs

Flagstaff: the Northern Arizona University Hiking Club offers field trips that "explore the wilderness of the Colorado Plateau and surrounding areas through various means of environmentally clean recreation. Contact NAU Hiking Club, Box 6100, Flagstaff, AZ 86011, (520) 523-4971.

Tucson: the Southern Arizona Hiking Club has monthly meetings and offers dozens of hikes each month. For membership information and a bulletin, write to Southern Arizona Hiking Club, P.O. Box 32257, Tucson, AZ 85751. No Phone. The club sells an excellent set of composite topographic maps showing the hiking trails (with mileages) in the Santa Catalina, Rincon, Santa Rita, and Chiricahua mountains.

The Tucson Audubon Society also sponsors hiking trips in areas noted for their bird life. For information on Audubon Society hikes and outdoor natural history education programs, write to the society at 34 N. Tucson Boulevard, Tucson, AZ 85716, (520) 323-9673.

UofA Ramblers Hiking Club - UA Associated Students Activities at the University of Arizona is an active hiking group. For information call (520) 621-8046.

Statewide: The Sierra Club is a national conservation organization with 360,000 members and 56 chapters nationwide. Within Arizona's Grand Canyon Chapter (based in Flagstaff), five local groups are active in the state: the Plateau group in Flagstaff, the Paloverde group in Phoenix, the Rincon group in Tucson, the Kofa group in Yuma, and the Chiricahua group in Sierra Vista. In addition to conservation activities and trail cleanup outings, the Sierra Club offers the most comprehensive list of club hikes in the state, from day hikes to extended overnighters. It's hikes are also rated A through D (A being the most difficult) so you have some idea what your getting into. For a complete list of chapter hikes and their newsletter call The Sierra Club, (520) 620-6401.

2. Instruction

Prescott College is an accredited, nationally recognized, four-year college that offers a diverse program in environmental education, with an emphasis on independent studies. It also offers month-long courses in rock climbing and mountaineering, taught by world-class climbers, as well as courses in white-water rafting and kayaking and wilderness travel. Many of the top outdoor educators in the country are graduates of Prescott College. Write Prescott College, 220 Grove Avenue, Prescott, AZ 86301, (520) 778-2090.

Friendly Pines Camp is an internationally known summer camp. As part of its summer camp curriculum, it also offers two four-week long programs called "Challenge" for those 10-13 years old. The Challenge program includes supervised camp and field instruction in hiking, overnight backpacking, rockclimbing, and camp skills. Their safety record is impeccable. Write: Friendly Pines Camp, 933 Friendly Pines Road, Prescott, AZ 86303, (520) 445-2128.

3. Programs

Phoenix: The Desert Botanical Garden offers botanical, ecological, and horticultural programs for both children and adults. The garden is in Papago Park. for further information, write: Desert Botanical Garden, 1201 N. Galvin Parkway, Phoenix, AZ 85008. Phone, 941-1225.

Tucson: The Arizona-Sonora Desert Museum offers theme hikes to its members throughout the year as part of its special events program: wildflower walks, botanical hikes, and geological excursions. for further information on membership and these special events, write Special Events Office, Arizona-Sonora Desert Museum, 2021 N. Kinney Rd. Tucson, AZ 85743, (520) 883-1380.

Summit Hut in Tucson sponsors an excellent series of lecture/slide programs. Summit Hut phone is (520) 325-1554 and its address is 5045 East Speedway, Tucson, AZ 85712.

Pima Trails Association is a private, non-profit organization. It is a multi-use trails advocacy organization for promoting and protecting trails in Pima County, AZ. The association has published a poster entitled, Trails of the Tucson Basin. You can contact the group at P.O. Box 41358, Tucson, AZ 85717.

Flagstaff: The Museum of Northern Arizona offers a variety of excursions and expeditions to the public. There are adventure trips, such as rafting on the San Juan and Colorado rivers, horsepacking in the Superstition Wilderness, backpacking in the Grand Canyon, cross-country skiing, and day hiking on the Colorado Plateau. Its education department also offers a Junior Science camp in the summer for children and teenagers. for further information write: Education Department Museum of Northern Arizona, Rt. 4, Box 720, Flagstaff, AZ 86001, (520) 774-5211.

Superior: The Boyce Thompson Southwestern Arboretum is a riparian desert sanctuary located at the base of 4375-foot Picket Post Mountain just west of Superior. Its 30 acres of lower and upper Sonoran desert are sliced by Queen Creek, offering a unique micro-habitat for a wide variety of avifauna mammals, reptiles, fish, and desert plants. Self-guiding nature trails provide access and education to those who are willing to make the one hour-plus drive east of Phoenix. Write Boyce Thompson Southwestern Arboretum, U.S. Route 60, Superior, AZ 85273, (520) 689-2811.

4. Reading List

Within the scope of this guide, it is impossible to cover every single aspect of wilderness travel in detail. the following is a list of books and references you'll find helpful.

Accidents in North American Mountaineering: Details and analyzes mountain climbing and travel related accidents: the lessons are applicable to wilderness travel in the canyons and deserts as well. Write American Alpine Club, 710 E. 10th St., Golden, CO 80401. Phone (303) 384-0110.

Arizona Natural Environment by Charles H. Lowe is a comprehensive introduction to the landscapes and habitats of Arizona and details the late James A. Wilkerson life zone concept. University of Arizona Press, Tucson. This book is out of print but it would be worth it to try your library.

Desert Survival edited by Lt. Col. AUS (Ret.) Louis E. Roninger is the most complete booklet on desert survival in Arizona. He has done his homework. And its free. Write the Maricopa County Department of Civil Defense and Emergency Services, 2035 North 52nd Street, Phoenix, AZ 85008, (602) 273-1411.

Deserts and *Western Forests,* Audubon Society Nature Guides, are two "must" comprehensive field guides for your library. The first is by James A. MacMahon and the latter by Stephen Whitney. They are *the* references to wildflowers, trees, birds, reptiles, mammals, insects, and "other natural wonders of North America." These recent publications are also illustrated with color plates. Alfred A. Knopf, New York.

Fit or Fat? A New Way to Health and Fitness Through Nutrition and Aerobic Exercise by Covert Bailey is excellent reading. Houghton Mifflin, Boston.

International Mountain Rescue Handbook by Hamish MacInnes will provide you with graphic insight into the details and planning necessary to effect a successful rescue. Charles Scribner's & Sons, New York.

Medicine for Mountaineering edited by James A. Wilkerson, M.D. is the recognized field source detailing the cause and treatment of traumatic injuries, environmental injuries, and nontraumatic diseases that may require treatment in the field. The Mountaineers, Seattle, WA.

Outdoor Survival Skills by Larry Dean Olsen is the source on primitive survival techniques by someone who has mastered these techniques in the wilderness. Brigham Young University, Provo, UT 84601.

Mountaineering: The Freedom of the Hills edited by Ed Peters is the most comprehensive source on mountain travel. The Mountaineers, Seattle, WA.

Van Aaken Method by Ernst Van Aaken, M.D. is a top source on endurance running and travel complemented with a no-nonsense approach to nutrition. World Publications, P.O. Box 66, Mountain View, CA 94040.

Walking Softly in the Wilderness by John Hart is probably the single best guide to backpacking. Sierra Club Books, San Francisco.

Weathering the Wilderness by William F. Reifsnyder is a practical guide to meteorology as it pertains to wilderness travel. Sierra Club Books, San Francisco.

Venomous Animals of Arizona by Robert L. Smith, illustrated by Joel Floyd, is the guide to your worst nightmares. Read this book and chances are you'll prevent those nightmares from occurring in the field. Cooperative Extension Service, College of Agriculture, The University of Arizona, Tucson, AZ 85721.

Tom Bean

Index

**Boldface type indicates
photograph.
"m" indicates map.**